MARK THE MESSIAH'S GOSPEL

CARROLL ROBERSON

WESTBOW
PRESS®
A DIVISION OF THOMAS NELSON
& ZONDERVAN

WestBow Press books may be ordered through booksellers or by contacting:

WestBow Press
A Division of Thomas Nelson & Zondervan
1663 Liberty Drive
Bloomington, IN 47403
www.westbowpress.com
1 (866) 928-1240

ISBN: 978-1-9736-5758-3 (sc)
ISBN: 978-1-9736-5759-0 (hc)
ISBN: 978-1-9736-5757-6 (e)

Library of Congress Control Number: 2019903383

Print information available on the last page.

WestBow Press rev. date: 03/25/2019

CONTENTS

INTRODUCTION

The most significant source of information about our precious Lord Jesus Christ is found in the four gospel accounts. Mark is the second gospel account we find in the New Testament, and as we will see, the four gospels are in the correct chronological order. Mark is also the shortest gospel with only sixteen chapters. When we compare the amount of words in each gospel they stack up like this:

Matthew – 18,346
Mark – 11,304
Luke – 19,482
John – 15,634

But we should not let the brevity of Mark's account cause us to think that it is less important. It is fast paced, and Mark uses the word *"immediately"* or the Greek *"euthus"* more than 17 times throughout his gospel. So Mark's gospel is explosive and action packed. He writes in a way that is sudden, abrupt, and with a sense of urgency.

The four gospels should not be read as an exhaustive narrative of the life and ministry of Jesus the Messiah.

For example, John explicitly states that there were many other signs and miracles that Jesus performed that were not recorded.

> *And there are also many other things which Jesus did, the which, if they should be written every one, I suppose that even the world itself could not contain the books that should be written. Amen.* John 21:25

Sometimes people ask, *"Why are there four gospels, and why do they sometimes seem to contradict each other?"* The answer lies in the fact that the four writers wrote their accounts at different times to a different audience. Through the guidance of the Holy Spirit, each writer arranged the factual historic data of the life of our Lord in a way that best suited their chosen audience. The chronology and exhaustive coverage of the specific events were secondary. Weaving the gospels together in harmony is possible, but they should never be taken as a biography. The ancient method was highlighting key events and themes, while giving a distinct perspective about Jesus' earthly ministry. Just one gospel account could never capture the complete picture, and that is why we need to study all four gospels. One writer may bring out something a little different about a specific miracle or the mention of someone's name in order to stir the hearts of their particular audience.

Like the other three gospels, the Jewish, Semitic nature of Mark's gospel is obvious. It is arrogant to say that the

Greek text of Mark is to be criticized or unreliable, but he is writing to a Gentile audience about a Jewish Messiah. So in my interpretations I am not trying to take away from the original Greek manuscript of Mark, but trying to convey the original Hebrew thought behind the text. As I have written many times before, Jesus the Messiah came to Israel and spoke the Hebrew of the religious Jews and the Aramaic of the Galileans. Language was certainly no problem for Jesus, who is the Word, but we need to understand Him within His early first century Jewish context. There is no language that is superior to the original Hebrew language of creation and the language of our Lord. Mark is communicating this Jewish message to a Greek and Latin speaking audience. Some Bible teachers are offended when someone tries to correct the Greek or English text, but it's the Person of Christ we worship, not the Greek, Latin, or English manuscripts. We want to know more about this Divine Person who came to walk this sin-cursed earth *to seek and to save that which was lost.* So in order to know more about the Jesus in the gospels, we need to go beyond the *communicative language* and see how He connects to the Old Testament, which were the only inspired scriptures they had in the early first century.

AUTHOR

Although the author does not identify himself, the earliest manuscripts attribute the gospel to John Mark. There is more biblical information about Mark than any other gospel writer. Mark was a Jewish-Christian, and according to Hippolytus was one of the 70 who our Lord sent out in **Luke 10:1:**

> *After these things the LORD appointed other seventy also, and sent them two and two before his face into every city and place, whither he himself would come.*

He was an African native of Jewish parents who belonged to the tribe of the Levites. His family lived in Cyrene until they were attacked by barbarians and lost their property. They moved to Jerusalem with their child, Mark. Apparently Mark received a good education and was conversant in Hebrew, Greek, and Latin, the three languages that are mentioned above the cross of Jesus.

*And a superscription also was written over him
in letters of Greek, and Latin, and Hebrew,
THIS IS THE KING OF THE JEWS.*

Luke 23:38.

Mark's family was very religious and became close followers of our Lord Jesus the Messiah. There is a strong tradition that Mark's father was also a cousin of Simon Peter, which would strongly connect Mark being with Peter in Rome. It is believed that Mark was present in Cana when Jesus turned the water into wine. Mark most likely was the one who was carrying the pitcher of water in **Mark 14:13**, who took the two disciples to the furnished large upper room belonging possibly to his immediate family.

We only find ten verses in the New Testament that mention John Mark, but they are sufficient enough to give us a brief biographical sketch of him.

Mark was the nephew of Barnabas.

*Aristarchus my fellowprisoner saluteth you,
and Marcus, sister's son to Barnabas, (touching
whom ye received commandments: if he come
unto you, receive him;)*

Colossians 4:10

Mark was the son of the woman named Mary who provided a meeting place for the early believers.

*And when he had considered the thing, he came
to the house of Mary the mother of John, whose*

surname was Mark; where many were gathered
together praying.

Acts 12:12

Many have speculated that Mark was the young man
at the Garden of Gethsemane during the betrayal of Jesus.

And there followed him a certain young man,
having a linen cloth cast about his naked body;
and the young men laid hold on him: And he
left the linen cloth, and fled from them naked.

Mark 14:51-52

We know that Mark accompanied Barnabas and Saul
on their first missionary journey.

And Barnabas and Saul returned from
Jerusalem, when they had fulfilled their
ministry, and took with them John, whose
surname was Mark.

Acts 12:25

Mark departed early from that first missionary journey
and returned to Jerusalem.

Now when Paul and his company loosed from
Paphos, they came to Perga in Pamphylia:
and John departing from them returned to
Jerusalem.

Acts 13:13

After the Jerusalem Council, Barnabas and Paul were planning their second missionary journey. Barnabas wanted to take Mark, but Paul opposed the idea because Mark had departed from them on their first journey. Barnabas took Mark, and Paul took Silas as they went on their separate ways.

> *And some days after Paul said unto Barnabas, Let us go again and visit our brethren in every city where we have preached the word of the LORD, and see how they do. And Barnabas determined to take with them John, whose surname was Mark. But Paul thought not good to take him with them, who departed from them from Pamphylia, and went not with them to the work. And the contention was so sharp between them, that they departed asunder one from the other: and so Barnabas took Mark, and sailed unto Cyprus; And Paul chose Silas, and departed, being recommended by the brethren unto the grace of God. And he went through Syria and Cilicia, confirming the churches.*
>
> Acts 15:36-41

But later Paul gave Mark a good name and even called him a co-worker.

Marcus, Aristarchus, Demas, Lucas, my fellowlabourers.

Philemon 24

Aristarchus my fellowprisoner saluteth you, and Marcus, sister's son to Barnabas, (touching whom ye received commandments: if he come unto you, receive him;)

Colossians 4:10

Only Luke is with me. Take Mark, and bring him with thee: for he is profitable to me for the ministry.

2 Timothy 4:11

The scriptures tell us that Mark was very close to Simon Peter. It is strongly believed that Mark was writing his gospel as a channel through Peter in Rome. Mark was writing down the things that Simon Peter actually witnessed firsthand. So it seems likely that Mark started writing his gospel in Rome and later finished it in Alexandria.

Early Church Fathers such as *Papias* (130AD), *Irenaeus* (180AD), *Clement of Alexandria* (200Ad), and *Tertullian* (200AD) all echo the tradition that Peter's authority stands behind the second gospel, and describe Mark as the interpreter.

The church that is at Babylon, (Rome) elected together with you, saluteth you; and so doth Marcus my son.   I Peter 5:13

DATE

I personally hold to an earlier writing for Mark than most. As a matter of fact, many of the books in the New Testament were written much earlier than scholars suppose. We must look at the scriptural facts and historical data carefully before placing any dates on when Mark was written. I believe that Matthew was the first gospel written, in 37AD, and then the Epistle of James, around 40-41AD, and next is the gospel of Mark, written between 42-49AD. Fragments of Mark's gospel have been found in the Dead Sea Scrolls, placing Mark's gospel around 50AD. Mark was with Simon Peter in Jerusalem between the years of 38-44AD and was his secretary. We need to keep in mind that Peter was not a very well educated man as Mark, who was a Levite. Try to imagine Simon Peter telling Mark about the days he walked with the very Son of God, with tear-filled eyes and a trembling lip, while Mark was writing with holy excitement and a shaky hand. I am reminded of this powerful verse shortly before Peter was executed:

> *For we have not followed cunningly devised fables, when we made known unto you the power and coming of our Lord Jesus Christ, but were eyewitnesses of his majesty.*
>
> 2 Peter 1:16

I am convinced when I study the chronology of the book of Acts, the ministry of Simon Peter, and the history of Alexandria that Mark wrote his gospel between 42-49AD. It is possible that Mark's account may not have been well circulated until the time Simon Peter was executed by the Roman Emperor Nero in 64AD. This is why many scholars place Mark's writing at a later time.

DESTINATION

Mark's purpose was to write down the gospel of Christ as Peter presented to the Romans. We can see the internal evidence that Mark was writing to Gentiles. Mark translates several Hebrew/Aramaic names:

> *And James the son of Zebedee, and John the brother of James; and he surnamed them Boanerges, which is, The sons of thunder:*
>
> Mark 3:17

> *And he took the damsel by the hand, and said unto her, Talitha cumi; which is, being interpreted, Damsel, I say unto thee, arise.*
>
> Mark 5:41

> *But ye say, If a man shall say to his father or mother, It is Corban, that is to say, a gift, by whatsoever thou mightest be profited by me; he shall be free.*
>
> Mark 7:11

And looking up to heaven, he sighed, and saith unto him, Ephphatha, that is, Be opened.

Mark 7:34

And they came to Jericho: and as he went out of Jericho with his disciples and a great number of people, blind Bartimaeus, the son of Timaeus, sat by the highway side begging.

Mark 10:46

And he said, Abba, Father, all things are possible unto thee; take away this cup from me: nevertheless not what I will, but what thou wilt.

Mark 14:36

And they bring him unto the place Golgotha, which is, being interpreted, The place of a skull.

Mark 15:22

And at the ninth hour Jesus cried with a loud voice, saying, Eloi, Eloi, lama sabachthani? which is, being interpreted, My God, my God, why hast thou forsaken me?

Mark 15:34

Mark mentions several Jewish customs:

And the first day of unleavened bread, when they killed the passover, his disciples said unto

him, Where wilt thou that we go and prepare
that thou mayest eat the passover?

Mark 14:12

And now when the even was come, because it
was the preparation, that is, the day before the
sabbath,

Mark 15:42

Mark only quotes from the Old Testament Law of
Moses one time. He even uses Latin terms and names in
several instances. Mark also wanted to show his Roman
readers the authority and power of Jesus the Messiah over
the Roman Emperor Caesar, who was Claudias (41–54AD)
at the time. **(Acts 18:2)**

And there came a certain poor widow, and she
threw in two mites (Greek lepton), *which make*
a farthing (Two mites, or leptons, made the
Latin quadran)

Mark 12:42

But that ye may know that the Son of man
hath power on earth to forgive sins, (he saith
to the sick of the palsy,)

Mark 2:10

And when he was gone forth into the way, there
came one running, and kneeled to him, and

asked him, Good Master, what shall I do that I may inherit eternal life?

Mark 10:17

And they compel one Simon a Cyrenian, who passed by, coming out of the country, the father of Alexander and Rufus, to bear his cross.

Mark 15:21 (Compare **Romans 16:13**)

And when the centurion, which stood over against him, saw that he so cried out, and gave up the ghost, he said, Truly this man was the Son of God.

Mark 15:39

It is very likely that Mark was writing to Gentile believers in Rome who were the target of fierce persecution at that time. By reminding them of the suffering that Jesus endured, he was encouraging them to remain faithful during their time of trial.

Mark uses Roman time, showing that his readers were probably Gentiles. We have even adopted the Roman method of time beginning the day at midnight and dividing it into 12-hour intervals.

And he saw them toiling in rowing; for the wind was contrary unto them: and about the fourth watch of the night he cometh unto them, walking upon the sea, and would have passed by them.

Mark 6:48

Watch ye therefore: for ye know not when the master of the house cometh, at even, or at midnight, or at the cockcrowing, or in the morning:

Mark 13:35

THEME

Mark's primary theme is Jesus being the Messiah, the sinless Son of God, and that also Jesus is the *"Servant Branch"* of **Zechariah 3:8**:

Hear now, O Joshua the high priest, thou, and thy fellows that sit before thee: for they are men wondered at: for, behold, I will bring forth my servant the BRANCH.

Mark's *Servant* gospel needs no genealogy because a Roman audience would not be so interested. There is no birth narrative, but he begins his account with the forerunner of Israel's Messiah that was prophesied in the old Hebrew scriptures. One notable theme in Mark is the mysterious, *messianic secret*. Jesus is more hidden in Mark's gospel than in Matthew, Luke, or John. He teaches His disciples in secret, He commands many who are healed not to tell anyone, He commands demons to be quiet, and His disciples seem to rarely understand what Jesus is talking about. We can hear and see the mystery that was in the mind of Simon Peter for over three years walking with

Jesus until everything was revealed to Him. Notice these verses containing the *messianic secret*:

> *And saith unto him, See thou say nothing to any man: but go thy way, shew thyself to the priest, and offer for thy cleansing those things which Moses commanded, for a testimony unto them.*
>
> Mark 1:44

> *And he straitly charged them that they should not make him known.*
>
> Mark 3:12

> *And he charged them straitly that no man should know it; and commanded that something should be given her to eat.*
>
> Mark 5:43

> *And he charged them that they should tell no man: but the more he charged them, so much the more a great deal they published it;*
>
> Mark 7:36

> *And he charged them that they should tell no man of him.*
>
> Mark 8:30

In Mark's gospel the disciples believe in Jesus as the Messiah being eyewitnesses of His super-heroic miracles, but the mystery lies in the fact that they could not understand that Israel's Messiah had to suffer and die in Jerusalem, especially at such a young age. While this truth is in all four gospels, it is more obvious in Mark's gospel. The death of Israel's Messiah seems to be central in identifying Jesus as the *Suffering Servant* of **Isaiah 52-53**.

Mark records five *Parables* in chapter 4, and the *Parable of the Growing Seed* (**4:26-29**) is unique to Mark alone. From **Mark 6:33-8:26**, the word *"bread"* is used 17 times, showing the importance of Jesus being *The Bread of Life*.

LEGACY

Mark served in Jerusalem and Judea, Antioch, Cyprus, Asia Minor, Colossae, Rome, and Venice. His major service was in North Africa while it was under Roman rule. Alexandria was the intellectual capital of its time, and Mark won countless people to Jesus and baptized many Egyptians, Greeks, Romans, and Jews. When Mark arrived in Alexandria, the strap of one of his sandals was broken and he went to a shoe cobbler named, Ananias. While working on Mark's sandal, the awl pierced Ananias' hand, and he cried "Oh, One God." Then Mark healed his hand, and preached to Ananias and his family. They believed in Christ and were all baptized, and the first church in Alexandria was born in the house of Ananias. In 44AD, Mark ordained Ananias as the first bishop, and the Coptic Church today claims its history all the way back to Mark.

Mark would later establish the Theological School of Alexandria where people studied theology, medicine, engineering, music, literature, and science. The 20th Coptic Patriarch, St. Athanasius, (328-373AD) was a graduate of that school.

The work of Mark in Egypt and his attacks on the local pagan gods were so successful that great hatred and vengeance was poured out on Mark. Mark was dragged through the streets of Alexandria by a rope tied around his neck on Easter Sunday in 68AD. They placed his wounded body in jail where he saw a vision of the Lord Jesus Christ who said, "Peace to you, Mark, my disciple and evangelist." Mark started to shout, "O My Lord Jesus," but the vision disappeared.

The next day Mark was dragged again through the city until his head was severed from his body. The pagans wanted to burn his body, but heavy rains prevented it. He was buried underneath the altar at the Church of Baucalis, in Alexandria. According to Coptic Church history, Mark was about 55 years of age. This is reckoned because Mark was born in 13AD, 15 years after Christ was born in 2BC, and was martyred in 68AD.

In 828AD, Venetians stole parts of his body and brought them to Venice. Some of his relics were later moved to the new Cathedral named after St. Mark in Cairo, Egypt, while the rest of his relics are in San Marco Cathedral in Venice, Italy.

MARK AND THE LION

The voice of the lion is the symbol for Mark. Why? For several reasons:

> *As for the likeness of their faces, they four had the face of a man, and the face of a lion, on the right side: and they four had the face of an ox on the left side; they four also had the face of an eagle.* Ezekiel 1:10

Irenaeus (140–202AD) began what is called a *tetramorph*, a symbolic arrangement of four different elements together. *Tetra* = four, and *morph* = shape, borrowing from Egyptian, Greek, and Assyrian art. So from the fifth century many Christian artists have painted where each of the four gospels represents each living creature in Ezekiel's vision. **Matthew** - *the man;* **Mark** - *the lion;* **Luke** - *the ox; and* **John** - *the eagle,* depicting four different facets of the Lord Jesus Christ.

Also, there is a famous story as was told by *Severus Ebn-El-Mokafa*, a Coptic Bishop from the tenth century.

Once a lion and lioness appeared to John Mark and his father, Arostalis, while they were traveling in Jordan. The father was very scared and begged his son to escape while he awaited his fate. John Mark assured his father that Jesus Christ would save them and began to pray. The two beasts fell dead and as a result of this miracle, the father believed in Christ.

Another reason why Mark is symbolized by the lion is

because he begins his gospel with the thundering of John the Baptist in the Judean wilderness as a lion. And the most important reason is because Jesus is the *Lion of the Tribe of Judah* who fought death and won. As a lion sleeps with its eyes open, Jesus arose from His sleep and walked out of the tomb!

CHAPTER ONE

Mark 1:1 - *The beginning of the gospel of Jesus Christ, the Son of God;*

This opening verse is the title for the rest of Mark's gospel. The *gospel* is the *good news* that the Savior has come into the world to rescue us from ourselves, from sin, from the world, and from Satan. Mark is one of the four narratives that started what we would later call the *Gospels*. Because most all commentators will only mention the Greek word *Euaggelion,* which does mean *good news*, it actually comes from the Hebrew *besorah*, which also means *good news*. The one who proclaims this *good news* is called a *mebaser,* which is the equivalent of *evangelist*. This is where we get the title of *Mark the evangelist*. Mark is announcing that the time has arrived for the *good news*, or the Hebrew *besorah tovah*, that the prophet Isaiah wrote about:

> *How beautiful upon the mountains are the feet of him that bringeth good tidings, that publisheth peace; that bringeth good tidings of*

good, that publisheth salvation; that saith unto
Zion, Thy God reigneth!

Isaiah 52:7

The long-awaited Messiah-King of Israel has arrived! This *good news* will be accomplished by none other than the *Christ*, or *Messiah* of Israel, the *Son of God*. Mark is not shy about stating that the Jewish *Yeshua* is Israel's Messiah, and that He is the second Person of the Triune Godhead. What a revolting way to start his gospel to a Roman audience who had always been told that Caesar was god and savior of the world. The rest of Mark's gospel will be spent exploring and validating his claim. Mark is begging his readers to examine the evidence. He wants them to *wrestle, to ponder, to consider, "Who is this revolutionary figure called Jesus?"* Each of us must answer the question for ourselves.

MINISTRY OF JOHN THE BAPTIST

Mark 1:2-3 - *As it is written in the prophets, Behold, I send my messenger before thy face, which shall prepare thy way before thee. The voice of one crying in the wilderness, Prepare ye the way of the Lord, make his paths straight.*

This is one of the few times that Mark quotes from the Old Testament, but it is a powerful stringing together of different passages from the Hebrew scriptures. In ancient times to search out the scriptures was called *darash*, much like a modern-day preacher will search out a text to fit his sermon. Except in Hebrew thought, the scriptures are inspired by the one true God to connect together in beautiful harmony.

Concerning John the Baptist, the *messenger* that would *prepare the way* for Israel's Messiah, watch how Mark blends these three passages together:

> **Behold, I send an Angel** *(Hebrew = malak, or messenger)* **before thee, to keep thee in <u>the way</u>, and to bring thee into the place which I have prepared.**
>
> Exodus 23:20

> **The voice of him that crieth in the wilderness, <u>Prepare ye the way</u> of the LORD, make straight in the desert a highway for our God.**
>
> Isaiah 40:3

> **Behold, I will send my <u>messenger</u>, and he shall <u>prepare the way</u> before me: and the LORD, whom ye seek, shall suddenly come to his temple, even the messenger of the covenant, whom ye delight in: behold, he shall come, saith the LORD of hosts.**
>
> Malachi 3:1

Keep in mind that in Bible times there were no chapters and verses, so sages would quote a few key words from several passages in order to refer to the larger picture. The forerunner of Israel's Messiah is not only going to *prepare the way* for Israel's Messiah, he is also being validated in the Torah and the Prophets of Israel.

In the Exodus passage God has appointed a messenger to lead the children of Israel from slavery into the Promised Land. The prophet Isaiah connects the distant past to the future announcing that both Israel and the nations will experience a new *Exodus.* Malachi's prophecy presents the darker side, warning Jerusalem that judgment will come if the shepherds of Israel do not welcome their Messiah. Elijah will be the *messenger* before the terrible day of the Lord's second coming, and John the Baptist is in the spirit of Elijah when he announces the first coming of Jesus the Messiah.

This deeper meaning goes even farther regarding John *preparing the way* of the Messiah. The first followers of Jesus were called *"people of the way."*

> **And desired of him letters to Damascus to the synagogues, that if he found any of <u>this way</u>, whether they were men or women, he might bring them bound unto Jerusalem.**
>
> Acts 9:2

One of the criteria for the 12 apostles was that they had heard the ministry of John the Baptist:

> **Beginning from the baptism of John, unto that same day that he was taken up from us, must one be ordained to be a witness with us of his resurrection.**
>
> Acts 1:22

4

John had *prepared the way* for men and women who would be called *"people of the way."* They were also referred to as people who followed *"the way of the Nazarene."* Jesus said that He was *"Haderek" or "The Way."* (John 14:6)

It is absolutely astounding how the sacred scriptures have so many hidden truths.

> **Mark 1:5-8 -** *And there went out unto him all the land of Judaea, and they of Jerusalem, and were all baptized of him in the river of Jordan, confessing their sins. And John was clothed with camel's hair, and with a girdle of a skin about his loins; and he did eat locusts and wild honey; And preached, saying, There cometh one mightier than I after me, the latchet of whose shoes I am not worthy to stoop down and unloose. I indeed have baptized you with water: but he shall baptize you with the Holy Ghost.*

Why did John baptize in water? Because it was a Jewish way of being identified with repentance. His baptism did not save anyone, but it pointed to a greater baptism of the Spirit that could only be given by Jesus the Messiah. Why the Jordan River? * Because it linked the people of Jesus' day with events of deliverance in the Old Testament:

> *And it came to pass, when the people removed from their tents, to pass over Jordan, and the*

*priests bearing the ark of the covenant before
the people; And as they that bare the ark were
come unto Jordan, and the feet of the priests
that bare the ark were dipped in the brim of
the water, (for Jordan overfloweth all his banks
all the time of harvest,) That the waters which
came down from above stood and rose up upon
an heap very far from the city Adam, that
is beside Zaretan: and those that came down
toward the sea of the plain, even the salt sea,
failed, and were cut off: and the people passed
over right against Jericho. And the priests that
bare the ark of the covenant of the LORD stood
firm on dry ground in the midst of Jordan, and
all the Israelites passed over on dry ground,
until all the people were passed clean over
Jordan.* Joshua 3:14-17

*Then went he down, and dipped himself seven
times in Jordan, according to the saying of the
man of God: and his flesh came again like unto
the flesh of a little child, and he was clean.*

2 Kings 5:14

*Every time this passage is read, this author thinks of the
many times he has been blessed to walk close to where John had
his ministry. One is so taken by the barrenness and the seclusion
of the Judean Wilderness. It is amazing that one of the most
powerful preachers the world has ever known was called by God to*

6

announce the coming of Israel's Messiah in such an isolated place. It's a very humbling experience, and it even sifted this writer of the pride in his own life. It's less than 20 miles due east of Jerusalem, descending from over 2,500 feet above sea level to over 1,300 feet below sea level, to the lowest point on planet earth. In Jesus' time this was in the middle of the desert, just north of the Dead Sea. And yet, people were coming from all around to be baptized of John. Why? Because he was a man sent from God, and the Holy Spirit was drawing people to him. The Temple worship in Jerusalem had turned into just ceremonialism, and John was showing that the God of Israel was going to do His kingdom work outside of the religious system of his day. Even though we read about him in the New Testament, John the Baptist was the last and the greatest prophet of the Old Testament.

John's ministry was ordained by God to occur at a specific location where Israel's forefathers had crossed over into the Promised Land. John's clothing is a clear reminder of the powerful prophet Elijah's clothing and the place where Elijah ascended to heaven:

> **And they answered him, He was an hairy man, and girt with a girdle of leather about his loins. And he said, It is Elijah the Tishbite.**
>
> 2 Kings 1:8

> **And Elijah said unto him, Tarry, I pray thee, here; for the LORD hath sent me to Jordan. And he said, As the LORD liveth, and as thy soul liveth, I will not leave thee. And they two went**

7

on. And fifty men of the sons of the prophets went, and stood to view afar off: and they two stood by Jordan. And Elijah took his mantle, and wrapped it together, and smote the waters, and they were divided hither and thither, so that they two went over on dry ground. And it came to pass, when they were gone over, that Elijah said unto Elisha, Ask what I shall do for thee, before I be taken away from thee. And Elisha said, I pray thee, let a double portion of thy spirit be upon me. And he said, Thou hast asked a hard thing: nevertheless, if thou see me when I am taken from thee, it shall be so unto thee; but if not, it shall not be so. And it came to pass, as they still went on, and talked, that, behold, there appeared a chariot of fire, and horses of fire, and parted them both asunder; and Elijah went up by a whirlwind into heaven.

2 Kings 2:6-11

"he did eat locusts and wild honey" – John's ministry highlighted his renunciation of worldly comforts. Scholars have debated if the locusts were pods from the carob tree or if they were real insects. While we cannot be certain about the carob tree, there was an insect that was kosher to eat in the Torah:

Even these of them ye may eat; the locust after his kind, and the bald locust after his kind, and the beetle after his kind, and the grasshopper after his kind.

Leviticus 11:22

Removing and carrying sandals was a menial task reserved for slaves. John's humility is seen in the fact that he considered himself unworthy to even perform a slave's task for the coming Messiah. Jesus, the Son of God, not only became human flesh, but His precious feet were placed in sandals made from animal skins. He wanted to be identified with humanity in every way. He clothed Himself with human nature in the incarnation, and the mystery was so mysterious that not even John was worthy to unfasten His sandals.

THE BAPTISM OF JESUS

Mark 1:9-11 - *And it came to pass in those days, that Jesus came from Nazareth of Galilee, and was baptized of John in Jordan. And straightway coming up out of the water, he saw the heavens opened, and the Spirit like a dove descending upon him: And there came a voice from heaven, saying, Thou art my beloved Son, in whom I am well pleased.*

Depending on which way Jesus walked, it was between 70-80 miles from Nazareth to where John was baptizing.

9

Jesus couldn't be baptized by just anyone; it had to be the *messenger* who was foretold. The sinless Christ was baptized? Yes, to be identified with us poor sinners. The immersion of Jesus in the Jordan River would also be a symbol of His own death, burial, and resurrection.

"he saw the heavens open" – The meaning here is much greater than a translation of the Bible can convey. The same verb is used depicting the tearing of the Temple veil in **Mark 15:38**:

> *And the veil of the temple was rent in twain from the top to the bottom.*

It was a *tearing open* of heaven itself. Notice what Isaiah said centuries before:

> *Oh that thou wouldest rend the heavens, that thou wouldest come down, that the mountains might flow down at thy presence,* Isaiah 64:1

"the Spirit like a dove descending upon him"– This imagery connects us to various associations in the Old Testament.

> *And the earth was without form, and void; and darkness was upon the face of the deep. And the Spirit of God moved upon the face of the waters.*
> Genesis 1:2

And he stayed yet other seven days; and again he sent forth the dove out of the ark; And the dove came in to him in the evening; and, lo, in her mouth was an olive leaf pluckt off: so Noah knew that the waters were abated from off the earth. And he stayed yet other seven days; and sent forth the dove; which returned not again unto him any more.

Genesis 8:10–12

Behold, thou art fair, my love; behold, thou art fair; thou hast doves' eyes.

Song of Solomon 1:15

Just like the Spirit of God that fluttered over creation in Genesis, bringing about a new creation, the Spirit of God came upon Jesus in the Jordan River inaugurating another new beginning for the world. Every person that embraced Jesus would be made new creatures by the same Holy Spirit that moved upon the Son of God. Wow!

"And there came a voice from heaven, saying, Thou art my beloved Son, in whom I am well pleased" – The voice of the *Father*, the baptism of the *Son*, and the descent of the *Holy Spirit* give us the revelation of the Triune Godhead. How could anyone deny this powerful truth?

Again, Mark is alluding to three different passages of scripture from the Old Testament:

I will declare the decree: the LORD hath said unto me, <u>Thou art my</u> Son; this day have I begotten thee.

Psalm 2:7

And he said, Take now thy son, thine only son Isaac, <u>whom thou</u> <u>lovest</u>, and get thee into the land of Moriah; and offer him there for a burnt offering upon one of the mountains which I will tell thee of.

Genesis 22:2

Behold my servant, whom I uphold; mine elect, <u>in whom my soul</u> <u>delighteth</u>; I have put my spirit upon him: he shall bring forth judgment to the Gentiles.

Isaiah 42:1

TEMPTATION OF JESUS

Mark 1:12-13 - *And immediately the Spirit driveth him into the wilderness. And he was there in the wilderness forty days, tempted of Satan; and was with the wild beasts; and the angels ministered unto him.*

The same Holy Spirit that gently descended upon the Messiah in the Jordan River now *drives* Him westward into the Judean wilderness. ★ The temptation of Jesus takes on a deeper meaning when we understand that before He

12

could start His public ministry in the Galilee, He had to go through a time of testing as a Man against the adversary Satan.

The Jordan River flows into the Dead Sea and is the present-day border between Israel and the country of Jordan. Going back west a few miles is the city of Jericho that gives way to the Judean mountains. They create over 15 miles of golden desert as they ascend to Jerusalem. Somewhere not far from Jericho is believed to be the place where the Spirit drove Jesus to be tempted by the devil. Today one can see a Greek Monastery on a high mountain over 1,200 feet high overlooking Jericho that is traditionally called The Mount of Temptation. The monastery was originally built in the fourth century by a monk named Saint Chariton, and is called the Lavra of Douka. A lavra-type monastery is a cluster of caves normally with the main church in the center.

The *first Adam* was tempted and fell, bringing sin into the human race. Jesus was the *last Adam* who would be tempted, but would resist the devil and restore mankind back to the Creator. The *first Adam* was tempted in a place where there were animals, and the *last Adam* was tempted among the wild beasts.

The people of Israel were led into the wilderness for 40 years of testing, and they did not follow the ways of the Lord. That generation would not enter into the Promised Land. Yeshua, *the Greater Israel,* was led into the wilderness for 40 days, and He would be obedient to the Father's will. His temptation took place within the Promised Land. Being tempted by Satan would initiate an extended campaign against demons, disease, and eventually against death that was brought into the world by Satan.

The temptation of the Messiah would also give the disciples and future followers of Jesus the example of how to overcome the devil. By staying in God's Holy Word and having no desire for the things of this world, we can be overcomers. Satan tempts us the same way he tempted Jesus: by the flesh, pride, and the world. We should not be surprised that after we start on our spiritual journey, we will be more aggressively attacked by the enemy.

THE TIME IS FULFILLED

> **Mark 1:14-15 -** *Now after that John was put in prison, * Jesus came into Galilee, preaching the gospel of the kingdom of God, And saying, The time is fulfilled, and the kingdom of God is at hand: repent ye, and believe the gospel.*

This marks a pivotal event turning the focus on the earthly ministry of the Messiah. Jesus could not begin His ministry some 70 miles north in the Galilee until John's ministry was completed.

"Accordingly John was sent as a prisoner, out of Herod's suspicious temper, to Macherus, the castle I already mentioned, and was put to death."* **(18.119, Jewish War, the Jewish Antiquities, Flavius Josephus) *This fortified castle was located on a hill just 16 miles south of where the Jordan River flows into the Dead Sea, on the present-day Jordanian side.*

Mark uses the term *kingdom of God,* while Matthew used the term the *kingdom of heaven.* The *kingdom of heaven* was synonymous with the *kingdom of God* when writing to a Jewish audience. But Mark was writing to a Gentile audience and did not want them to miss the meaning. The time had arrived for God's rule to be in the hearts of all of those who would *repent and believe the gospel.* This belief in Jesus as the Messiah, the Son of God, would bring God's spiritual kingdom ★ into their lives.

★The physical kingdom would be offered to Israel, but the all-knowing God of the universe knew that they would reject Jesus as their Messiah, and the physical kingdom would be delayed. But this was all part of the plan in the gospel leaving Israel and going to the Gentiles. **(Romans 9–11)**

THE FISHERMEN OF GALILEE

Mark 1:16-20 - *Now as he walked by the sea of Galilee, he saw Simon and Andrew his brother casting a net into the sea: for they were fishers. And Jesus said unto them, Come ye after me, and I will make you to become fishers of men. And straightway they forsook their nets, and followed him. And when he had gone a little farther thence, he saw James the son of Zebedee, and John his brother, who also were in the ship mending their nets. And straightway he called them: and they left*

their father Zebedee in the ship with the hired
servants, and went after him.

So now the scene moves north to the shoreline of the Sea of Galilee outside the fishing village of Capernaum. ★ Jesus deliberately chooses men of modest education to prove to the world that God's wisdom is wiser than men. **(I Cor.1:20-21)** The breaking away immediately from their father Zebedee, the hired servants, and their fishing business showed the power in the call of Jesus. The call of Jesus surpasses the desire of all worldly pursuits.

★*There is much more to this calling of Jesus than to just two sets of brothers, Simon and Andrew, and James and John. When we study the other gospel accounts we can fill in with some of the background that Mark leaves out. Peter and Andrew were from Bethsaida,* **(John 1:44),** *which was about seven miles from Capernaum on the other side of the lake, in the territory of Herod Philip. Bethsaida was later raised from a village to a city in 30AD. James and John were also fishermen in Capernaum, in the territory of Herod Antipas. Scholars speculate that they were all in the fishing business together because the taxes on the fish that were caught on the other side might be less, since Bethsaida was only a village. We do not know all of the specifics as to where they paid their taxes on the fish, either in the territory of Herod Antipas (Naphthali) or Herod Philip (Gaulanitis), but the Jewish fishermen may have been avoiding some Roman taxes any way they could. After some time, Peter married a girl from Capernaum, and they relocated. Peter and Andrew lived in the same house in Capernaum.* **(Mark 1:29)** *But all of this was happening at the*

16

right time, because Jesus' earthly ministry headquarters would be in Capernaum, which was on the major trade route, the Via Maris, that ran from Damascus, Syria, to Cairo, Egypt. When we carefully study the other three gospels, we see that Mark's account of Jesus calling them to be a disciple came <u>after</u> they had heard the ministry of John the Baptist, and after they had witnessed some of Jesus' first miracles. So this was not the first time they saw Jesus. This was the call to be one of His closest disciples.

JESUS CAST DEMONS OUT IN CAPERNAUM

Mark 1:21-28 - *And they went into Capernaum; * and straightway on the sabbath day * he entered into the synagogue, * and taught. And they were astonished at his doctrine: for he taught them as one that had authority, and not as the scribes. And there was in their synagogue a man with an unclean spirit; and he cried out, Saying, Let us alone; what have we to do with thee, thou Jesus of Nazareth? art thou come to destroy us? I know thee who thou art, the Holy One of God. And Jesus rebuked him, saying, Hold thy peace, and come out of him. And when the unclean spirit had torn him, and cried with a loud voice, he came out of him. And they were all amazed, insomuch that they questioned among themselves, saying, What thing is this? what new doctrine is this? for with authority commandeth he even the*

unclean spirits, and they do obey him. And immediately his fame spread abroad throughout all the region round about Galilee.

Capernaum in Hebrew is, "Kefar Nachum" which means, "Village of Comfort." It was a seaside village on the northern shore of the Sea of Galilee during the time of Jesus' earthly ministry. The population was less than 2,000, and was a Jewish village under Roman occupation. Capernaum commanded a beautiful view of the lake and was a natural harbor for the fishing industry. It was also a village that enjoyed heavy traffic from caravans passing through on the Via Maris that skirted just north of the village. Capernaum was surrounded by fertile fields that sloped down to the Sea of Galilee. These fields provided wheat, barley, olives, figs, as well as vineyards. The village was also noted for olive oil production, and several olive presses have been discovered from Jesus' time. Less than a mile away there were seven springs that poured into the sea that attracted large schools of fish.

Bargil Pixner, a Franciscan archaeologist, discovered the remains of a Roman military garrison at Capernaum. The Roman garrison was probably supervised by the Roman Centurion in **Luke 7:1-10**, *who showed great faith in Jesus. Because Capernaum was a border town, there was a tax station there, and Herod Antipas, the tetrarch, lived across the lake in Tiberias.*

This was not just another day in everyday Jewish life; it was the Sabbath Day. A reverent hush fell over the little village as even the morning sun shown differently across the water. The fishermen were not cleaning their nets, and there were no hammers and chisels sounding in the streets. The animals were in the stalls and pastures.

There was no hustle in the market places and no women grinding at the mills. This was the day when the voices of men and women were occupied with prayers and scripture reading.

★Synagogues were started during the Babylonian captivity because the religious Jews were away from their homeland. The synagogues were no substitute for the Temple in Jerusalem, but did provide a Jewish place for worship on the Sabbath Day. They could be started with only ten men (a minyan), and they got that idea from Abraham asking God not to destroy Sodom and Gomorrah if there were only ten righteous people. **(Gen.18:32–33)** *The earliest archaeological evidence was found in Egypt from the third century BC. Synagogues were all over Israel during Jesus' earthly ministry and were the center of Jewish life for civil and religious affairs.*

In Capernaum today there stands the remains of a white limestone synagogue that sits on a black basalt foundation. Interesting! Most guides and scholars believe the white synagogue was built in the third or fourth century over the original, first-century foundation. After doing research and discussing this with some retired guides over the years, it is a possibility that the white limestone synagogue was built by the Roman Centurion in **Luke 7:5**. *This is why it is recorded in the gospels; it was a very unusual act for a Roman Centurion to build a Jewish synagogue. Major earthquakes from 32 AD (crucifixion of Jesus), 115 AD, and 363 AD destroyed the synagogue, and it was later reconstructed. The large stones had to be quarried miles away from the top of Mount Arbel. It took someone who had the resources and authority to chisel those stones and bring them on a cart all the way down to Capernaum. The problem with teaching that the synagogue was* *built in the later centuries is that there are no Christian symbols anywhere on the capitals or relief carvings. The only symbols that have been found are Roman and Jewish. All worship buildings built in the Byzantine period had crosses and other Christian symbols from that period. This is an ongoing debate among scholars.*

The teaching of our Master brought strange looks on the faces of the people because He taught them as one having authority, unlike what they had been used to hearing from the scribes. The people were used to hearing the same repetitive prayers and interpretations from different rabbis. The teaching of the Master was so powerful and so authentic that it brought out the violent sound of a demon-possessed man. Because the places of worship were not following in the true ways of the God of Israel, the demons found refuge there. If they had been proclaiming the scriptures in the power of the Holy Spirit, the demons would not have been there. Not only did the demons, *plural*, know who Jesus was, they obeyed His Words and came out of the man. No lengthy incantations, no odorous roots to expel the demons; Jesus simply commands the unclean spirits and they leave. Wow!

"Jesus rebuked him, saying, Hold thy peace" - Jesus did not want the demons to declare who He was because of two reasons: 1) *It was not the ordained time for Jesus to go to Jerusalem* and 2) *Jesus, the sinless Christ, did not want demons from hell declaring who He was.* This Sabbath-Day would not be forgotten, and the events are even recorded in the golden pages of the Holy Bible. The fame of Jesus spread immediately around the Galilee. The region and the world would never be the same.

JESUS HEALS PETER'S MOTHER-IN-LAW

> **Mark 1:29-31** - *And forthwith, when they were come out of the synagogue, they entered into the house of Simon and Andrew, with James and John. But Simon's wife's mother lay sick of a fever, and anon they tell him of her. And he came and took her by the hand, and lifted her up; and immediately the fever left her, and she ministered unto them.*

Simon Peter's house * was less than 200 feet just south of the synagogue, not far from the shoreline of the Sea of Galilee. Notice that Simon and Andrew both lived in the same house. The scriptures do not tell us about wives of any of the other disciples, but we do know that Peter was married, and this was also mentioned in the letters of the apostle Paul.

> *Have we not power to lead about a sister, a wife, as well as other apostles, and as the brethren of the Lord, and Cephas?*
> I Corinthians 9:5

The fifth century remains of an octagonal Byzantine church was discovered over what is believed to be the house of Simon Peter. Underneath the little church was the foundation of a simple, first-century dwelling of several rooms with a courtyard in the center. Italian excavators tell us that the original had coarse walls and a ceiling made of earth and straw. This house was probably the scene for many of the miracles and teachings of Jesus our Lord that were written in the gospels. Peter's house became one of the first places of worship for some of the Jewish Christians in the first century. Over 100 graffiti were found on the walls with words like "Lord Jesus Christ help thy servant" and "Christ have mercy." They were written in Syriac, Greek, and Hebrew. Peter's name was also found on the walls. There is no strong evidence of the name of Peter's wife, but the possible names of Concordia and Perpetua were mentioned in the following centuries. There is a rather solid legend that Peter had one daughter named Petronilla.

Our Catholic friends have a serious problem with this passage because they teach that Peter was the first Pope, and the Pope cannot have a wife. So they just try to ignore these verses. But our Lord Jesus certainly placed His approval on marriage many times.

Peter's mother-in-law had a distinct fever that was not like the fever that people get today from various illnesses. In the times of Jesus it was referred to as a *"fire"* and led to physical death most of the time. Jesus has just rebuked the demons out of a man while in the synagogue a few feet away, and the same day one touch from the Master sends a fiery fever immediately out of a woman.

Jesus also stayed in Peter's house while He lived in Capernaum. Try to imagine how this family must have felt when they lay down to sleep that night knowing the Lord of glory was in their house! Wow!

THE STREETS OF CAPERNAUM

> **Mark 1:32-34 -** *And at even, when the sun did set, they brought unto him all that were diseased, and them that were possessed with devils. And all the city was gathered together at the door. And he healed many that were sick of divers diseases, and cast out many devils; and suffered not the devils to speak, because they knew him.*

After the sunset on that particular Sabbath, the streets of Capernaum were filled with sick and demon-possessed people. It was a gathering in the little village like the people had never seen before. Diseases and mental illness were very common in Jesus' time, many times caused by demonic powers. Galilee was a long way from the modern cities of Rome where there were educated physicians or hospitals. The village people had to cope with things like poor sanitation, dysentery, and bacteria in the drinking water. The common thing to do was use herbs, poultices, wine, and olive oil, but this would help only temporarily. But that evening in Capernaum the people met the Great Physician!

JESUS PRAYING AND PREACHING

> **Mark 1:35-39 -** *And in the morning, rising up a great while before day, he went out, and departed into a solitary place, and there*

prayed. And Simon and they that were with him followed after him. And when they had found him, they said unto him, All men seek for thee. And he said unto them, Let us go into the next towns, that I may preach there also: for therefore came I forth. And he preached in their synagogues throughout all Galilee, and cast out devils.

Before the sun came up ★ our Lord Yeshua rose and slipped out of the house and found a *solitary* place to pray somewhere up in the mountains north of Capernaum. As a Man, Jesus knew the importance of praying to the Father before starting another busy day. He knew the needs of the people were overwhelming, and He wanted to be focused on the Father's will before the day started. This writer has often thought about how Jesus would have prayed, but a lot can be said about Him walking to a private place to get away from the people.

★To be effective in God's kingdom, we all need time away from others and time spent with the Lord. There have been many times over the years while leading a group in the Galilee, that the same sunrise was seen over the Golan Heights. My heart would be moved deeply when talking to the Lord before starting our daily pilgrimage around the Sea of Galilee. One does not have to be in Israel to enjoy those quite times with our Lord. A public witness for Christ is much more powerful after a private talk with the Lord.

The hills command a beautiful view of the lake just before the golden sun creeps over the Golan Heights. Local tradition says that Jesus often withdrew to a place called the *Eremos Cave*, which is about a mile away, the same area where He gave the Sermon on the Mount. The cragginess of the hillside there was uncultivated and enabled our Lord to gather large crowds without causing damage to the farmland.

When Simon Peter and his family arose, they realized that Jesus was gone, they hurried to find Jesus. After they found where Jesus was, they wanted Him to know that everyone was searching to find Him. After that revolutionary, life-changing Sabbath Day, the common people wanted to be where Jesus was.

From Bethsaida and Chorazin to the east, to Tabgha, Gennesaret, and Magdala to the west, and other towns in the Galilee, Jesus and His disciples start walking. Wherever there was a Jewish synagogue, Jesus would preach and cast out demons. The words that Isaiah wrote centuries before were being fulfilled:

> *Nevertheless the dimness shall not be such as was in her vexation, when at the first he lightly afflicted the land of Zebulun and the land of Naphtali, and afterward did more grievously afflict her by the way of the sea, beyond Jordan, in Galilee of the nations. The people that walked in darkness have seen a great light: they that dwell in the land of the shadow of death, upon them hath the light shined.*
>
> Isaiah 9:1-2

THE LEPER AND THE CROWDS

Mark 1:40–45 – *And there came a leper to him, beseeching him, and kneeling down to him, and saying unto him, If thou wilt, thou canst make me clean. And Jesus, moved with compassion, put forth his hand, and touched him, and saith unto him, I will; be thou clean. And as soon as he had spoken, immediately the leprosy departed from him, and he was cleansed. And he straitly charged him, and forthwith sent him away; And saith unto him, See thou say nothing to any man: but go thy way, shew thyself to the priest, and offer for thy cleansing those things which Moses commanded, for a testimony unto them. But he went out, and began to publish it much, and to blaze abroad the matter, insomuch that Jesus could no more openly enter into the city, but was without in desert places: and they came to him from every quarter.*

We must not confuse the modern day *leprosy*, or Hansen's disease, with the biblical condition of leprosy. In the Old Testament it was called *tsara'ath,* which is a ritualistic word for various types of uncleanness, defilement, skin, clothes, and certain stones. This Hebrew term is used over two dozen times in the Old Testament. The New Testament term is the Greek *aphe lepras*, and when Jerome translated the Bible into Latin in 383AD, he used the word *leprosy*. This is where we got the idea that all *leprosy* was the same type. It is believed that the *leprosy* in Jesus' time was a different type than in Moses' time. Many scholars believe that this type was brought into Israel by Alexander the Great's army in the fourth century BC from other countries. So we cannot be certain that the Old Testament definition for *leprosy* is the same as the New Testament. The most important thing that we need to know is that this kind of *leprosy* in Jesus' time was still considered *unclean* and could not be allowed in the Jewish community. Even if the physical condition was not contagious, the spiritual uncleanness was certainly contagious. Study **Leviticus 13-14** to see the ritual impurity of *leprosy*.

No one could *touch* a leper, otherwise they would become *unclean* themselves. But the Holy Christ touched this *unclean leper* and made the *leper clean*! Jesus reaches across the great religious divide and does what no one else could do. Jesus knew that He could heal any disease, but He was even more concerned about restoring a person to the joy of life that He created everyone to have. What compassion! What love! Dear reader, Jesus wants to restore you so you can have the abundant life that He came to give you!

Here once again we find the *messianic secret;* **"See thou say nothing to any man."** Jesus told the leper not to tell anyone, but the leper could not control himself. It doesn't say if the healed leper went to the priests like Jesus told him to do, but he began to run across the hills of Galilee showing people that his leprosy was gone. The Galileans thought that leprosy was incurable, and this carpenter from

Nazareth has just healed a leper! People started running out of the houses and villages to see the whereabouts of this man Jesus. Jesus could no longer be seen publicly in the streets of the cities because of the press, but people began to follow Him even in the deserted places. There was only a small window of time for Jesus to do His work before going to the cross in Jerusalem, and now He would have to carefully select His time and places to teach and to perform miracles. The cleansing of the leper was a major transition in the multitudes coming to Jesus.

CHAPTER TWO

Jesus Heals and Forgives

Mark 2:1-12 – *And again he entered into Capernaum after some days; and it was noised that he was in the house. And straightway many were gathered together, insomuch that there was no room to receive them, no, not so much as about the door: and he preached the word unto them. And they come unto him, bringing one sick of the palsy, which was borne of four. And when they could not come nigh unto him for the press, they uncovered the roof where he was: and when they had broken it up, they let down the bed wherein the sick of the palsy lay. When Jesus saw their faith, he said unto the sick of the palsy, Son, thy sins be forgiven thee. But there was certain of the scribes sitting there, and reasoning in their hearts, Why doth this man thus speak blasphemies? who can forgive sins but God only? And immediately* *when Jesus perceived in his spirit that they so reasoned within themselves, he said unto them, Why reason ye these things in your hearts? Whether is it easier to say to the sick of the palsy, Thy sins be forgiven thee; or to say, Arise, and take up thy bed, and walk? But that ye may know that the Son of man hath power on earth to forgive sins, (he saith to the sick of the palsy,) I say unto thee, Arise, and take up thy bed, and go thy way into thine house. And immediately he arose, took up the bed, and went forth before them all; insomuch that they were all amazed, and glorified God, saying, We never saw it on this fashion.*

Mark continues to prove that Jesus is truly the Messiah of Israel through His miracles. This miracle is truly messianic and is so important that it is recorded in three of the four gospel accounts.

"it was noised that he was in the house" – This is believed to be the house of Simon Peter. Because the cleansed leper had blazed it abroad about Jesus healing power, the people were searching anywhere and everywhere to know where Jesus was. When they heard that He was back in *the* house, there was standing room only, even outside the house. This miracle of our Lord holds so many truths that this writer has decided to list some of the major points of interest so we can understand things more clearly.

<u>Roof</u> - In Jesus' time they used the flat roofs of their

houses as much as they did the bottom floor. While they did place earth and straw on the very top of the roof, they had to place strong support underneath. They were commanded under Jewish law to make sure that the roof was fortified to keep others from falling and being held accountable for their death.

> *When thou buildest a new house, then thou shalt make a battlement for thy roof, that thou bring not blood upon thine house, if any man fall from thence.*
>
> Deuteronomy 22:8

There were many things that happened on the *roofs* in the Old Testament. Examples of one positive and one negative follow. Let's start with the time *Rahab* hid the two spies coming into the Promised Land.

> *But she had brought them up to the roof of the house, and hid them with the stalks of flax, which she had laid in order upon the roof.*
>
> Joshua 2:6

Israel was condemned and punished for worshipping the pagan god Baal from the tops of their roofs. When king David committed adultery, it all started from his roof.

> *And the Chaldeans, that fight against this city, shall come and set fire on this city, and burn it with the houses, upon whose roofs they have*

offered incense unto Baal, and poured out drink offerings unto other gods, to provoke me to anger.

Jeremiah 32:29

And it came to pass in an eveningtide, that David arose from off his bed, and walked upon the roof of the king's house: and from the roof he saw a woman washing herself; and the woman was very beautiful to look upon.

2 Samuel 11:2

The reason these Old Testament stories are mentioned is because that helps us better understand that *roofs* were a very important part of everyday Jewish life. And during this miracle of Christ, they had to take off the earth and straw and tear open the fortified timbers and tiles in order to get the palsied man down to Jesus. It wasn't as simple as one might think.

<u>*Reason*</u> - **(Mark 2:4)** The reason why they went to so much trouble was because these men had the faith that if they could only get their friend to Jesus, he would be healed. They knew if Jesus could cleanse a leper, he could certainly take care of a crippled man.

<u>*Remedy*</u> - **(Mark 2:5, 9-11)** The remedy was found when Jesus *saw* their faith and made the revolutionary announcement, **"Son, thy sins be forgiven thee."** Not only did Jesus heal this man physically, He healed him of his sinful condition. Jesus used this miracle to show what power

He possessed. Think of Mark writing to the believers in Rome where forgiveness of sins was never mentioned in the Roman mind. Rome had the goddess *Clementia* who offered clemency, but the idea of *sin* and being forgiven for your sins was unthinkable. This miracle showed that Jesus the Messiah could do what no pagan god could do.

Religion - **(Mark 2:6-7)** The scribes said, ***"Who can forgive sins but God only?"*** In the Jewish religious view of Jesus' time, only the God of the Old Testament could forgive sins. Here are a few examples:

> ***Who forgiveth all thine iniquities; who healeth all thy diseases;*** Psalm 103:3

> ***I, even I, am he that blotteth out thy transgressions for mine own sake, and will not remember thy sins.*** Isaiah 43:25

Blasphemy was a capital crime in ancient Israel.

> ***And he that blasphemeth the name of the LORD, he shall surely be put to death, and all the congregation shall certainly stone him: as well the stranger, as he that is born in the land, when he blasphemeth the name of the Lord, shall be put to death.*** Leviticus 24:16

Redeemer - **(Mark 2:8-11)** Jesus knew the inward thoughts of the religious leaders. Jesus was showing through this miracle and forgiving this man of his sins that

He was the God of the Old Testament, the long-awaited Messiah that the prophets had written about who had come to His people. Wow! Think about the Jewish believers in the church at Rome who were going through severe persecution. Mark was comforting them with the profound truth that *Yeshua* truly was the Jewish Messiah!

Results - **(Mark 2:11-12)** Jesus demonstrated His power to heal and to forgive by asking the man to ***"Arise, take up thy bed, and walk."*** This healed and forgiven man took up his bed and walked back to his own house. He walked before the crowd of people so they could see clearly that he was a walking miracle.

Response - **(Mark 2:12)** *"amazed, and glorified God, we never saw it on this fashion."* The people had never heard a man say *"thy sins be forgiven thee."* This miracle also connects us to the signs of the *Messianic Kingdom*:

> ***Then shall the lame man leap as an hart, and the tongue of the dumb sing: for in the wilderness shall waters break out, and streams in the desert.***
>
> Isaiah 35:6

The Call of Levi (Matthew)

> **Mark 2:13-14 - *And he went forth again by the sea side; and all the multitude resorted unto him, and he taught them. And as he passed by, he saw Levi * the son of Alphaeus * sitting***

34

**at the receipt of custom, and said unto him,
Follow me. And he arose and followed him.**

*Levi was not a chief publican like Zacchaeus in **Luke 19**, *but he was working across the Sea of Galilee from Tiberias, the capital of Galilee in those days. Herod Antipas, the tetrarch of Galilee, had a custom station in Capernaum because it was on the border of the territory of Trachonitis where his brother Herod Philip ruled. The Via Maris went just north of Capernaum as well, so Levi was collecting taxes from everyone who passed out of and into Herod Antipas's domain.*

*Alphaeus comes through translating the Aramaic name into Greek and then into English. Alphaeus was the father of two of Jesus' disciples, Matthew and James. **(Mark 3:18)** *Alphaeus is also believed to be the same person as Cleophas in* **Luke 24:18** and **John 19:25.**

The remains of a small harbor were discovered underwater at Capernaum where the little ships would bring in their fish. Somewhere close by is where Jesus was walking when He called *Levi*, or also called *Matthew*, the tax collector. Jewish sources call him *"Mattityahu Levi."* What a contradiction of terms! Being a descendant from the tribe of Levi, and then becoming a tax collector must have brought many terrible nicknames and slanderous remarks from the village people. It was a despicable job! Here are three reasons:

*   *Tax collectors were ritually defiled with being in contact with the pagan Gentiles*

* *Tax Collectors Were Considered Traitors To Israel By Working For Rome*
* *Tax Collectors Were Guilty Of Extortion, Collecting More Than What Was Due*

But there was something that Jesus saw in *Levi* that could be great for God's kingdom. Jesus wanted to call this tax collector while there was a multitude of people listening. There was no doubt that *Levi* had heard about the miracles of Jesus in Capernaum. His heart had already been stirred about what was going on in the little seaside village. The call of Jesus was so strong that *Levi* immediately arose from working for Herod and starting working for Jesus. Hallelujah! *Levi* would not only become one of the 12 disciples, he would leave his gospel of *Matthew* that would be the first book of the New Testament and help to change the course of the world. Once we feel this divine call, our paradigms change and our pathway in life changes as well.

Jesus Eating with Publicans and Sinners

> **Mark 2:15-20 -** *And it came to pass, that, as Jesus sat at meat in his house, many publicans and sinners sat also together with Jesus and his disciples: for there were many, and they followed him. And when the scribes and Pharisees saw him eat with publicans and sinners, they said unto his disciples, How is it that he eateth and drinketh with publicans and sinners? When*

Jesus heard it, he saith unto them, They that are whole have no need of the physician, but they that are sick: I came not to call the righteous, but sinners to repentance. And the disciples of John and of the Pharisees used to fast: and they come and say unto him, Why do the disciples of John and of the Pharisees fast, but thy disciples fast not? And Jesus said unto them, Can the children of the bridechamber fast, while the bridegroom is with them? as long as they have the bridegroom with them, they cannot fast. But the days will come, when the bridegroom shall be taken away from them, and then shall they fast in those days.

It was the *compassion* of our Lord that healed the leper, forgave the man with the palsy, called Levi, and started eating with what the religious leaders called *publicans and sinners*. Eating and drinking with people was considered to be personal acceptance and mutual friendship in Jesus' time. But Jesus was violating the standards of the Pharisees.

"They that are whole have no need of the physician, but they that are sick: I am come not to call the righteous, but sinners to repentance" - Jesus did not come to avoid the sinners, but to call them into His service. Jesus came to transform people's lives and to bring in the New Covenant:

Behold, the days come, saith the LORD, that I will make a new covenant with the house of Israel, and with the house of Judah: Not according to the covenant that I made with their fathers in the day that I took them by the hand to bring them out of the land of Egypt; which my covenant they brake, although I was an husband unto them, saith the LORD: But this shall be the covenant that I will make with the house of Israel; After those days, saith the LORD, I will put my law in their inward parts, and write it in their hearts; and will be their God, and they shall be my people. And they shall teach no more every man his neighbour, and every man his brother, saying, Know the LORD: for they shall all know me, from the least of them unto the greatest of them, saith the LORD: for I will forgive their iniquity, and I will remember their sin no more.

Jeremiah 31:31–34

The scribes and Pharisees were not ready to receive their Messiah. They wanted to live in isolation from the rest of the world. Jesus the Messiah came not only for the lost sheep of the house of Israel, but for the Gentiles as well. This was a radical and revolutionary moment in the life of Israel.

"Why do the disciples of John and of the Pharisees fast, but thy disciples fast not?" – Non-followers of Jesus do not rejoice when others are being changed by the love of God,

but are always looking for ways to judge and criticize. Jesus uses marital imagery to reveal who He was.

"And Jesus said unto them, Can the children of the bridechamber fast, while the bridegroom is with them? as long as they have the bridegroom with them, they cannot fast. But the days will come, when the bridegroom shall be taken away from them, and then shall they fast in those days" - Jesus is identifying Himself as the *bridegroom* who is married to Israel in the Old Covenant and will be married to His church in the New Covenant. **(Jeremiah 3:20, Eph.5:25)**

Fasting symbolizes mourning, and while the disciples were with their *bridegroom,* it was a time for rejoicing. A Jewish wedding was the most festive event in everyday Jewish life, and Jesus wanted His followers to be joyful. There would come a time when the *bridegroom* would be taken away, and then they could fast, but not now!

What it must have been like to have seen Jesus the Son of God, but also to have been able to sit down and eat with Him! What a day that will be! We must all watch and be mindful that religion tries to take away our joy, while Jesus gives us true joy.

Parable of the Cloth and the Bottles

> **Mark 2:21-22 -** *No man also seweth a piece of new cloth on an old garment: else the new piece that filled it up taketh away from the old, and the rent is made worse. And no man putteth*

*new wine into old bottles: else the new wine
doth burst the bottles, and the wine is spilled,
and the bottles will be marred: but new wine
must be put into new bottles.*

The religious leaders were patching up their religious lives in order to look good in front of the people. But Jesus is saying that He has to start with a *new cloth* and *new bottles*. The people in God's kingdom do not consist of repaired or reformed lives, but a transformation into a new life. Jesus was calling people like tax collectors, lepers, and demon-possessed who knew they needed a new beginning. They were ready to hear the message of repentance that Jesus was giving. The religious leaders thought they were righteous by outward ceremonialism. We must come to the end of our old selves before Jesus can make us new!

What comforting words these must have been to the believers in Rome to whom Mark was writing to. The believing Jews who were away from their homeland didn't need to feel like they had to be a part of the religious system in Jerusalem to be saved. They needed to know that the Jewish religion within itself was not the answer. It had hindered many of their ancestors from knowing that Jesus was the Messiah when He came to Israel. The Gentile believers needed to know that while they came out of paganism, Jesus takes people and gives them a new beginning.

Jesus is the Lord of the Sabbath

> **Mark 2:23-28** - *And it came to pass, that he went through the corn fields on the sabbath day; and his disciples began, as they went, to pluck the ears of corn. And the Pharisees said unto him, Behold, why do they on the sabbath day that which is not lawful? And he said unto them, Have ye never read what David did, when he had need, and was an hungred, he, and they that were with him? How he went into the house of God in the days of Abiathar the high priest, and did eat the shewbread, which is not lawful to eat but for the priests, and gave also to them which were with him? And he said unto them, The sabbath was made for man, and not man for the sabbath: Therefore the Son of man is Lord also of the sabbath.*

The Torah did permit the Israelites to pluck a *qamah*, or a *stalk of grain*.

> *When thou comest into the standing corn of thy neighbour, then thou mayest pluck the ears with thine hand; but thou shalt not move a sickle unto thy neighbour's standing corn.*
> Deuteronomy 23:25

The Pharisees were condemning Jesus and His disciples for plucking the grain on the *Sabbath Day*.

41

> *Six days thou shalt work, but on the seventh day thou shalt rest: in earing time and in harvest thou shalt rest.*
>
> Exodus 34:21

"Have ye never read" – This was a stinging insult to the supposedly educated Pharisees. Jesus recalls a passage concerning the life of king David.

> *Then came David to Nob to Ahimelech the priest: and Ahimelech was afraid at the meeting of David, and said unto him, Why art thou alone, and no man with thee? And David said unto Ahimelech the priest, The king hath commanded me a business, and hath said unto me, Let no man know any thing of the business whereabout I send thee, and what I have commanded thee: and I have appointed my servants to such and such a place. Now therefore what is under thine hand? give me five loaves of bread in mine hand, or what there is present. And the priest answered David, and said, There is no common bread under mine hand, but there is hallowed bread; if the young men have kept themselves at least from women. And David answered the priest, and said unto him, Of a truth women have been kept from us about these three days, since I came out, and the vessels of the young men are holy, and the*

bread is in a manner common, yea, though it were sanctified this day in the vessel. So the priest gave him hallowed bread: for there was no bread there but the shewbread, that was taken from before the LORD, to put hot bread in the day when it was taken away.

I Samuel 21:1-6

David was permitted to override the Mosaic Law by letting his hungry companions eat the sacred bread that was reserved for the priests. Is Israel's Messiah not greater than David? The Messiah of Israel should not be condemned for suspending the Sabbath to meet a legitimate need for His own disciples. If the Pharisees denounced Jesus, they would also be denouncing king David.

"in the days of Abiathar" – The priest who provided David with bread was actually *Ahimelech*, *Abiathar's* father. Jesus was probably using the name *Abiathar* because he was the last priest of his line, and he was banished from Jerusalem and the priesthood for going against king Solomon.

And unto Abiathar the priest said the king, Get thee to Anathoth, unto thine own fields; for thou art worthy of death: but I will not at this time put thee to death, because thou barest the ark of the LORD God before David my father, and because thou hast been afflicted in all wherein my father was afflicted. So Solomon thrust out Abiathar from being priest unto the LORD; that he might fulfil the word of the LORD, which he spake concerning the house of Eli in Shiloh.

I Kings 2:26-27

Jesus was saying that the Pharisees were figures like *Abiathar*, and they would lose their positions because of their unbelief. Because of their unbelief, God would allow the Romans to destroy the Temple in 70AD.

But most likely Jesus was also referring to something much more profound and deeper. *Abiathar* was one of the last priests to use the two gemstones, *Urim and Thummim,* that were hidden in the breastplate of the high priest.

And thou shalt put in the breastplate of judgment the Urim and the Thummim; and they shall be upon Aaron's heart, when he goeth in before the LORD: and Aaron shall bear the judgment of the children of Israel upon his heart before the LORD continually.

Exodus 28:30

These two gemstones had Hebrew lettering written on them and were used in critical times throughout Israel's history to make the right judgment. It was believed that the stones would light up to help the high priest make the right decision concerning Israel. Sometimes the word *ephod* is used, where the breastplate was attached, or just the single word, *Urim,* when the scriptures refer to making a decision.

The Hebrew names *Urim and Thummim* mean *"lights and perfections"* or also *"cursed or innocent."* When the Pharisees condemned Jesus their Messiah for eating grain on the Sabbath Day, this was the wrong decision because Jesus was the *Innocent One* who instituted the Sabbath Day in the first place. The Pharisees could not see that they were standing in front of their *Supreme Judge!* He designed the Sabbath Day to benefit His people and to be a blessing. The Sabbath Day was supposed to be a day of *rest* to acknowledge their total dependence upon God. Jesus the Messiah would fulfill the Sabbath Day and be the complete *rest* for His people.

> *Let no man therefore judge you in meat, or in drink, or in respect of an holyday, or of the new moon, or of the sabbath days: Which are a shadow of things to come; but the body is of Christ.*
>
> Colossians 2:16–17

> *There remaineth therefore a rest to the people of God. For he that is entered into his rest, he also hath ceased from his own works, as God did from his. Let us labour therefore to enter into that rest, lest any man fall after the same example of unbelief.*
>
> Hebrews 4:9–11

But the Pharisees built fences around the true meaning of the Sabbath Day and turned it into a legalistic test of being faithful to their brand of Judaism. It was in this world of outward hypocrisy that our Lord came.

"Therefore the Son of man is Lord also of the sabbath" – When we place more emphasis on a religious day or a religious ordinance than we do on the Person of Christ, we are treading in dangerous waters. Notice that Jesus uses the term *Son of man* in this context because the religious authorities are condemning the God of Israel who had come to them as a *Man,* in order to save them. But their traditions blinded them from knowing who He was. Not only is God in heaven the Lord over everything, but when Jesus walked this earth, He was also Lord over everything. This reminds us of what Paul would later write about the Lord Jesus Christ:

> *Which in his times he shall shew, who is the blessed and only Potentate, the King of kings, and Lord of lords.*
>
> I Timothy 6:15

CHAPTER THREE

Jesus Heals a Withered Hand on the Sabbath

> **Mark 3:1-5** - *And he entered again into the synagogue; and there was a man there which had a withered hand. And they watched him, whether he would heal him on the sabbath day; that they might accuse him. And he saith unto the man which had the withered hand, Stand forth. And he saith unto them, Is it lawful to do good on the sabbath days, or to do evil? to save life, or to kill? But they held their peace. And when he had looked round about on them with anger, being grieved for the hardness of their hearts, he saith unto the man, Stretch forth thine hand. And he stretched it out: and his hand was restored whole as the other.*

Jesus implies that doing *good* for the sake of mercy or necessity does not violate the Sabbath Day. Jesus could have also been alluding to a Jewish writing from the *Hasmonean*

Dynasty, (140-116BC) where they believed in suspending the Sabbath to permit warfare.

> *And they determined in that day, saying: Whosoever shall come up against us to fight on the sabbath day, we will fight against him: and we will not all die, as our brethren that were slain in the secret places.*
>
> I Maccabees 2:41

"Stretch forth thine hand" – This act of stretching out the hand was symbolic of releasing the power of God. It is used seven times throughout the book of Exodus where God instructs Moses and Aaron.

> *And the LORD spake unto Moses, Say unto Aaron, Take thy rod, and stretch out thine hand upon the waters of Egypt, upon their streams, upon their rivers, and upon their ponds, and upon all their pools of water, that they may become blood; and that there may be blood throughout all the land of Egypt, both in vessels of wood, and in vessels of stone.*
>
> Exodus 7:19

This poor man in the synagogue had lost his power to perform almost any physical task. Notice that the religious leaders were watching Jesus to see what He would do, and Jesus deliberately had this man to *stand forth* in front of them. Jesus healing a man on the Sabbath was also the fulfillment of the eighth benediction prayer of the Jewish *Amidah*, a prayer for *refuah*, or healing:

> *Heal us Lord, and we will be healed. Save us and we will be saved, for you are our praise. Bring complete recovery for all our ailments, for you are God and King, the faithful and merciful healer. Blessed are you Lord who heals the sick of his people Israel.*

This Jewish prayer is actually coming from a scriptural passage in Jeremiah.

> *Heal me, O LORD, and I shall be healed; save me, and I shall be saved: for thou art my praise.*
>
> Jeremiah 17:14

Why did Jesus heal this man on the Sabbath? Could He not have waited until the next day? Jesus is teaching these Jewish leaders a Hebrew *kol v'chomer*, from the light to the heavy. *"If it is permissible to violate the Sabbath in order to do good to animals, how much more it is permissible to do good to human beings?"*

"And when he had looked around about on them with anger" – These words need to find an echo in all of our hearts. When religious traditions supersede the need of people, it *angers* the Lord. The God of heaven is not impressed with ceremonialism or outward show. Our duty as followers of *Yeshua* is to love Him supremely and to love others as ourselves.

Jesus Draws a Multitude by the Sea of Galilee

Mark 3:6-12 - *And the Pharisees went forth, and straightway took counsel with the Herodians against him, how they might destroy him. But Jesus withdrew himself with his disciples to the sea: and a great multitude from Galilee followed him, and from Judaea, And from Jerusalem, and from Idumaea, and from beyond Jordan; and they about Tyre and Sidon, a great multitude, when they had heard what great things he did, came unto him. And he spake to his disciples, that a small ship should wait on him because of the multitude, lest they should throng him. For he had healed many; insomuch that they pressed upon him for to touch him, as many as had plagues. And unclean spirits, when they saw him, fell down before him, and cried, saying, Thou art the Son of God. And he straitly charged them that they should not make him known.*

It's very interesting that here we see a *religious* group and a *political* group who normally were enemies joining hands against our dear Lord. We know that the *Pharisees* were the religious rulers over the synagogues, but the *Herodians* we know less about. The *Herodians* were a group of Jewish people who supported *Herod Antipas* and *Herod Philip,*

(Luke 3:1) who inherited different territories of Israel from their wicked father, *Herod the Great*. **(Matthew 2:1)**

Capernaum was built along the northern seashore, where Jesus started withdrawing Himself from the people. But notice that the crowds kept coming from *Galilee, Judea, Jerusalem, Idumea, (territory of Herod Philip) beyond Jordan (Perea),* and even as far away as *Tyre and Sidon* in the north. There were so many people that Jesus asked for a small ship so He could at least be on the water to get a little separation. Just think! No marketing was needed. Jesus didn't go to one of the large amphitheaters to start an evangelistic campaign. Jesus was not impressed with large crowds; He just wanted people to follow Him because they loved Him. He was seeking just a few good men and women to be His disciples. Notice the contrast between the common people running to Jesus and the religious and political people opposing Him.

"And he straitly charged them that they should not make him known" – Here we find the messianic secret once again. *The unclean spirits knew who Jesus was, the Son of God!* As already stated, Jesus only had a small window of time before His final passion in Jerusalem. Jesus certainly did not want demons of hell to proclaim His deity and hinder His mission. Since the religious and political establishments were after Jesus any way, it was going to take divine wisdom in using the time He had left to fulfill the Father's will.

Choosing the Twelve Disciples

Mark 3:13-21 - *And he goeth up into a mountain, and calleth unto him whom he would: and they came unto him. And he ordained twelve, that they should be with him, and that he might send them forth to preach, And to have power to heal sicknesses, and to cast out devils: And Simon he surnamed Peter; And James the son of Zebedee, and John the brother of James; and he surnamed them Boanerges, which is, The sons of thunder: And Andrew, and Philip, and Bartholomew, and Matthew, and Thomas, and James the son of Alphaeus, and Thaddaeus, and Simon the Canaanite, And Judas Iscariot, which also betrayed him: and they went into an house. And the multitude cometh together again, so that they could not so much as eat bread. And when his friends heard of it, they went out to lay hold on him: for they said, He is beside himself.*

It is very likely that Jesus ascended to what is called today the *Eremos Hill* that overlooks the Sea of Galilee, the same hill where He preached the Sermon on the Mount. Think of being one of the 12 disciples and hearing the Master call out your name! Why 12? Why not ten? Or 20? Twelve is symbolic of the 12 sons of Jacob who represented the Old

Covenant. Jesus was calling 12 disciples to represent the New Covenant.

> *All these are the twelve tribes of Israel: and this is it that their father spake unto them, and blessed them; every one according to his blessing he blessed them.*
>
> Genesis 49:28

We also find that the New Jerusalem will have 12 gates, 12 angels, the names of the 12 tribes of Israel, and 12 foundations named after the 12 apostles of the Lamb. Wow!

> *And had a wall great and high, and had twelve gates, and at the gates twelve angels, and names written thereon, which are the names of the twelve tribes of the children of Israel: On the east three gates; on the north three gates; on the south three gates; and on the west three gates. And the wall of the city had twelve foundations, and in them the names of the twelve apostles of the Lamb.*
>
> Revelation 21:12–14

We know that Jesus had more than 12 disciples, but these 12 men would be His closest students. These 12, other than Judas Iscariot, would be trained by our Lord to take the message of the gospel for the very first time into the known world. What an honor and what a responsibility! They would be the primary eyewitnesses of the resurrection of the Messiah! They were even given the power to *cast out demons and to heal people of their sicknesses.*

"that they should be with him" – This "circle of friends" or *chaverim*, would be taught by Jesus and would imitate Him. One of the customs of the day was for the students to listen carefully to the interpretations of their rabbi. They would hear Jesus pray! They would eat with Jesus! They would walk behind Jesus as they traveled along the dusty roads of Galilee to Jerusalem! They would see His compassion for the people! They would learn how to understand the Old Testament as it related to the coming of Israel's Messiah! The difference between Jesus and His disciples and the traditional Pharisees was that Jesus would teach them how to have fellowship with others outside of their little band. The idea of a monk-like asceticism was quite foreign to the teachings of *Yeshua.*

"he surnamed them Boanerges" – Why Jesus gave *James and John* this name has baffled scholars for years. While the common interpretation of *James and John* being impetuous may be a good way to interpret it, this author has an added thought after careful research. While Jesus spoke Hebrew/Aramaic, He may have called them *"Benay ragash,"* but there is no exact Semitic equivalent for *"Boanerges."* Mark could have translated it in such a way to interest his Latin/Greek-speaking audience in Rome. The word *"Boanerges"* is actually taken from the Greek or Latin wording meaning, *"roaring energy."*

When we think about the worldview at that time, there were Greco/Roman gods and goddesses all along the streets of the entire Roman world for just about everything one could imagine. In mythology, the Greek god *Zeus* or the Roman god *Jupiter* held a thunderbolt in his right hand and was thought to have had many sons and daughters who were called *"sons and daughters of thunder."* Mark may have been telling His Roman audience that Jesus the Son of God is the only one who controls the thunder, not *Zeus* or *Jupiter*. *James and John* would be the sons of Almighty God by following Jesus the Messiah! *James and John* held very significant positions among the disciples. *James* would be the first martyr in **Acts 12:1-2**, and John would be the last disciple to die, but not before Jesus gave him the last Revelation to complete the canonization of scripture. We must remember that Jesus is the one who gave them the original title, so He gave them the supernatural power of the Holy Spirit to accomplish what they were called to do.

When we scan over the names of these disciples, we do not know the occupations of all of them. But we do know that some were fishermen like *Peter and Andrew, James and John, Bartholomew* (Nathanael), and Thomas **(John 21:1-2)** Others include a tax collector, *Matthew;* a zealot, *Simon the Canaanite;* and a lover of money, *Judas Iscariot* who would later betray the Son of God. This ragtag group of men had no idea what the months would hold, and their lives would be forever changed. They were not tainted with the traditions of the scribes and Pharisees, and while they were uneducated, they were people in who our Lord saw something special. They were teachable! The Lord knows that we all will fail along the journey, but if we have a meek, teachable spirit, then He can use us in His kingdom.

Judas Iscariot remains a mystery to many, but he was the only disciple from Jerusalem, or from *Kerioth*, in southern Judea. This author does believe that he was chosen to fulfill the scriptures. Scholars have debated over the centuries if Judas Iscariot found grace at the end of His life. ★ While we cannot say for certain about his eternal destiny, we can say that Judas is a picture of all of us who have betrayed our Lord from one time or the other.

> *Yea, mine own familiar friend, in whom I trusted, which did eat of my bread, hath lifted up his heel against me.*
>
> Psalm 41:9

> *And I said unto them, If ye think good, give me my price; and if not, forbear. So they weighed for my price thirty pieces of silver.*
>
> Zechariah 11:12

★In 1874 the Greek Monastery of St. Onuphrius was built over an earlier church in the Valley of Hinnom where Judas hanged himself. The place is called Aceldama, or "Field of Blood" from **Acts 1:19.** *Onuphrius was a monk who lived in the third or fourth century. The Greek Orthodox Church believes that Judas was chosen to fulfill the scriptures and that he repented and found grace at his death. They believe also that his name will be among*

the 12 names of the apostles written on the foundations of the New Jerusalem in **Revelation 21**.

"And the multitude cometh together again, so that they could not so much as eat bread. And when his friends heard of it, they went out to lay hold on him: for they said, He is beside himself " - The scriptures do not say which house they entered into, but it may have been where Jesus lived in Capernaum about a mile away. The multitude followed Jesus and His disciples so much that it created a major problem; *they could not eat bread.* The family of Jesus lived in Nazareth, about 18 miles away, and they heard about what was going on with Jesus at the Sea of Galilee. Probably the mother of Jesus and His brethren panicked, and when they saw how large the crowds were, they thought Jesus wasn't thinking straight. *"He has created a monster for himself. What's He thinking!"* It helps to remember that the earthly family of Jesus thought of him as being only the simple carpenter from Nazareth at this point.

Major Transition in the Ministry of Jesus

> **Mark 3:22-30 -** *And the scribes which came down from Jerusalem said, He hath Beelzebub, ★ and by the prince of the devils casteth he out devils. And he called them unto him, and said unto them in parables, How can Satan cast out Satan? And if a kingdom be divided against itself, that kingdom cannot stand. And if a house be divided against itself, that house*

cannot stand. And if Satan rise up against himself, and be divided, he cannot stand, but hath an end. No man can enter into a strong man's house, and spoil his goods, except he will first bind the strong man; and then he will spoil his house. Verily I say unto you, All sins shall be forgiven unto the sons of men, and blasphemies wherewith soever they shall blaspheme: But he that shall blaspheme against the Holy Ghost hath never forgiveness, but is in danger of eternal damnation. Because they said, He hath an unclean spirit.

The god Baal Zevuv came from a god of the Philistines and was later worshipped in Ekron. Baal Zevuv is also associated with the god Baal. In demonology he was the prince of the demons. He was considered the "lord of the flies" and was thought to have been able to fly. Baal Zevuv is also another name for the devil, or Satan.

And Ahaziah fell down through a lattice in his upper chamber that was in Samaria, and was sick: and he sent messengers, and said unto them, Go, enquire of Baalzebub the god of Ekron whether I shall recover of this disease. But the angel of the LORD said to Elijah the Tishbite, Arise, go up to meet the messengers of the king of Samaria, and say unto them, Is

it not because there is not a God in Israel, that
ye go to enquire of Baalzebub the god of Ekron?

2 Kings 1:2-3

The scribes from Jerusalem calling the works of Jesus the works of *Beelzebub* mark a major transition in the earthly ministry of the Messiah. In the minds of the Jewish leaders, the prince of the demons had power over the weaker demons. So here they are saying that Jesus was casting out demons because He was the prince demon, *Beelzebub*. This episode reveals the wickedness of the scribes and Pharisees. They were part of the devil's kingdom, and Jesus the Son of God would defeat their evil kingdom. Jesus casting out demons was *binding the strong man* first, and then He would *spoil his house* on the cross. This was one of the primary reasons why Jesus came into the world. The devil brought death into the world, and Jesus would reverse the law of sin and death for His people.

He that committeth sin is of the devil; for the
devil sinneth from the beginning. For this
purpose the Son of God was manifested, that
he might destroy the works of the devil.

I John 3:8

Forasmuch then as the children are partakers of
flesh and blood, he also himself likewise took
part of the same; that through death he might

> *destroy him that had the power of death, that*
> *is, the devil.*

Hebrews 2:14

While this certainly was no surprise to our Lord, He came into the world at a time when He knew the nation would reject Him. But the physical kingdom would be postponed, the Temple would be destroyed in 70AD, and the gospel would be launched into the world. The religious leaders in Jerusalem represented the nation of Israel. Many common people received Jesus as their Messiah, but the nation as a whole rejected Him. Their rebellion was *blaspheming the Holy Ghost;* which was unforgivable. They were blinded by their own traditions so much that they did not see their need for forgiveness. A parallel to this sin was when the Israelites fashioned the golden calf:

> *And when the people saw that Moses delayed*
> *to come down out of the mount, the people*
> *gathered themselves together unto Aaron, and*
> *said unto him, Up, make us gods, which shall*
> *go before us; for as for this Moses, the man*
> *that brought us up out of the land of Egypt,*
> *we wot not what is become of him. And Aaron*
> *said unto them, Break off the golden earrings,*
> *which are in the ears of your wives, of your*
> *sons, and of your daughters, and bring them*
> *unto me. And all the people brake off the golden*
> *earrings which were in their ears, and brought*

60

them unto Aaron. And he received them at their hand, and fashioned it with a graving tool, after he had made it a molten calf: and they said, These be thy gods, O Israel, which brought thee up out of the land of Egypt. And when Aaron saw it, he built an altar before it; and Aaron made proclamation, and said, To morrow is a feast to the LORD. And they rose up early on the morrow, and offered burnt offerings, and brought peace offerings; and the people sat down to eat and to drink, and rose up to play.

Exodus 32:1-6

We are reminded of how Pharaoh, in the book of Exodus, could not comprehend how the God of the enslaved Hebrews could have power over the gods of Egypt. But the God of Moses had come in the form of a Man named *Yeshua*! These passages where Jesus of Nazareth has power over the underworld powers showed the believers in Rome that Jesus was the true God of the afterlife, not *Osiris* of Egypt or *Pluto* of Greece.

"eternal damnation" – Strong words coming from Jesus the Messiah to some of His own nation. There have been some famous scholars over the years who have taught *annihilationism, (total extinction or destruction for the lost)* but here is one instance where our Lord taught *eternal existence* after the judgment for the lost. We oftentimes only think about *eternal life*, but the scriptures also teach *eternal hell*.

The New Family of God

> **Mark 3:31-35 -** *There came then his brethren and his mother, and, standing without, sent unto him, calling him. And the multitude sat about him, and they said unto him, Behold, thy mother and thy brethren without seek for thee. And he answered them, saying, Who is my mother, or my brethren? And he looked round about on them which sat about him, and said, Behold my mother and my brethren! For whosoever shall do the will of God, the same is my brother, and my sister, and mother.*

The mother of Jesus and His family probably wanted to take Him back to Nazareth. Not only did they see tension between Jesus and the scribes, they could not understand why Jesus was spending so much time with fishermen and tax collectors. They still had not understood why Jesus left Nazareth and made His home in Capernaum. The earthly family of our Lord was outside the house and sent word that they wanted to see Him.

Mary and the family wanted Jesus to follow them, and instead Jesus was calling people to follow Him! Jesus' earthly family had not yet put on the sandals of being a disciple, and they could not fully see that Jesus was the true Messiah of Israel. The reconciliation between the earthly family of our Lord and His spiritual family would happen later in Jerusalem. But for now Jesus is using the moment to teach a powerful lesson to His disciples and to His earthly family. Jesus states that it is more important to be obedient to the Father than it is to be related to Him biologically. Those who *do the will of God* are all brothers and sisters! Wow! How we need to be reminded of this truth! Jesus is not excluding His earthly family. He knows that they will understand and one day become part of His heavenly family. His brothers, *James* and *Jude,* would later refer to themselves as *"servants of Jesus Christ."* **(James 1:1, Jude 1)**

What joy this must have brought to the Jews and Gentile believers in Rome to whom Mark was writing. They were across the Mediterranean Sea in another country, but if they did the will of God, they could call themselves *brethren* of Jesus the Messiah!

> *For both he that sanctifieth and they who are sanctified are all of one: for which cause he is not ashamed to call them brethren, Saying, I will declare thy name unto my brethren, in the midst of the church will I sing praise unto thee.*
> Hebrews 2:11-12, Psalm 22:22

The family of *Yeshua* has always been a matter of speculation and embellishment. During the first three or four centuries with the rise of the Catholic Church, the church found itself in an awkward position trying to teach the perpetual virginity of Mary, while the scriptures taught that she did have other children after Jesus was born. *Mariology* ★ became official in 431AD. But as we will see,

Jesus did have brothers *and sisters*. Joseph and Mary went on to have several children after the birth of our Lord which was the norm for Jewish families in the early first century.

At the Ecumenical Council of Ephesus in 431AD, Mary was called "Theotokos", or "Mother of God." The council determined this because Jesus was Man and He was God, and the woman who birthed Him should be deified as well. This has led to centuries of worshipping and praying to Mary. They claim that Jesus' brethren were only His cousins because the Hebrew word for "brothers" is "ach" and has a broad definition. We will look at this subject in more detail in **Mark 6**.

CHAPTER FOUR

Parable of the Sower

Mark 4:1-8 - *And he began again to teach by the sea side: and there was gathered unto him a great multitude, so that he entered into a ship, and sat in the sea; and the whole multitude was by the sea on the land. And he taught them many things by parables, and said unto them in his doctrine, Hearken; Behold, there went out a sower to sow: And it came to pass, as he sowed, some fell by the way side, and the fowls of the air came and devoured it up. And some fell on stony ground, where it had not much earth; and immediately it sprang up, because it had no depth of earth: But when the sun was up, it was scorched; and because it had no root, it withered away. And some fell among thorns, and the thorns grew up, and choked it, and it yielded no fruit. And other fell on good ground, and did yield fruit that sprang up and* *increased; and brought forth, some thirty, and some sixty, and some an hundred.*

Since the nation as a whole rejected Jesus and called His works the works of Beelzebub, the message of the kingdom would now be brought through *parables,* and Jesus would explain them to His disciples when they were alone. Jesus would give spiritual lessons by using word pictures from everyday Jewish life. It would also conceal the message of the kingdom from His enemies until it was time to die on the cross. It was prophesied that the Messiah of Israel would speak in *parables*, or *maschal*:

> *Give ear, O my people, to my law: incline your ears to the words of my mouth. I will open my mouth in a parable: I will utter dark sayings of old: Which we have heard and known, and our fathers have told us. We will not hide them from their children, shewing to the generation to come the praises of the LORD, and his strength, and his wonderful works that he hath done.*
>
> Psalm 78:1-4

After traveling to the Sea of Galilee dozens of times over the years, there is a very vivid picture in this writer's mind of Jesus sitting in a boat and teaching the multitude along the shore. ★

★*The Sea of Galilee was created in the shape of a harp, or the Hebrew kinnor. It is also called the Lake of Kinneret. It was designed in such a way that it sits over 650 feet below sea level surrounded by mountains. The shape of a harp is very fitting because as the west wind sweeps over the lake every day, the sounds from the water are blown up on the hillsides. The voice of Jesus our Lord would have carried easily on the hillsides without the need of any microphone. Sound carries seven times louder on water than on land. There is a traditional location called the "Cove of the Sower" where possibly Jesus would have been sitting. The little circular cove lies just beneath the Eremos Hill, slightly to the west between Capernaum and the place where Jesus appeared to His disciples after the resurrection in* **John 21**. *From this cove there could have been thousands who could have heard the voice of the Master. Experiments have been performed, and people could hear the person talking in a boat from hundreds of feet away.*

The parable of the sower is one of the most famous that Jesus gave because He explained the meaning of each type of soil. We would be wise to study the interpretations that Jesus gave:

> *"fell by the wayside"* - **And these are they by the way side, where the word is sown; but when they have heard, Satan cometh immediately, and taketh away the word that was sown in their hearts.** Mark 4:15

> *"fell on stony ground"* - **And these are they likewise which are sown on stony ground; who, when they have heard the word, immediately receive it with gladness; And have no root**

*in themselves, and so endure but for a time:
afterward, when affliction or persecution
ariseth for the word's sake, immediately they
are offended.*   Mark 4:16-17

"fell among thorns" - *And these are they which
are sown among thorns; such as hear the word,
And the cares of this world, and the deceitfulness
of riches, and the lusts of other things entering
in, choke the word, and it becometh unfruitful.*
          Mark 4:18-19

"fell on good ground" - *And these are they which
are sown on good ground; such as hear the
word, and receive it, and bring forth fruit, some
thirtyfold, some sixty, and some an hundred.*
          Mark 4:20

Notice the graphic language of Jesus: *devoured, scorched,*
and *choked.* These words describe the hearts of the people
who reject the message of the gospel. In contrast, the *good
soil* yields an abundant harvest. There will always be a
remnant that will receive the good seed and bring forth
good fruit.

Mark 4:9-12 - *And he said unto them, He
that hath ears to hear, let him hear. And when
he was alone, they that were about him with
the twelve asked of him the parable. And he
said unto them, Unto you it is given to know*

the mystery of the kingdom of God: but unto them that are without, all these things are done in parables: That seeing they may see, and not perceive; and hearing they may hear, and not understand; lest at any time they should be converted, and their sins should be forgiven them.

Sometimes we fail to see the connection of the Jews in Jesus' day and the Jews during the days of the prophets Isaiah and Ezekiel. Many of the people of Israel long ago are like many of the Jews and Gentiles of today. They were and still are a stubborn and rebellious people. Read these verses and notice how the hearts of the people were very similar:

And he said, Go, and tell this people, Hear ye indeed, but understand not; and see ye indeed, but perceive not. Make the heart of this people fat, and make their ears heavy, and shut their eyes; lest they see with their eyes, and hear with their ears, and understand with their heart, and convert, and be healed.
                            Isaiah 6:9-10, John 12:40

Son of man, thou dwellest in the midst of a rebellious house, which have eyes to see, and see not; they have ears to hear, and hear not: for they are a rebellious house.
                            Ezekiel 12:2

When the Apostle Paul arrived in Rome, there were some Jews who received his message and some who did not. Interestingly enough this same truth was given to Paul when it was time to take the gospel to the Gentiles:

> *And when they agreed not among themselves, they departed, after that Paul had spoken one word, Well spake the Holy Ghost by Esaias the prophet unto our fathers, Saying, Go unto this people, and say, Hearing ye shall hear, and shall not understand; and seeing ye shall see, and not perceive: For the heart of this people is waxed gross, and their ears are dull of hearing, and their eyes have they closed; lest they should see with their eyes, and hear with their ears, and understand with their heart, and should be converted, and I should heal them. Be it known therefore unto you, that the salvation of God is sent unto the Gentiles, and that they will hear it.*
>
> Acts 28:25-28

Parable of the Lamp

> **Mark 4:21-25 -** *And he said unto them, Is a candle brought to be put under a bushel, or under a bed? and not to be set on a candlestick? For there is nothing hid, which shall not be manifested; neither was any thing kept secret,*

70

but that it should come abroad. If any man have ears to hear, let him hear. And he said unto them, Take heed what ye hear: with what measure ye mete, it shall be measured to you: and unto you that hear shall more be given. For he that hath, to him shall be given: and he that hath not, from him shall be taken even that which he hath.

While the meaning of the kingdom is being hidden from the enemies of Jesus for a while, the message will eventually be manifest to everyone. The translation *candle* comes from the *olive oil lamp*, or the Hebrew *nerah*, which means *"to glisten."* In the village houses of Galilee, they would place small olive oil lamps in the windowsill or on a stand in the middle of the house. Placing a basket over the lamp would easily blow out the lamp. There could also be a direct correlation to Jesus being the *Light*, and the message of His *Light* would permeate the dark world through the disciples being filled with the Holy Spirit. By the time of Mark's gospel, the *Light* of Jesus had already shown into parts of the world, like to the believers in Rome.

"If any man have ears to hear, let him hear. And he said unto them, Take heed what ye hear: with what measure ye mete, it shall be measured to you: and unto you that hear shall more be given. For he that hath, to him shall be given: and he that hath not, from him shall be taken even that which he hath" – Those who heard the message of the kingdom needed to obey the message. The people needed

to carefully consider how blessed they were to hear the message coming from the lips of Jesus. This is a powerful warning, as well as a powerful promise from our Lord. By using the language of weighing grain in a market, Jesus was saying that if the people obey the *measure* of truth that they had heard, then a greater *measure* would be given to them. But if they did not obey the *measure* of truth they had been given, then a greater *measure* of judgment would be upon them.

Parable of the Growing Seed

> **Mark 4:26-29 -** *And he said, So is the kingdom of God, as if a man should cast seed into the ground; And should sleep, and rise night and day, and the seed should spring and grow up, he knoweth not how. For the earth bringeth forth fruit of herself; first the blade, then the ear, after that the full corn in the ear. But when the fruit is brought forth, immediately he putteth in the sickle, because the harvest is come.*

This parable, referring to the agrarian culture of the Galilee, is used again by Jesus and is only recorded in Mark's gospel. The mysterious growth of a seed in the earth while people are sleeping is compared to the mysterious growth of God's kingdom once the seed is planted in the hearts of the people. There is an invisible Spirit that is at work even after the seed is planted. The kingdom of God would not happen all at once, and universal peace would not come to the earth anytime soon. The Messiah wasn't going to fix a fallen world's problems all at one time. His kingdom would start small in the Galilee, but in time it would spread all over the world. The responsibility of the disciples was to be sure they sowed the seed of God's Word. The disciple's message about Jesus the Son of God would be empowered by the Holy Spirit. The Holy Spirit would take the Word and cause a mysterious growth to take place even when the disciples were not aware of it. The day of harvest will come!

As we plant God's Word into the hearts of people, we need to be reminded that while our efforts may seem weak and may not be without problems, the Spirit of God is at work. We just need to make sure that we give people the sound doctrine that Jesus left us to bring. It's not based on our ingenuity or our talents. Its effectiveness is based on the power of the Word of God! God knows the spiritual condition of every individual person, and He takes the Word of God that we sow and brings forth a harvest. God's Word is so powerful that the same message will bring forth a harvest of people who are at different levels in their spiritual life. They may hear the Word of God one day and the harvest may come forth weeks or months later. All of the praise and glory go to the Lord of the harvest!

Parable of the Mustard Seed

Mark 4:30-34 - *And he said, Whereunto shall we liken the kingdom of God? or with*

what comparison shall we compare it? It is like a grain of mustard seed, * which, when it is sown in the earth, is less than all the seeds that be in the earth: But when it is sown, it groweth up, and becometh greater than all herbs, and shooteth out great branches; so that the fowls of the air may lodge under the shadow of it. And with many such parables spake he the word unto them, as they were able to hear it. But without a parable spake he not unto them: and when they were alone, he expounded all things to his disciples.

*The mustard tree in Israel is called "Brassica nigra" and grows wild or can be cultivated. True stories have been told of a man planting a small mustard seed and then later being able to climb the tree. They also have yellow flowers with a pungent fragrance.

As we close this section on the parables, it was the Hebrew style of the day for a rabbi, in this case the Great Rabbi *Yeshua*, to teach in two different styles, *Haggadah and Halachah*. *Haggadah* is telling stories, while *Halachah* is explaining how to live out the stories. Jesus used *Haggadah* when speaking to the crowds and *Halachah* when speaking to His disciples.

This picture of a tree growing so large that its branches can lodge birds is a parallel of several stories given in the Old Testament:

Thus saith the Lord GOD; I will also take of the highest branch of the high cedar, and will set it; I will crop off from the top of his young twigs a tender one, and will plant it upon an high mountain and eminent: In the mountain of the height of Israel will I plant it: and it shall bring forth boughs, and bear fruit, and be a goodly cedar: and under it shall dwell all fowl of every wing; in the shadow of the branches thereof shall they dwell. And all the trees of the field shall know that I the LORD have brought down the high tree, have exalted the low tree, have dried up the green tree, and have made the dry tree to flourish: I the LORD have spoken and have done it.

Ezekiel 17:22–24

Thus were the visions of mine head in my bed; I saw, and behold a tree in the midst of the earth, and the height thereof was great.

Daniel 4:10

Whose leaves were fair, and the fruit thereof much, and in it was meat for all; under which the beasts of the field dwelt, and upon whose branches the fowls of the heaven had their habitation:

Daniel 4:21

The *mustard seed* imagery depicts how Christ's kingdom begins with a small band of disciples in the Galilee and grows to be such a large tree that even Gentiles could lodge in the branches. Think of Mark writing to the believers in Rome who were lodging under the branches of the kingdom of God that started a few years earlier in the Galilee. Although it started small, the Roman Empire could not stop what God had started. The world has had many nations and conquerors that tried to stop the spread of Christianity, but no earthly kingdom can stop God's kingdom. There are less than 15 million Jews today in the world, and yet over 7 billion Gentiles live on planet earth. So try to think how many believing Gentiles there must be in the world who are lodging in the branches of the kingdom that was started by the Jewish Messiah! And the scriptures make it clear that one day Christ will return and to His kingdom there will be no end.

Jesus is the God of the Sea

> **Mark 4:35-41 -** *And the same day, when the even was come, he saith unto them, Let us pass over unto the other side. And when they had sent away the multitude, they took him even as he was in the ship. And there were also with him other little ships. And there arose a great storm of wind, and the waves beat into the ship, so that it was now full. And he was in the hinder part of the ship, asleep on a pillow: and they awake him, and say unto him, Master, carest thou not that we perish? And he arose,*

and rebuked the wind, and said unto the sea,
Peace, be still. And the wind ceased, and there
was a great calm. And he said unto them, Why
are ye so fearful? how is it that ye have no
faith? And they feared exceedingly, and said
one to another, What manner of man is this,
that even the wind and the sea obey him?

"Let us pass over unto the other side" - This meant that
Jesus wanted the disciples to go with Him outside of Jewish
territory. The *other side* was the Roman *Decapolis* where
Jews dared not to enter. Was the Jewish Messiah going
to take the message of the kingdom of God to a Gentile
world?

"And the same day, when the even was come" - A lot
had transpired during this day of the Messiah as He had
taught by the lake. The scriptures want us to know that
without having time to rest, Jesus entered into a ship *"even*
as he was."

"great storm of wind, and the waves beat into the ship, so
that it was now full" - Mark writes the Greek word *megas*
for *great*, but the Hebrew word for *great* is *gadol* and is used
to describe the dramatic story of Jonah the prophet from
Galilee. Notice in this miracle of Jesus calming the storm
that the same word is used to describe the *great storm* and the
great calm. It wasn't a normal storm; it was a *great storm*! The
boats in those days were made out of several different types
of wood that caused the bottom of the boat to hold water.
This served as a natural live-well for the fish they caught.

The little ships were less than 30 feet long, so try to imagine being out in the middle of a raging sea in such a small vessel. Not that we have to have a scientific explanation, but cold air sweeps down from Mount Hermon about 40 miles north. Mount Hermon is 9,200 feet above sea level. The cold air meets the hot air at the Sea of Galilee, and a storm can build in a matter of minutes.

"And he was in the hinder part of the ship, asleep on a pillow" - Jesus was exhausted from the busy day of pouring out His heart to the people and dealing with His enemies from Jerusalem. They kept floating cushions on the boats made out of leather. What a scene! The same Person who has power over nature also needs to sleep!

"Master, carest thou not that we perish?" - One can vision the disciples trying to bail water out of the ship and their faces and hearts were filled with fear, and they looked over and saw Jesus sleeping! The disciples did not know at this point that Jesus was the very God of Creation! So they cry out as though Jesus didn't care if they drowned. This frustration about God not caring is expressed many times in the Old Testament. **(Psalm 10:1, 44:23-26)**

"And he arose, and rebuked the wind, and said unto the sea, Peace, be still" - This is one of the most powerful verses in the life and ministry of Jesus the Messiah. He has the power to rebuke sickness, the power to rebuke demons, and now He has the power to rebuke a raging storm! Wow! Jesus calmed the storm quicker than it started. The first thing Jesus did when He awoke was talk to the storm! The

Hebrew word would have been *"Shalom"* that Jesus said to the sea. We are reminded of this beautiful psalm:

> **Be still, and know that I am God.**
> Psalm 46:10

"And the wind ceased, and there was a great calm" – The sea became like a piece of smooth glass as the waters obeyed the Master's voice. Not only did the wind obey, but also the waters of the sea obeyed. This reminds us of several powerful psalms:

> **Thou rulest the raging of the sea: when the waves thereof arise, thou stillest them.**
> Psalm 89:9

> **The LORD on high is mightier than the noise of many waters, yea, than the mighty waves of the sea.**
> Psalm 93:4

> **They that go down to the sea in ships, that do business in great waters; These see the works of the LORD, and his wonders in the deep. For he commandeth, and raiseth the stormy wind, which lifteth up the waves thereof. They mount up to the heaven, they go down again to the depths: their soul is melted because of trouble. They reel to and fro, and stagger like a drunken man, and are at their wit's end. Then they cry**

unto the L<small>ORD</small> in their trouble, and he bringeth them out of their distresses. He maketh the storm a calm, so that the waves thereof are still.
Psalm 107:23-29

"Why are ye so fearful? how is it that ye have no faith?" – Jesus understands the disciples being afraid of the storm, but He wanted them to know that His power was greater than the storm. In other words, *"You will face many different kinds of storms, but your fear for God needs to be greater!"* Jesus had just told them that very same day that some would hear the Word of God and when tribulations arise, they would drop out. **(Mark 4:17)** The power of Christ that calmed a raging storm would go with the disciples when they left Israel to go into the known world.

"And they feared exceedingly, and said one to another, What manner of man is this, that even the wind and the sea obey him?" – This happens to be one of this author's favorite verses in the life and ministry of Jesus. Jesus is in a storm with His disciples, and if the ship goes down, He goes down with them. The disciples were afraid of the storm, afraid for their physical life, and now they were afraid because the God of Israel was standing in their boat! The Bible doesn't say, but maybe Jesus went back to sleep while they talked nervously among themselves. Before they could know the God-Man, Jesus the Messiah, they had to experience the fear of the storm. They must see His power over their fears before they can realize how great He

really is! We succumb to our fears of life because we do not understand the glorious power of Christ!

These disciples would go through many struggles, but in the end they would persevere even in the face of death. Jesus didn't tell them that He would protect them from all the storms of life, but that He would be *with them* through all their troubles, just like He will be with us through all of our troubles. He will never leave us!

What powerful words this miracle of Jesus must have been to the Jew and Gentile believers in Rome who were facing persecution. The gods *Poseidon and/or Neptune* were not the gods of the sea. Jesus was the God of the sea!

CHAPTER FIVE

There are those, *(including this writer at one time)* who preach that when we study the scriptures, all we need to know is *how the text applies to the reader* and do not have to know all of the background to a particular passage. Sometimes people say in a pious way, *"all I need is Jesus, and I'm not interested in the history behind the text."* While that may sound flattering and religious, those people are missing a great treasure by not studying the customs, the culture, and the worldview during the time of Jesus our Lord. Of course Jesus is all we need, but we should desire to know more about why He said what He did and why He performed certain miracles in specific places. Knowing more about the culture behind the text will help us know more about our precious Lord. We are about to enter into a strange passage of scripture where we need to spend a little time and space trying to analyze some of the reasons why our Lord would even take the time to cross over the Sea of Galilee and enter into a non-Jewish territory.

What was the political situation in this area where the Romans ruled? Are there any pagan religious beliefs that might form and indeed shape the context? What were the Jewish and Roman beliefs of the first century? Was there a particular message that Mark was trying to convey to his readers? Are there any extra biblical sources that we might compare with the scriptures? What was the message that Jesus was giving to His disciples in Galilee?

In this passage that we are leading up to, there is a plethora of information on the subject of demons, pigs, exorcisms, and Jewish traditions. While we are not going to cover all of them, there are certain points of interests that will hopefully help us to see this miracle in a fresh and different light. But let's first simply read this strange and captivating story without losing the overall significance of the miracle, then look at a few points of interest.

Jesus in Non-Jewish Territory (Maniac of Gadara)

Mark 5:1-20 - *And they came over unto the other side of the sea, into the country of the Gadarenes. * And when he was come out of the ship, immediately there met him out of the tombs a man with an unclean spirit, Who had his dwelling among the tombs; and no man could bind him, no, not with chains: Because that he had been often bound with fetters and chains, and the chains had been plucked asunder by him, and the fetters broken in pieces: neither could any man tame him. And always, night and day, he was in the mountains, and in the*

tombs, crying, and cutting himself with stones.
But when he saw Jesus afar off, he ran and
worshipped him, And cried with a loud voice,
and said, What have I to do with thee, Jesus,
thou Son of the most high God? I adjure thee
by God, that thou torment me not. For he said
unto him, Come out of the man, thou unclean
spirit. And he asked him, What is thy name?
And he answered, saying, My name is Legion:
for we are many. And he besought him much
that he would not send them away out of the
country. Now there was there nigh unto the
mountains a great herd of swine feeding. And
all the devils besought him, saying, Send us
into the swine, that we may enter into them.
And forthwith Jesus gave them leave. And
the unclean spirits went out, and entered into
the swine: and the herd ran violently down a
steep place into the sea, (they were about two
thousand;) and were choked in the sea. And
they that fed the swine fled, and told it in the
city, and in the country. And they went out
to see what it was that was done. And they
come to Jesus, and see him that was possessed
with the devil, and had the legion, sitting, and
clothed, and in his right mind: and they were
afraid. And they that saw it told them how it
befell to him that was possessed with the devil,
and also concerning the swine. And they began

to pray him to depart out of their coasts. And when he was come into the ship, he that had been possessed with the devil prayed him that he might be with him. Howbeit Jesus suffered him not, but saith unto him, Go home to thy friends, and tell them how great things the Lord hath done for thee, and hath had compassion on thee. And he departed, and began to publish in Decapolis how great things Jesus had done for him: and all men did marvel.

It is called "Gaderenes" or "Gergesenes" which refers to the same area. One reason may be because of the names of two important cities, Jerash and Gadara. This was the land of the Decapolis, or the place of ten cities. The closest city to where Jesus would have landed by ship on the other side of the Galilee was Hippos, which stood on top of a tall mountain that everyone could see from all around the sea. The capital of the Decapolis was the ornate, beautiful Scythopolis, (Old Testament Beth Shean) south of the Galilee, the only city on the west side of the Jordan River. This territory had a Greco-Roman culture and was under the control of Rome since the invasion of Pompey in 63BC. This territory was not part of the Herodian Dynasty, and each city was autonomous but under Roman protection.

There is a traditional place where this miracle took place, called Kursi, where the ruins of a fifth century Byzantine Monastery were found during road construction in 1970. In recent years part of a synagogue has also been discovered that lead archaeologists to believe that this may have been an early Judeo-Christian worship site. It lies at the bottom of the Golan Heights, not far from the shore of the Galilee.

1) To the Jewish-minded disciples this was unclean territory with an unclean man living among unclean tombs with unclean swine
2) The demons knew that Jesus was the Son of God
3) The demons begged Jesus for mercy *(The fallen angels begged Enoch for mercy after the terrible sin of* **Genesis 6:4.** *This sin took place on Mount Hermon in the Golan Heights)* **And Enoch went and said: Azazel, thou shalt have no peace: a severe sentence has gone forth against thee to put thee in bonds: And thou shalt not have toleration nor request granted to thee, because of the unrighteousness which thou hast taught, and because of all the works of godlessness and unrighteousness and sin which thou hast shown to men. Then I went and spoke to them all together, and they were all afraid, and fear and trembling seized them. And they besought me to draw up a petition for them that they might find forgiveness, and to read their petition in the presence of the Lord of heaven. For from thenceforward they could not speak (with Him) nor lift up their eyes to heaven for shame of their sins for which they had been condemned. Then I wrote out their petition, and the prayer in regard to their spirits and their deeds individually and in regard to their requests that they should have forgiveness and length (of days) And I went off and sat down at the**

waters of Dan, in the land of Dan, to the south of the west of Hermon: I read their petition till I fell asleep. And behold a dream came to me, and visions fell down upon me, and I saw visions of chastisement, and a voice came bidding me to tell it to the sons of heaven, and reprimand them. And when I awaked, I came unto them, and they were all sitting gathered together, weeping in Abelsjail, which is between Lebanon and Seneser, with their faces covered. And I recounted before them all the visions which I had seen in sleep, and I began to speak the words of righteousness, and to reprimand the heavenly Watchers.

I Enoch 13

4) Demons are territorial, and Jesus showed His power in the midst of a demonic territory

5) Legion was also the name of 6,000 Roman soldiers

6) Other rabbis cast out demons by incense, incantations, praying, and music, but they were not always successful

7) Jesus was always successful in casting out demons with only His command

8) Pigs were used by the Romans to disturb horses and elephants of other invading armies

9) Pigs were offered to the Greek goddess Demeter, who was the goddess of agriculture and grain

10) There were enough demons in one man to destroy 2,000 pigs. Jesus proved that He was not only the God of the sea, but also the God of the underworld – *That at the name of Jesus every knee should bow,*

of things in heaven, and things in earth, and things under the earth.

Philippians 2:10

11) The pigs being drowned in the sea was a reminder of Pharaoh's army being drowned in the Red Sea in the book of Exodus

12) Jesus was the God of Moses in human form

13) The people in the area thought more of the pigs than they did the man who was set free

14) Jesus showed the disciples how to have compassion on the heathen

15) Jesus showed the disciples that even a demon-possessed pagan could be rescued and used in God's kingdom

16) Gentile region was evangelized by this one man who was set free by the power of the Jewish Messiah of Israel

17) The man told the people what *Jesus the Lord* had done for him- Mark 5:19

18) Jesus was preparing the disciples to go into the Roman world and confront the demonic powers of mythology and false gods

19) With the power of Jesus the Son of God, there is nothing to fear

20) The disciples of Jesus would never forget the storm on the sea and the maniac of Gadara being set free

21) Try to imagine the expressions that were on the faces of the disciples in the boat as they started back across the Sea of Galilee

22) The wind knows who Jesus is; the sea knows who Jesus is; the demons know who Jesus is; death knows who Jesus is; and they all have to bow in His presence

One Touch of the Master *(Over Sickness)*

Mark 5:21-34 - *And when Jesus was passed over again by ship unto the other side, much people gathered unto him: and he was nigh unto the sea. And, behold, there cometh one of the rulers of the synagogue, Jairus by name; and when he saw him, he fell at his feet, And besought him greatly, saying, My little daughter lieth at the point of death: I pray thee, come and lay thy hands on her, that she may be healed; and she shall live. And Jesus went with him; and much people followed him, and thronged him. And a certain woman, which had an issue of blood twelve years, And had suffered many things of many physicians, and had spent all that she had, and was nothing bettered, but rather grew worse, When she had heard of Jesus, came in the press behind, and touched his garment. For she said, If I may touch but his clothes, I shall be whole. And straightway the fountain of her blood was dried up; and she felt in her body that she was healed of that plague. And Jesus, immediately knowing in himself that virtue had gone out of him, turned him*

about in the press, and said, Who touched my
clothes? And his disciples said unto him, Thou
seest the multitude thronging thee, and sayest
thou, Who touched me? And he looked round
about to see her that had done this thing. But
the woman fearing and trembling, knowing
what was done in her, came and fell down
before him, and told him all the truth. And he
said unto her, Daughter, thy faith hath made
thee whole; go in peace, and be whole of thy
plague.

By His miracles, Mark continues to verify that Jesus of Nazareth is the long-awaited Messiah. In this one chapter Mark gives us three powerful miracles back-to-back: *the demon-possessed man, the woman with the issue of blood, and the daughter of Jairus who had died.*

The miracle of the woman with the issue of blood has touched many hearts over the centuries, and it shows the power of *touching Jesus with great faith.* Jesus and His disciples have ridden in a small boat back across the Sea of Galilee, which would have been about seven to eight miles. The pagan people from the Decapolis asked Jesus to depart, but when they arrive back in Jewish territory, we find a Jewish leader falling down at His feet. This was *Jairus,* or *Yair,* a Jewish ruler of *the synagogue,* which tells us that it was in Capernaum. While most of the Jewish establishment did not embrace Jesus as the Son of God, there were a few who did. His dying daughter brought him to Jesus, and He

MARK THE MESSIAH'S GOSPEL

believed that Jesus could heal her. Again, remember this is a Jewish *ruler* of the synagogue in Capernaum!

While Jesus was going with *Jairus,* a great crowd of people started following. A *certain woman* ★ who had an *issue of blood* for 12 years made her way through the crowd and touched the clothes of Jesus. Her touch of faith caused the issue of blood to stop immediately. Here are a few things to help us better understand this poor woman's condition and her healing:

We cannot say for sure if this woman was a Gentile or a Jew, but Eusebius (260-340AD) writes in his Historica Ecclesiastica (vii) that she was a Gentile who lived in Caesarea Philippi, which was about 40 miles north of the Galilee. He writes that her name was Berenice in Greek, and a statue of her stood in Caesarea Philippi even into the fourth century. There was a strong church tradition that she followed Jesus all the way to Jerusalem and offered him her veil as He carried His cross on the Via Dolorosa. The image of the face of Jesus was left on her veil, and her name was changed to the Latin, Veronica, which means, "true image."

Relationships – In the Jewish mind, this woman had been *unclean* for 12 years. ***And if a woman have an issue of her blood many days out of the time of her separation, or if it run beyond the time of her separation; all the days of the issue of her uncleanness shall be as the days of her separation: she shall be unclean.*** Leviticus 15:25

Considering the life span in those days was only about 40 years, she had spent almost half of her life as an unclean woman. If she was married, her husband may have divorced her for being unclean. If she had children, they also would be unclean if they touched her. Every place she touched was also unclean.

Finances – She spent all that she had on many physicians and was getting worse. No security, no resources.

Expectations – This woman had heard about the power of Jesus and began to talk within herself. She knew that if she could touch the garment ★ of Jesus, she would be made whole. What courage and what faith this woman had.

Restoration – Her touch of faith was so great that Jesus felt the power come out of Him. Wow!

Position – Her touch of great faith not only made her physically whole, this woman went from being called a *"certain woman"* to being called a *"daughter"* by Jesus.

★*This is believed to have been the tassels on the Hebrew kanaph on the prayer shawl that Jesus may have worn. This makes a powerful connection to passages like:*

> **And he said, Who art thou? And she answered, I am Ruth thine handmaid: spread therefore thy skirt (kanaph) over thine handmaid; for thou art a near kinsman.**
>
> Ruth 3:9

> **But unto you that fear my name shall the Sun of righteousness arise with healing in his wings (kanaph); and ye shall go forth, and grow up as calves of the stall.**
>
> Malachi 4:2

One Touch of the Master *(Over Death)*

Mark 5:35-43 - *While he yet spake, there came from the ruler of the synagogue's house certain which said, Thy daughter is dead: why troublest thou the Master any further? As soon as Jesus heard the word that was spoken, he saith unto the ruler of the synagogue, Be not afraid, only believe. And he suffered no man to follow him, save Peter, and James, and John the brother of James. And he cometh to the house of the ruler of the synagogue, and seeth the tumult, and them that wept and wailed greatly. And when he was come in, he saith unto them, Why make ye this ado, and weep? the damsel is not dead, but sleepeth. And they laughed him to scorn. But when he had put them all out, he taketh the father and the mother of the damsel, and them that were with him, and entereth in where the damsel was lying. And he took the damsel by the hand, and said unto her, Talitha cumi; which is, being interpreted, Damsel, I say unto thee, arise. And straightway the damsel arose, and walked; for she was of the age of twelve years. And they were astonished with a great astonishment. And he charged them straitly that no man should know it; and commanded that something should be given her to eat.*

"James, Peter and John" – Three of the closest disciples who were also allowed to be with Jesus at the Mount of Transfiguration **(Mark 9:2)** and in the Garden of Gethsemane **(Mark 14:33).** It is interesting that these three disciples are the only ones that Jesus renamed. Simon Peter to *Cephas*, which means *"rock"* and James and John to *"Boanerges"* which means *"sons of thunder."*

"and seeth the tumult, and them that wept and wailed greatly" – Childhood deaths were very common in Israel during Jesus' time, perhaps half of the children born did not survive. It was a strong Jewish tradition to have flutists and mourners to be at the house even of a poor family. If the family were more prominent, like the house of *Jairus*, then more mourners would assemble. Because of the climate in Israel, the bodies would decompose rapidly and mourners had to be ready quickly. So in the little village of Capernaum sadness filled the streets, wailing and mournful music was being heard, and people who lived close by knew that the 12-year old daughter of the ruler of the synagogue had died. Young girls at the age of 12 were looking forward to a joyous wedding event in their near future, and to die unmarried was lamented as a greater tragedy.

"the damsel is not dead, but sleepeth" – This is a biblical euphemism for biological death. **(Matt.27:52, John 11:11, I Cor.15:6)** Jesus is saying that the little girl's condition is only temporary and reversible.

"And he took the damsel by the hand" – Within the Jewish culture when Jesus was touched by the bleeding woman, He would have been considered *unclean* for one day.

(Leviticus 15:19-33) Here Jesus reaches forth His hand and deliberately touches the dead girl, and even takes her by the hand. Touching a corpse led to *seven days* of uncleanness.

> *He that toucheth the dead body of any man*
> *shall be unclean seven days.*
>
> Numbers 19:11

"Talitha Cumi" – *"Talitha"* is the Aramaic, ★ feminine form of *"young"* and *"cumi"* or *"koum"* means *"to rise, or get up."* The little girl not only arose, she started *walking*. Mark translates the Aramaic language of Jesus to his Roman audience who probably spoke mostly Greek.

★ *The Aramaic language was a Galilean dialect of Hebrew of the village people in Jesus' time. Jesus probably spoke in the Jerusalem dialect of Hebrew when He taught in the synagogues and the Temple in Jerusalem. While they look very similar when written, the Galilean dialect does not have the strong guttural sounds of the original Hebrew. Greek was the common language of the street people and was used on the road signs of the Roman Empire. Latin was the language of the Roman officials.*

"and commanded that something should be given her to eat" – Jesus is *Life*, and He brought *Life* not only to this little girl, but Jesus brought *Life* to Capernaum that day. The Hebrew word for *"life"* is *"chay,"* and two of the other meanings of "chay" are *"alive"* or *"appetite."* While it may sound simple to Gentiles today, Jesus wanted to show the family that this little girl was *truly alive*, physically and spiritually. Eating had a much deeper meaning in Jesus'

time than it does today. God created the earth to bring forth the food to nourish His people! Then God created man to have the appetite to enjoy the food from the earth! Jesus is our *Bread of Life* that gives us the spiritual nourishment that results in everlasting life! Amen and Amen!

CHAPTER SIX

Mark 6:1-6 - *And he went out from thence, and came into his own country; and his disciples follow him. And when the sabbath day was come, he began to teach in the synagogue: and many hearing him were astonished, saying, From whence hath this man these things? and what wisdom is this which is given unto him, that even such mighty works are wrought by his hands? Is not this the carpenter, the son of Mary, the brother of James, and Joses, and of Juda, and Simon? and are not his sisters here with us? And they were offended at him. But Jesus said unto them, A prophet is not without honour, but in his own country, and among his own kin, and in his own house. And he could there do no mighty work, save that he laid his hands upon a few sick folk, and healed them. And he marvelled because of their unbelief. And he went round about the villages, teaching.*

According to Mark's account, Jesus left Capernaum and walked about 18 to 20 miles southwest to Nazareth, ★ *his own country.* It was the Jewish custom to have a guest speaker on the *Sabbath day.* For a better rendering of exactly what Jesus said in the synagogue, one needs to study **Luke 4:15–30.**

★Nazareth was such a small village in Jesus' time that it is not mentioned in any Jewish writings. Today the city of Nazareth is over 75,000 people and is a mixture of Arab/Jewish population, mostly Arabs. Nazareth is about 70 percent Muslim and 30 percent Christian.

The importance of the town comes from the prophecy concerning the coming Messiah in **Isaiah 11:1 - And there shall come forth a rod out of the stem of Jesse, and a Branch (netzer) shall grow out of his roots.** *The name "netzer" is connected to a Hebrew word pun and Jesus being called a "Nazarene." The first followers of Jesus were called "people of the way of the Nazarene." There was a small group of the descendants of David who moved back to Nazareth after the Babylonian captivity, and it was referred to as the "Branch Village." This is where the angel, Gabriel, would be sent to give the annunciation to the virgin girl Mary. Today, the Hebrew word for "Christian" is "notzrim" that comes from the title "Yeshua ha Noztri" or "Jesus of Nazareth."*

"and what wisdom is this which is given unto him, that even such mighty works are wrought by his hands?" - The local residents of the little town of Nazareth did not know that in their presence was the Almighty God that the prophets wrote about in human flesh:

Who hath measured the waters in the hollow of his hand, and meted out heaven with the span, and comprehended the dust of the earth in a measure, and weighed the mountains in scales, and the hills in a balance? Who hath directed the Spirit of the LORD, or being his counsellor hath taught him? With whom took he counsel, and who instructed him, and taught him in the path of judgment, and taught him knowledge, and shewed to him the way of understanding? Behold, the nations are as a drop of a bucket, and are counted as the small dust of the balance: behold, he taketh up the isles as a very little thing.

Isaiah 40:12-15

"Is not this the carpenter" – The first Adam was created as a grown man without ever having been a babe in a manger or a young boy growing up in Nazareth. But the second Adam came into this world to know all of the sufferings of His people and to be identified with those who were looked down upon. The cave in Bethlehem heard His cry! The hills of Nazareth heard the sound of the hammer as He worked as a *carpenter*! The Greek word *"tekton"* and the Hebrew word *"charash"* for *carpenter* are very similar in meaning; however, the Hebrew word for *carpenter* carries more weight. Jesus could have worked as an artisan, a blacksmith, a carpenter, and a stonemason. Jesus no doubt built wooden plows, doors, as well as helped to construct some of the stone dwellings in and around Nazareth. It was

a strong Jewish custom for a child to learn a trade from his father.

"the son of Mary, the brother of James, and Joses, and of Juda, * and Simon? - Church history records that the grandsons of Jude lived until the time of the Emperor Trajan. (98-117AD) It is recorded that they were hardworking men who showed their calloused hands to the Emperor Domitian. (81-96AD) These words are recorded by the historian Eusebius:

*For Domitian feared the coming of Christ as Herod also had feared it....And when they (Jude's grandsons) were asked concerning Christ and his kingdom, of what sort it was and where and when it was to appear, they answered that it was not a temporal nor an earthly kingdom, but a heavenly and angelic one, which would appear at the end of the world, when he should come in glory to judge the quick and the dead, and to give unto every one according to his works. Upon hearing this, Domitian did not pass judgment against them but despising them as of no account, he let them go, and by a decree put a stop to the persecution of the Church. Eusebius Church History 3.19,20

"brothers and sisters" - This passage in Mark has caused a lot of debate over the centuries, especially between the Catholic Church and the Protestant Church. The truth can be found when we study the Hebrew meanings. The Hebrew word for *"brother"* is *"ach"* and it can mean *"brothers, relatives, or kinsmen."* This is where the Catholic Church tries to prove the perpetual virginity of Mary and that Jesus did not have any *brothers*, that they were only *cousins*. The problem lies in the Hebrew word for *"sisters"*

or *"achoth."* The word has to mean *"sisters."* Mary did have other children after Jesus was born, and the people in the family village of Nazareth knew them all.

When Jesus taught in the synagogue that He was the one Isaiah wrote about, the people were *offended.* What were they offended about in Jesus?

* *Jesus was just the son of a carpenter*
* *Jesus said that He was the one the prophets wrote about*
* *Jesus said that the message of the gospel would be sent to the Gentiles*

"A prophet is not without honour, but in his own country, and among his own kin, and in his own house" - The family of Jesus did not believe that He was the Messiah until after the resurrection. **(Acts 1:14)** As today, hometown people have a difficult time believing that God calls simple people for His kingdom work. Jesus referred to Himself as *a prophet*, but of course He was not just a prophet. He was that great *Prophet* that God promised Moses would come.

> **The LORD thy God will raise up unto thee a Prophet from the midst of thee, of thy brethren, like unto me; unto him ye shall hearken;**
> Deuteronomy 18:15, Acts 7:37

Jesus Sends Forth the Twelve

Mark 6:7-13 - *And he called unto him the twelve, and began to send them forth by two and*

two; and gave them power over unclean spirits; And commanded them that they should take nothing for their journey, save a staff only; no scrip, no bread, no money in their purse: But be shod with sandals; and not put on two coats. And he said unto them, In what place soever ye enter into an house, there abide till ye depart from that place. And whosoever shall not receive you, nor hear you, when ye depart thence, shake off the dust under your feet for a testimony against them. Verily I say unto you, It shall be more tolerable for Sodom and Gomorrha in the day of judgment, than for that city. And they went out, and preached that men should repent. And they cast out many devils, and anointed with oil many that were sick, and healed them.

As Jesus sent forth the 12 disciples *two-by-two* to preach that the people needed to *repent*, He was training them how to place their trust in Him to provide for their everyday needs. The idea of sending them out *two- by-two* reminds us of this passage:

Two are better than one; because they have a good reward for their labour. For if they fall, the one will lift up his fellow: but woe to him that is alone when he falleth; for he hath not another to help him up.

Eccl.4:9-10

When someone has all of the luxuries of life at his fingertips, he seems to forget his need of faith. Their message was so revolutionary that He gave them the power over *unclean spirits* and the power to *heal the sick.* The *anointing with oil* * was more than just a ritual; it was for medicinal purposes. This would set the precedence for the early church:

> *Is any sick among you? let him call for the elders of the church; and let them pray over him, anointing him with oil in the name of the Lord: And the prayer of faith shall save the sick, and the Lord shall raise him up; and if he have committed sins, they shall be forgiven him.*
>
> James 5:14–15

In 1963 a Greek monk discovered over 60 artifacts in a cave on Mount Zion, close to the Upper Room in Jerusalem. One artifact was a marble stone that had the inscriptions of the Messianic Seal and the words "For the oil of the Spirit." It is strongly believed that James was the leader of that first church who met in this cave and practiced the anointing of oil. The Israeli authorities have kept this a secret over the years and refused to have the artifacts displayed. This author has had the privilege of being given access into the cave on two occasions. The first Jewish Christians not only worshipped in this cave, but many were baptized here. It is under the tight control of the Greek Orthodox today because it was a Greek monk who made the discovery.

So the disciples would *preach the message of the kingdom,*

drive out the demons, pray for the sick, administer the medicine of oil, all in the Name of the Master. This first journey would be something the disciples would never forget. And the best was yet to come!

"shake the dust under your feet for a testimony against them" – When the people rejected the message of the apostles, they were rejecting Jesus as well. The symbolic act of shaking the dust off of their feet was a sign of severe judgment that would follow.

The Death of John the Baptist and the Troubled Conscience of Herod Antipas

> **Mark 6:14-29 -** *And king Herod * heard of him; (for his name was spread abroad:) and he said, That John the Baptist was risen from the dead, and therefore mighty works do shew forth themselves in him. Others said, That it is Elias. And others said, That it is a prophet, or as one of the prophets. But when Herod heard thereof, he said, It is John, whom I beheaded: he is risen from the dead. For Herod himself had sent forth and laid hold upon John, and bound him in prison for Herodias' sake, his brother Philip's wife: for he had married her. For John had said unto Herod, It is not lawful for thee to have thy brother's wife. Therefore Herodias had a quarrel against him, and would have killed him; but she could not: For Herod*

feared John, knowing that he was a just man and an holy, and observed him; and when he heard him, he did many things, and heard him gladly. And when a convenient day was come, that Herod on his birthday made a supper to his lords, high captains, and chief estates of Galilee; And when the daughter of the said Herodias came in, and danced, and pleased Herod and them that sat with him, the king said unto the damsel, Ask of me whatsoever thou wilt, and I will give it thee. And he sware unto her, Whatsoever thou shalt ask of me, I will give it thee, unto the half of my kingdom. And she went forth, and said unto her mother, What shall I ask? And she said, The head of John the Baptist. And she came in straightway with haste unto the king, and asked, saying, I will that thou give me by and by in a charger the head of John the Baptist. And the king was exceeding sorry; yet for his oath's sake, and for their sakes which sat with him, he would not reject her. And immediately the king sent an executioner, and commanded his head to be brought: and he went and beheaded him in the prison, * And brought his head in a charger, and gave it to the damsel: and the damsel gave it to her mother. And when his disciples heard of it, they came and took up his corpse, and laid it in a tomb.

When Herod the Great died in 1 BC, the Roman Emperor Augustus Caesar divided the kingdom of Israel among the three of Herod's sons, called a tetrarchy. Herod Antipas is the one mentioned in this text, who was the tetrarch (not king) of Galilee and Perea until 39AD. Herod Archelaus was given Judea and Jerusalem. Herod Philip was given the land in the northeast which included Ituraea, Trachonitis, and the territory of Caesarea Philippi below Mount Hermon. **(Luke 3:1)**

Now some of the Jews thought that the destruction of Herod's [Antipas's] army came from God, and that very justly, as a punishment of what he did against John, that was called the Baptist: for Herod slew him, who was a good man, and commanded the Jews to exercise virtue, both as to righteousness towards one another, and piety towards God, and so to come to baptism; for that the washing [with water] would be acceptable to him, if they made use of it, not in order to the putting away [or the remission] of some sins [only], but for the purification of the body; supposing still that the soul was thoroughly purified beforehand by righteousness. Now when [many] others came in crowds about him, for they were very greatly moved [or pleased] by hearing his words, Herod, who feared lest the great influence John had over the people might put it into his power and inclination to raise a rebellion, (for they seemed ready to do any thing he should advise) thought it best, by putting him to death, to prevent any mischief he might cause, and not bring himself into difficulties, by sparing a man who might make him repent of it when it would be too late. Accordingly he was sent a prisoner, out of Herod's suspicious temper, to <u>Macherus</u>, the castle I before mentioned, and was there put to death. Now the Jews had an

opinion that the destruction of this army was sent as a punishment upon Herod, and a mark of God's displeasure to him.[64]
Flavius Josephus (37-100AD) Antiquities of the Jews, Book 18, 5:2

The fame of our Lord Jesus had spread throughout the Galilee. When Herod Antipas heard about Jesus, he thought that John the Baptist had risen from the dead. Herod Antipas knew that John was a godly man, and he was convicted when he heard him speak. But the lust that Herod had for his brother Philip's wife *Herodias*, and *Salome*, *(Antiquities of the Jews, Book 18, Chapter 5:4)* her daughter, led to his ultimate downfall. ★ The seductive dance of the daughter of Herodias caused Herod to offer her half of his kingdom. With a heart full of wickedness and hatred, she asked for the head of John the Baptist. Because of the promise that he made to her and the people that were at his birthday party, Herod sorrowfully sent an executioner and beheaded John in prison.

★The history is rather lengthy and complicated, but Herod Antipas' former wife, Phasaelis, was a daughter to the Nabatean king Aretas. After Herod cheated on his daughter, and some territorial differences, eventually king Aretas raised up an army and wiped out Herod Antipas' army. Because of pride and the lust of power, Herodias still persuaded Herod to become a king. Herod then went to Rome with his wife Herodias to request the title of king from then Caesar Gaius Calligula. (37-41AD) But Herod's nephew, Agrippa, had already sent letters to Caesar accusing his brother of treason. Herod Antipas was deposed to Gaul and his

territories were given to Agrippa. Herod Antipas should have stayed with his Nabatean wife.

"Herod, it is not lawful for thee to have thy brother's wife" - John was warning Herod that God's laws in the Torah were more than just words. Herod was living a life of debauchery, and John had the courage to stand up to him.

> **Thou shalt not uncover the nakedness of thy daughter in law: she is thy son's wife; thou shalt not uncover her nakedness. Thou shalt not uncover the nakedness of thy brother's wife: it is thy brother's nakedness. Thou shalt not uncover the nakedness of a woman and her daughter, neither shalt thou take her son's daughter, or her daughter's daughter, to uncover her nakedness; for they are her near kinswomen: it is wickedness.**
>
> Leviticus 18:15-17

In contrast to this troubling birthday party of Herod Antipas is the parallel story of the banquet scene in **Esther 5-7.** When *Queen Esther* was giving a feast for the *Persian King Ahasuerus*, he promised to give her half of his kingdom. Esther requested that the king spare the life of the Jews throughout the Persian Empire. This is a mirror opposite of Herodias and her daughter begging for the execution of John the Baptist.

The Apostles Return

> **Mark 6:30-31 -** *And the apostles gathered themselves together unto Jesus, and told him all things, both what they had done, and what they had taught. And he said unto them, Come ye yourselves apart into a desert place, and rest a while: for there were many coming and going, and they had no leisure so much as to eat.*

After the first missionary journey of the apostles, the apostles couldn't wait to inform Jesus about what they had done and what they had preached to the people. As though Jesus didn't already know! We have to understand that the ministry of the Messiah happened during a time in the history of Israel when there was great darkness but also great anticipation. When the crowds heard the preaching of the apostles, they were hoping that the long-awaited Messiah had arrived to set them free from Roman oppression. They wanted to see and to hear the Master themselves. The crowds were so overwhelming that Jesus and His disciples didn't have time to eat. Jesus took His disciples to a private place that would result in one of the greatest miracles of the Messiah.

Feeding the Five Thousand

> **Mark 6:32-34 -** *And they departed into a desert place by ship privately. And the people saw them departing, and many knew him, and*

*ran afoot thither out of all cities, and outwent
them, and came together unto him. And Jesus,
when he came out, saw much people, and was
moved with compassion toward them, because
they were as sheep not having a shepherd: and
he began to teach them many things.*

As Jesus and His disciples were traveling across the
northern part of the Sea of Galilee by ship, the multitudes
were outrunning them across the hills. What a sight that
must have been! Sometimes we focus so much on the
supernatural miracles of the Messiah that we forget about
His compassion for humanity. He became one of His
people so He could know what they were experiencing.
Their everyday needs were His everyday needs. When
Jesus saw the crowds, His heart was broken. He knew that
the common people were caught in the crossways of the
Roman power and the corrupt religious establishment. The
am ha eretz, or *people of the land*, were just existing with the
bare necessities of life. But Jesus saw them also in a spiritual
sense not having anyone to lead them. They were like
scattered sheep with no shepherd. Jesus, *the Good Shepherd*,
is using a familiar simile that He used hundreds of times
before throughout the history of Israel:

*Which may go out before them, and which
may go in before them, and which may lead
them out, and which may bring them in; that*

the congregation of the LORD be not as sheep which have no shepherd.

Numbers 27:17

And he said, I saw all Israel scattered upon the hills, as sheep that have not a shepherd: and the LORD said, These have no master: let them return every man to his house in peace.

I Kings 22:17

Woe be unto the pastors that destroy and scatter the sheep of my pasture! saith the LORD. Therefore thus saith the LORD God of Israel against the pastors that feed my people; Ye have scattered my flock, and driven them away, and have not visited them: behold, I will visit upon you the evil of your doings, saith the LORD. And I will gather the remnant of my flock out of all countries whither I have driven them, and will bring them again to their folds; and they shall be fruitful and increase.

Jeremiah 23:1-3

For the idols have spoken vanity, and the diviners have seen a lie, and have told false dreams; they comfort in vain: therefore they went their way as a flock, they were troubled, because there was no shepherd.

Zechariah 10:2

And I will set up one shepherd over them, and he shall feed them, even my servant David; he shall feed them, and he shall be their shepherd.

Ezekiel 34:23

The LORD is my shepherd; I shall not want. He maketh me to lie down in green pastures: he leadeth me beside the still waters. He restoreth my soul: he leadeth me in the paths of righteousness for his name's sake. Yea, though I walk through the valley of the shadow of death, I will fear no evil: for thou art with me; thy rod and thy staff they comfort me. Thou preparest a table before me in the presence of mine enemies: thou anointest my head with oil; my cup runneth over. Surely goodness and mercy shall follow me all the days of my life: and I will dwell in the house of the LORD for ever.

Psalm 23

Mark 6:35-44 - *And when the day was now far spent, his disciples came unto him, and said, This is a desert place, and now the time is far passed: Send them away, that they may go into the country round about, and into the villages, and buy themselves bread: for they have nothing to eat. He answered and said unto them, Give ye them to eat. And they say unto him, Shall we go and buy two hundred pennyworth of* *bread, and give them to eat? He saith unto them, How many loaves have ye? go and see. And when they knew, they say, Five, and two fishes. And he commanded them to make all sit down by companies upon the green grass. And they sat down in ranks, by hundreds, and by fifties. And when he had taken the five loaves and the two fishes, he looked up to heaven, and blessed, and brake the loaves, and gave them to his disciples to set before them; and the two fishes divided he among them all. And they did all eat, and were filled. And they took up twelve baskets full of the fragments, and of the fishes. And they that did eat of the loaves were about five thousand men.*

This miracle is so important that it is mentioned in all four of the gospels. When visiting the Sea of Galilee, the memory of this miracle sinks into one's mind forever. The feeding of the multitude looks to the past history of Israel and to the future where we, as believers today, internalize the Son of God into our lives by faith. It's easy to dissect each individual verse and overspiritualize the miracle. To keep the continuity of this beautiful miracle in the context of Mark's narrative, here are a few important nuggets:

* *They were in a deserted place*
* *It was late in the day*
* *The people were hungry*

* *Two hundred denarius = (over half of a year's wages)*
* *Five loaves and two fishes*
* *It was green grass = (spring time)*
* *Ranks of fifties and hundreds = (Moses in **Exodus 18:21**)*
* *Jesus looked up to heaven and blessed and broke the bread*
* *Jesus gave it to the disciples to distribute*
* *Twelve baskets = (12 tribes of Israel)*
* *The Greek word in Mark for "baskets" is "kophinoy" (Jewish baskets)*
* *Five thousand men (not counting women and children)*

The Sinless Messiah Walks on the Sea

Mark 6:45-52 - *And straightway he constrained his disciples to get into the ship, and to go to the other side before unto Bethsaida, ★ while he sent away the people. And when he had sent them away, he departed into a mountain to pray. And when even was come, the ship was in the midst of the sea, and he alone on the land. And he saw them toiling in rowing; for the wind was contrary unto them: and about the fourth watch of the night he cometh unto them, walking upon the sea, and would have passed by them. But when they saw him walking upon the sea, they supposed it had been a spirit, and cried out: For they all saw him, and were* *troubled. And immediately he talked with them, and saith unto them, Be of good cheer: it is I; be not afraid. And he went up unto them into the ship; and the wind ceased: and they were sore amazed in themselves beyond measure, and wondered. For they considered not the miracle of the loaves: for their heart was hardened.*

*The miracle of the Feeding of the Five Thousand took place on the northeastern shore of the Galilee near the fishing village called Beth-saida. The ruins were first discovered in the 1930's by Edward Robinson and later excavated more thoroughly in 1987. It was the home of three of Jesus' disciples; Peter, Andrew, and Philip. **(John 1:44)** The village was changed to a polis, or city, by Herod Philip in 30AD, and renamed Bethsaida-Julias, after the wife of Caesar Augustus, the mother of Tiberias Caesar, who died in 29AD. Herod Philip was buried here in 34AD. Scholars still debate the exact location of Bethsaida, as the present ruins are well over a mile from the seashore. But the answer may be found in the fact that several huge earthquakes over the centuries changed the course of the Jordan River a little westward, and sedimentation and silt have filled in where the water used to come up to the hill of Bethsaida. Soil samples reveal that the land between the village and the Jordan River was underwater during the time of Jesus.

The miracle of *Yeshua* walking on the water has captivated this author for many years. It's not just the sentimentality of visualizing our Master walking on water, but it is the deep truths that our Lord was conveying to His disciples. Again, let's do not overspiritualize the text; it's much too beautiful and powerful for that. But let's mention a few points of interest that might help us better understand what happened during another stormy night out on the Sea of Galilee:

* *Jesus sent the disciples out on the sea*
* *Jesus went up into the mountain to pray*
* *Jesus saw the disciples struggling even in the darkness of the night*
* *It was the fourth watch of the night =* *(between 3:00 a.m. - 6:00 a.m.)*
* *Jesus walked on the sea =* (**Job 9:8**, *"Only God treads on the waves of the sea."*) *Jesus had no weight of sin as He strides safely across the water without sinking*
* *He would have passed by them =* *(The mysterious Person of the Messiah had no intention of passing them by but made them think that He would* (Read **Luke 24:28**) *because He wanted them to reach out to Him)*
* *The disciples saw Jesus walking on the water even in the darkness because of His glory*
* *Jesus started talking to the disciples while standing on the water*
* *Footsteps of Jesus, Psalm 77:19*
* *Be of good cheer: it is I; be not afraid – (Jesus is the "I Am" of Moses. Teaching the disciples not to be afraid once He is out of their sight)*
* *Jesus climbed into the ship and the storm ceased*
* *The disciples had been so afraid that they forgot about the miracle of Jesus feeding the multitude*

As we think about the impact this miracle would have had on the church in Rome that Mark was writing to, they were being assured that there was only one true God who had dominion over the powers of the sea, *The Lord Jesus Christ*! They could have the faith that He would take care of them in their hours of persecution. The truth that Jesus walked on the water tells us today that He knows where we are at all times. He is the Almighty God who will watch after His children in a fallen world!

Jesus and His Disciples Cross Over the Sea

> **Mark 6:53-56 -** *And when they had passed over, they came into the land of Gennesaret, ★ and drew to the shore. And when they were come out of the ship, straightway they knew him, And ran through that whole region round about, and began to carry about in beds those that were sick, where they heard he was. And whithersoever he entered, into villages, or cities, or country, they laid the sick in the streets, and besought him that they might touch if it were but the border of his garment: and as many as touched him were made whole.*

★*The town named "Gennessaret" is the Grecian form of the name "Kinneret" or "Chinnereth" found in* **Joshua 19:35, Numbers 34:11,** *and* **Deuteronomy 3:17.** *The town has such prominence that one of the names of the sea would be the*

Lake of Kinnereth (Sea of Galilee). Perched high on a hill on the northern shore of the lake, the people could view the entire, fertile plain below. The site has been located as Tell-Kenrot and excavations started in 2002 and are ongoing. The location sits directly behind the private hotel where this author has stayed on numerous occasions. One pilgrim walked behind the hotel one day and discovered a piece of pottery from the archaeology dig. Needless to say, he was elated and brought home a treasured piece of history.

Jesus continues to train His disciples by showing them His deity by His miracles: from feeding thousands, walking on the water, and even the *touch of His garments*. There were no words to explain this Man from Galilee. He was not Elijah, He was not John the Baptist raised from the dead, He was not one of the prophets of old. He was truly the God-Man, *Yeshua Ha Mashiach,* Jesus the Messiah! Jesus used tangible things such as clothes, spittle, clay, and water as channels of His power to flow through.

CHAPTER SEVEN

The Messiah and the Traditions of the Pharisees

Mark 7:1-5 - *Then came together unto him the Pharisees, and certain of the scribes, which came from Jerusalem. And when they saw some of his disciples eat bread with defiled, that is to say, with unwashen, hands, they found fault. For the Pharisees, and all the Jews, except they wash their hands oft, eat not, holding the tradition of the elders. And when they come from the market, except they wash, they eat not. And many other things there be, which they have received to hold, as the washing of cups, and pots, brasen vessels, and of tables. Then the Pharisees and scribes asked him, Why walk not thy disciples according to the tradition of the elders, but eat bread with unwashen hands?*

The fame of our Lord had reached 80 miles south to Jerusalem. The religious leaders deemed it necessary to dispatch a delegation to investigate the matter. Their hypocrisy caused them to live in fear of losing their positions. To hear that the multitudes were following a preacher from Galilee was a severe threat. Was this preacher from Nazareth living according the *tradition of the elders?* ★ Was He keeping kosher? Their jealous hearts would find something to accuse Jesus of.

★*The oral laws, or the tradition of the elders, were self-manufactured and added to the Mosaic Law by the scribes and Pharisees. This even started before Jesus' time. They were designed to supplement God's written law and to intensify the requirements of ritual purity. These oral laws were handed down from the Rabbi Shammai and Rabbi Hillel. These oral laws were eventually written down by 120 rabbis called the tannaim, around 200AD, in Hebrew and Aramiac. This is known as the Mishnah.*

It is interesting and ironic that Tiberias was considered an impure city during Jesus' time because Herod Antipas had built the city in 20AD over a Jewish cemetery. In the second century, a famous Rabbi, Simeon bar Yochai, moved the corpses from the cemetery and declared the city ritually pure in 145AD. After the Jewish Revolt of 135AD, the Jews had to flee from Jerusalem and many went to live in Tiberias. Rabbi Judah haNassi is credited with finalizing the Mishnah in Tiberias. For this reason Tiberias today is one of the four most religious cities to religious Jews; the other three are Jerusalem, Hebron, and Safed.

"but eat with unwashen hands?" – This was not specifically in the Mosaic Law but was a strong tradition within the Pharisees of Jesus' time. They believed that eating with unwashed hands was as unclean as having sex with a prostitute. Eating with unwashed hands meant that the bread they are eating is unclean. So it wasn't about good hygiene, it was about ritual purity. By the way, have you ever wondered where the disciples of our Lord got their bread? Could it have been from the 12 baskets that were left over from the feeding of the 5,000?

> **Mark 7:6-9 -** *He answered and said unto them, Well hath Esaias prophesied of you hypocrites, as it is written, This people honoureth me with their lips, but their heart is far from me. Howbeit in vain do they worship me, teaching for doctrines the commandments of men. For laying aside the commandment of God, ye hold the tradition of men, as the washing of pots and cups: and many other such like things ye do. And he said unto them, Full well ye reject the commandment of God, that ye may keep your own tradition.*

Jesus is using a passage from Isaiah to rebuke the Pharisees:

> *Wherefore the Lord said, Forasmuch as this people draw near me with their mouth, and with their lips do honour me, but have removed their heart far from me, and their fear toward me is taught by the precept of men:*
>
> Isaiah 29:13

In simple terms, the religious leaders were using their traditions as a substitute for genuine faith and obedience to

God. They had rather have their traditions than to believe in their Messiah, who was walking in their midst. This is how blind religious traditions can become. Morality and church attendance can hinder people from walking in the blessed Holy Spirit. Someone may be clean on the outside and speak religious clichés while his heart is full of evil and wickedness. We still have the spirit of the Pharisees with us today.

> **Mark 7:10-13 -** *For Moses said, Honour thy father and thy mother; and, Whoso curseth father or mother, let him die the death: But ye say, If a man shall say to his father or mother, It is Corban,* that is to say, a gift, by whatsoever thou mightest be profited by me; he shall be free. And ye suffer him no more to do ought for his father or his mother; Making the word of God of none effect through your tradition, which ye have delivered: and many such like things do ye.*

Jesus gives them an example of setting aside God's Word in order to keep their traditions. It was written in the Torah that a person must honor his father and mother:

> *Honour thy father and thy mother: that thy days may be long upon the land which the* LORD *thy God giveth thee.*
> Exodus 20:12

And he that curseth his father, or his mother, shall surely be put to death.

Exodus 21:17

For every one that curseth his father or his mother shall be surely put to death: he hath cursed his father or his mother; his blood shall be upon him.

Leviticus 20:9

Corban, or Qorban, is a Hebrew word for many of the sacrificial "offerings" in the Old Testament. The word simply means to "be near." Sacrificial offerings brought the children of Israel nearer to God. But the Pharisees of Jesus' time had invented a strong tradition that instead of giving money to help their parents, they could just pronounce their money as "Qorban." In other words, they had hypocritically dedicated their money to give to God to keep from honoring their father and mother. It was a religious sly way, that sounded pious, but Jesus saw through their covetous hearts.

In 1997, a first-century ossuary was found with an inscription on the top lid. It reads, "All that a man may find-to-his-profit in this ossuary is korban to God." The result of the vow is that if anyone should feel free to steal the valuables within the ossuary, he would be robbing from God, and hopefully that would dissuade him from taking it.

Jesus and the Parable of the Unclean Heart

> **Mark 7:14-23 -** *And when he had called all the people unto him, he said unto them, Hearken unto me every one of you, and understand: There is nothing from without a man, that entering into him can defile him: but the things which come out of him, those are they that defile the man. If any man have ears to hear, let him hear. And when he was entered into the house from the people, his disciples asked him concerning the parable. And he saith unto them, Are ye so without understanding also? Do ye not perceive, that whatsoever thing from without entereth into the man, it cannot defile him; Because it entereth not into his heart, but into the belly, and goeth out into the draught, purging all meats? And he said, That which cometh out of the man, that defileth the man. For from within, out of the heart of men, proceed evil thoughts, adulteries, fornications, murders, Thefts, covetousness, wickedness, deceit, lasciviousness, an evil eye, blasphemy, pride, foolishness: All these evil things come from within, and defile the man.*

This passage of scripture caused controversy in the early church and has caused religious debates down through the centuries. Did Jesus abrogate the dietary laws of the Old Testament? The context of this chapter will help clear up the problem. Jesus is talking about the Pharisees who pronounced that He and His disciples were *ceremonially unclean* by not washing their hands before they ate. Notice the spiritual sins that Jesus is mentioning: *evil thoughts, adulteries, fornications, murders, thefts, covetousness, wickedness, deceit, lasciviousness, evil eye, blasphemy, pride, and foolishness.* Jesus is not referring to what animals to eat or not eat. ✱ The Pharisees were keeping their oral traditions about being *ceremonially clean,* and yet their hearts were filled with sin. It's the heart of man that needs washing through the blood of the Messiah. A major part of living the kingdom life is a matter of the heart. The children of the kingdom realize that their hearts need to be made pure:

> **Blessed are the pure in heart: for they shall see God.**
>
> Matthew 5:8

✱*The Apostle Paul addressed meat issues in places such as* **Romans 14:14, "I know, and am persuaded by the Lord Jesus, that there is nothing unclean of itself."** *Paul was referring to this same passage in* **Mark 7**, *and he is not saying that Jesus spoke against the dietary laws of the Old Testament. Paul was addressing a major issue in Rome about eating meat that part of it had been offered up to idols in the pagan world. The meat was not unclean within itself, but if it violated a person's conscience, or if it offended the Jewish believers in Jesus to eat it, then they should not. It was a matter of the conscience or offending a brother in the Lord. For example: while it is not a sin for a Gentile to eat a ham sandwich, one should follow his* *or her own conscience about eating healthy or offending someone who doesn't believe in eating pork. There are those who become legalistic about eating and try to act pious, instead of obeying their conscience or thinking about causing an offense.*

Jesus and the Syrophenician Woman

> **Mark 7:24-30 -** *And from thence he arose, and went into the borders of Tyre and Sidon, and entered into an house, and would have no man know it: but he could not be hid. For a certain woman, ★ whose young daughter had an unclean spirit, heard of him, and came and fell at his feet: The woman was a Greek, a Syrophenician by nation; and she besought him that he would cast forth the devil out of her daughter. But Jesus said unto her, Let the children first be filled: for it is not meet to take the children's bread, and to cast it unto the dogs. And she answered and said unto him, Yes, Lord: yet the dogs under the table eat of the children's crumbs. And he said unto her, For this saying go thy way; the devil is gone out of thy daughter. And when she was come to her house, she found the devil gone out, and her daughter laid upon the bed.*

★*There is a statement that has been found in the pseudo-Jewish (cannot be proven to be true) writings of one named Clement, who traveled with Simon Peter. He writes that this woman's name was Justa and her daughter's name was Berenice.*

The pressure was mounting for our Lord Jesus and His disciples. Jesus took His disciples 35 to 40 miles north to escape the crowds and the religious leaders. There were deep spiritual lessons that Jesus wanted to teach His disciples, and He took them into a Gentile region that was considered contemptible by the Jews. **(Ezekiel 26, Joel 3)** *Tyre and Sidon* were two Phoenician cities on the Mediterranean coast north of Israel. Jesus tried to hide Himself, but the news had already spread about His mighty works even to that region.

> *And from Jerusalem, and from Idumaea, and from beyond Jordan; and they about Tyre and Sidon, a great multitude, when they had heard what great things he did, came unto him.*
>
> Mark 3:8

The miracle of Jesus performing an exorcism on this Gentile woman's daughter is a very underrated and overlooked miracle. To keep the context flowing, a few important truths of the miracle follow:

* *Whose young daughter had an unclean spirit* – *Her daughter was demon possessed.*
* *Came and fell at his feet* - *The humility and urgency of the mother to leave her daughter back at the house to go and fall down before Jesus.*

* ***The woman was a Greek*** *- A non-Jewish woman from either Syria or Africa.*

* ***Let the children first be filled*** *— The children of Israel hold the first claims to the blessings of the Messiah.*

* ***For it is not meet to take the children's bread, and to cast it unto the dogs*** *- The gospel was to the Jew first. The Gentiles were considered to be dogs by the Jews. The message would eventually go to the Gentiles, but Jesus the Messiah was sent first to the lost sheep of the house of Israel.*

* ***Yes, Lord: yet the dogs under the table eat of the children's crumbs*** *- Shows the faith, humility and the persistence of the Gentile woman.*

* ***For this saying go thy way; the devil is gone out of thy daughter*** *- Because of the woman's great faith, Jesus cast the demons out of her Gentile daughter.*

* ***And when she was come to her house, she found the devil gone out, and her daughter laid upon the bed*** *- The facts were that her prayer to Jesus was heard, and what Jesus told her really happened. Her daughter was no longer tormented, but lying down with peace that prefigures the peace Jesus would give to everyone who places faith in Him.*

This beautiful miracle must have been a great blessing to the Gentile believers in Rome seeing that Jesus showed mercy to a Gentile even during His earthly ministry to Israel. It may have also helped the Gentile believers to see the pattern of the gospel of Christ being spread to the Jew first.

For I am not ashamed of the gospel of Christ: for it is the power of God unto salvation to every one that believeth; to the Jew first, and also to the Greek.

Romans 1:16

Jesus Sighs and Heals the Deaf and Dumb in the Decapolis

Mark 7:31-37 - *And again, departing from the coasts of Tyre and Sidon, he came unto the sea of Galilee, through the midst of the coasts of Decapolis. And they bring unto him one that was deaf, and had an impediment in his speech; and they beseech him to put his hand upon him. And he took him aside from the multitude, and put his fingers into his ears, and he spit, and touched his tongue; And looking up to heaven, he sighed, and saith unto him, Ephphatha, that is, Be opened. And straightway his ears were opened, and the string of his tongue was loosed, and he spake plain. And he charged them that they should tell no man: but the more he charged them, so much the more a great deal they published it; And were beyond measure astonished, saying, He hath done all things well: he maketh both the deaf to hear, and the dumb to speak.*

Jesus and His disciples walked the long way southward and went through the eastern side of the Galilee through the Decapolis. They brought to Jesus a man who was *deaf and who had a speech impediment.* One could say that he was deaf and dumb. ★ There are several unusual truths about this miracle that show the humanity of our Lord, as well as His supernatural power:

★ ***Put his fingers into his ears*** *– The finger of God is mentioned in* **Exodus 31:18,** ***"And he gave unto Moses, when he had made an end of communing with him upon mount Sinai, two tables of testimony, tables of stone, written with the finger of God."***

★ ***He spit*** *– The sinless spit, or raqaq, from Jesus the Son of God was a purposeful action of healing. The opposite use of sinful spit would be used as a mockery at Jesus later in Jerusalem.* **(Mark 10:34)**

★ ***Touched his tongue*** *- The sinless spit of Jesus on His holy finger touching the tongue of a sinful man who could not speak.*

★ ***Looking up to heaven*** *– Jesus knew where He had come from there would be no more sickness or suffering. He was God, but was so human that He felt the need to pray.*

★ *He sighed – In the Hebrew language the word "anach" means "to mourn or groan." Jesus was probably sighing about the results of sin coming into the world and the suffering it had brought to His people.*

★ **Saith unto him, Ephphatha, that is, Be opened –** *Mark was writing to a Greek-speaking audience in Rome, and he interprets the Master's Aramaic language for them.*

There seems to be a strange irony in Jesus loosing the man's *tongue* and then telling His disciples and the people around not to *tell* anyone about the miracle. We can understand how the healed man, who now could plainly speak, could not keep quiet. Jesus knew what would happen!

★A prophecy about the deaf and dumb being healed in the future kingdom age also pointed to the earthly ministry of the Messiah. **Isaiah 35:5-6, "Then the eyes of the blind shall be opened, and the ears of the deaf shall be unstopped. Then shall the lame man leap as an hart, and the tongue of the dumb sing: for in the wilderness shall waters break out, and streams in the desert."**

CHAPTER EIGHT

Feeding of the Four Thousand

Mark 8:1-9 - *In those days the multitude being very great, and having nothing to eat, Jesus called his disciples unto him, and saith unto them, I have compassion on the multitude, because they have now been with me three days, and have nothing to eat: And if I send them away fasting to their own houses, they will faint by the way: for divers of them came from far. And his disciples answered him, From whence can a man satisfy these men with bread here in the wilderness? And he asked them, How many loaves have ye? And they said, Seven. And he commanded the people to sit down on the ground: and he took the seven loaves, and gave thanks, and brake, and gave to his disciples to set before them; and they did set them before the people. And they had a few small fishes: and he blessed, and commanded*

*to set them also before them. So they did eat,
and were filled: and they took up of the broken
meat that was left seven baskets. And they that
had eaten were about four thousand: and he
sent them away.*

To keep our thoughts within the context and note the similarities and differences of the feeding of the 5,000 **(Mark 6:32-44)** a few obvious, as well as hidden facts, follow:

* ★ *The location is the east side of Galilee in the Decapolis (Gentiles) instead of* the north side of Galilee at Bethsaida (Jewish)
* ★ *Three days without food instead of just* one day
* ★ *Fasting is mentioned instead of sending them away* to buy bread
* ★ *The multitude had traveled from a far instead of* across the lake
* ★ *Seven loaves and a few small fishes instead of* five loaves and two fishes
* ★ *The ground instead of* green grass
* ★ *Seven baskets instead of* 12 baskets
* ★ *Greek word for "baskets" is "spuris" (Large Gentile baskets) instead of "kophinoy" (Small Jewish baskets)*
* ★ *Four thousand instead of* 5,000
* ★ *Seven baskets symbolize the seven Gentile nations when Israel entered into the Promised Land.* **Joshua 3:10** *- Canaanites, Hittites, Hivites, Perizzites,*

Girgashites, Amorites, and Jebusites. The 12 baskets symbolize the 12 tribes of Israel; Reuben, Simeon, Levi, Judah, Issachar, Zebulon, Dan, Naphtali, Gad, Asher, Joseph,(including Manasseh and Ephraim) and Benjamin

The Jewish Messiah would offer *Living Bread* to the Jews and to the Gentiles. This is a major miracle for the Jewish disciples of Jesus to see this truth. This also marks a major transition in the earthly ministry of the Messiah. He had taken the disciples to the Gentile territory of Tyre and Sidon, and now He feeds a Gentile multitude in a Gentile territory, *the Decapolis.* ★

★Region of ten cities controlled by Rome on the east-southeast side of the Sea of Galilee. The cities were: Gerasa, Scythopolis, (west of the Jordan River and the largest of the ten cities, the capital) Hippos, Gadara, Pella, Philadelphia, Dion, Canatha, Raphana, and Damascus.

Jesus Sighs Deeply When the Pharisees Seek a Sign

Mark 8:10-12 - *And straightway he entered into a ship with his disciples, and came into the parts of Dalmanutha. ★ And the Pharisees came forth, and began to question with him, seeking of him a sign from heaven, tempting him. And he sighed deeply in his spirit, and saith, Why doth this generation seek after a sign? verily I say unto you, There shall no sign be given unto this generation.*

Dalmanutha was a Greek name of a village between Magdala and Genneseret along the northwest side of the lake. **Matthew 15:39** *calls the place Magdala. Flavius Josephus mentions there were over 200 villages and towns clustered around the Galilee during the first century.*

Leaving the Decapolis region Jesus and His disciples entered into a small ship and sailed back across the lake, northwest toward Magdala. It's interesting that the Pharisees were keeping such a close watch on Jesus that they knew when He reached the Jewish side of the lake. They not only had heard about the miracles of Jesus, but they were trying to find some way to trap Him with *their* messianic questions. Did they want Jesus to give them a *sign from heaven*? Did they want something like the voice of God, or the *Bat Kol*, from heaven like Moses heard?

> **And God said unto Moses, I AM THAT I AM:
> and he said, Thus shalt thou say unto the
> children of Israel, I AM hath sent me unto you.**
> Exodus 3:14

Maybe they wanted to see fire come down out of heaven like the prophet Elijah?

> **Hear me, O LORD, hear me, that this people
> may know that thou art the LORD God, and
> that thou hast turned their heart back again.
> Then the fire of the LORD fell, and consumed
> the burnt sacrifice, and the wood, and the**

stones, and the dust, and licked up the water that was in the trench. And when all the people saw it, they fell on their faces: and they said, The LORD, he is the God; the LORD, he is the God.

I Kings 18:37-39

It's interesting that Jesus did say that there would be signs in the heavens before His second coming as a sign that judgment was coming:

And there shall be signs in the sun, and in the moon, and in the stars; and upon the earth distress of nations, with perplexity; the sea and the waves roaring;

Luke 21:25

During His earthly ministry, Jesus was more concerned about the needs of the people and equipping His disciples. He had performed enough miracles on earth that the religious people should have known who He was. If they had known the old Hebrew scripture better, they would have known that Jesus had to be the Messiah. Jesus had already given them plenty of *signs*. The religious leaders of the villages of Israel asking Jesus to give them a *sign* causes Him to *sigh deeply*. Jesus *sighed* when He saw what the physical results of sin had brought into the world **(Mark 7:34),** and here He *sighs deeply* at the spiritual results of unbelief. Interesting!

Jesus and His Disciples in the Boat with One Loaf of Bread

> **Mark 8:13-21** - *And he left them, and entering into the ship again departed to the other side. Now the disciples had forgotten to take bread, neither had they in the ship with them more than one loaf. And he charged them, saying, Take heed, beware of the leaven of the Pharisees, and of the leaven of Herod. And they reasoned among themselves, saying, It is because we have no bread. And when Jesus knew it, he saith unto them, Why reason ye, because ye have no bread? perceive ye not yet, neither understand? have ye your heart yet hardened? Having eyes, see ye not? and having ears, hear ye not? and do ye not remember? When I brake the five loaves among five thousand, how many baskets full of fragments took ye up? They say unto him, Twelve. And when the seven among four thousand, how many baskets full of fragments took ye up? And they said, Seven. And he said unto them, How is it that ye do not understand?*

From the northern shore Jesus and His disciples use a boat again to get away from the people. It's difficult for us to imagine how important bread was to the village people of Galilee is Jesus' time. They were not used to sitting down to a three- or four-course meal as we do today. The

137

disciples forgot to bring enough bread, but they did bring one round *loaf* of bread. The Greek word that Mark used here is *"artos"* which comes from the word *"airos"* which means *"to raise."* Similar to what we would call *pita bread*, it was most likely made out of barley that contained yeast. Jesus being the master teacher used the one loaf of yeasted bread to teach the disciples about the *leaven*, or the *yeast of the Pharisees and the yeast of Herod*:

* ★ *Leaven of the Pharisees* = religion
* ★ *Leaven of Herod* = Politics

As leaven permeates bread, the hypocrisy of the Pharisees had permeated and corrupted many of the people. Herod Antipas was not concerned about religion, but he was concerned about gaining power and control over the people in a political way. He was a mere puppet of Caesar, and he saw the crowds following Jesus as a threat to his position. If a messianic revolt were to break out, Caesar would depose Herod because of his lack of leadership in the Galilee. There was truly a messianic fever in the air because the true Messiah of Israel was walking the hills of Galilee.

"And they reasoned among themselves, saying, It is because we have no bread" - We know that the hearts of the disciples were hardened because of what Mark told us in chapter six:

> *For they considered not the miracle of the loaves: for their heart was hardened.*
>
> Mark 6:52

MARK THE MESSIAH'S GOSPEL

The disciples were in the boat with the *Bread of Life* Himself who had just fed thousands across the lake. They didn't need to worry about physical bread. Many times we are in the same boat as the disciples. We become so consumed with the everyday needs of the physical bread of life that we miss the *spiritual bread*. Sometimes the theology that we have been taught causes us to miss the message that Jesus is giving to us. Many believers today cannot see the deeper things of God because they get so involved in religion or politics.

Jesus Touches a Blind Man *Twice*?

> **Mark 8:22-26 -** *And he cometh to Bethsaida; and they bring a blind man unto him, and besought him to touch him. And he took the blind man by the hand, and led him out of the town; and when he had spit on his eyes, and put his hands upon him, he asked him if he saw ought. And he looked up, and said, I see men as trees, walking. After that he put his hands again upon his eyes, and made him look up: and he was restored, and saw every man clearly. And he sent him away to his house, saying, Neither go into the town, nor tell it to any in the town.*

They had crossed back over the lake close to the place where He fed the 5,000. Maybe Jesus was trying to bring the miracle back to the minds of the disciples? They are traveling back through Bethsaida on the way north into the territory of Herod Philip. This unusual and powerful miracle that Jesus performs in Bethsaida is only given to us in the gospel of Mark. Why did Jesus take the man outside of Bethsaida? Why did Jesus touch the blind man twice? What does the spittle of Jesus have to do with the miracle? This miracle not only shows the compassion of our Lord, but carries with it a fourfold message:

* *Jesus had already pronounced judgment on the town of Bethsaida*
* *Jesus still offered salvation to individuals*
* *Jesus was teaching His disciples who He was*
* *Jesus told the healed man not to tell it to any in the town*

Just as Jesus took the deaf and dumb man away from the crowds in **Mark 7:33**, here He takes him outside of *Bethsaida*. Because most of the miracles of the Messiah had occurred in *Bethsaida, Chorazin, and Capernaum*, Jesus pronounced judgment on those towns:

> *Then began he to upbraid the cities wherein most of his mighty works were done, because they repented not: Woe unto thee, Chorazin! woe unto thee, Bethsaida! for if the mighty works, which were done in you, had been done in Tyre and Sidon, they would have repented*

*long ago in sackcloth and ashes. But I say
unto you, It shall be more tolerable for Tyre
and Sidon at the day of judgment, than for
you. And thou, Capernaum, which art exalted
unto heaven, shalt be brought down to hell: for
if the mighty works, which have been done in
thee, had been done in Sodom, it would have
remained until this day. But I say unto you,
That it shall be more tolerable for the land of
Sodom in the day of judgment, than for thee.*

Matthew 11:20-24

Jesus used His own spit to heal the deaf and dumb in
Mark 7:33, and He made *spittle* when He mixed His spit
with clay in **John 9:6** to heal a blind man in Jerusalem.
Here Jesus uses His spit again to put on this blind man's
eyes. The *spit* of the firstborn male child was considered to
have healing powers. Jesus could have just spoken the word,
and the man would have been healed. Living among His
people during the early first century, Jesus used some of
the customs the people had been taught to teach who He
really was. He didn't have to use those customs, but He was
a Galilean Jew living among His people. Here is just one of
the many Jewish customs about the firstborn:

*There was a certain man who came before Rabbi
Hanina and said to him: I know that this man is a
firstborn. Rabbi Hanina said to him: From where
do you know? He said to Rabbi Hanina: Because*

141

> *when people would come before his father to obtain*
> *a cure for their ailing eyes, he would say to them:*
> *Go to my son Shikhhat, as he is a firstborn and his*
> *saliva heals this ailment.*
>
> Bava Batra 126b

Jesus was saying that He truly was the only begotten Son of God!! The power was believed to have come from the father, not the mother.

"After that he put his hands <u>again</u> upon his eyes" - Jesus didn't have to touch the man *twice*. We believe that there is a hidden lesson here that Jesus was teaching His disciples. They were on their way to Caesarea Philippi where Peter would make that life-changing confession that Jesus was the Son of God. Then three of the disciples were going to experience the Mount of Transfiguration not far from there. So little by little, *touch by touch*, Jesus was showing the disciples who He really was.

There could also be a spiritual lesson to the nation of Israel as a whole. When Jesus came the first time, only a few believed in Him as the Messiah, and there is *still* a partial blindness on Israel. But there is coming a day when all of Israel will see clearly that *Yeshua* is their Messiah:

> **For I would not, brethren, that ye should be**
> **ignorant of this mystery, lest ye should be wise**
> **in your own conceits; that blindness in part**
> **is happened to Israel, until the fulness of the**
> **Gentiles be come in. And so all Israel shall**

be saved: *as it is written, There shall come out of Sion the Deliverer, and shall turn away ungodliness from Jacob:*

Romans 11:25-26

Peter's Confession "Thou Art the Christ"

Mark 8:27-30 - *And Jesus went out, and his disciples, into the towns of Caesarea Philippi: * and by the way * he asked his disciples, saying unto them, Whom do men say that I am? And they answered, John the Baptist; but some say, Elias; and others, One of the prophets. And he saith unto them, But whom say ye that I am? And Peter answereth and saith unto him, Thou art the Christ. And he charged them that they should tell no man of him.*

Caesarea Philippi was literally Herod's Philip's Caesarea, built after the death of his father. His father, Herod the Great, had built the Mediterranean seacoast city of Caesarea. Caesarea Philippi was named after Caesar and after Herod Philip and was built at the base of Mount Hermon, about 40 miles north of the Sea of Galilee. Across the town of Caesarea Philippi was a Paneion temple where they worshipped the half- shepherd, half-man Greek mythology god, Pan. The Roman counterpart was called Faunus. This grotesque looking fertility god was worshipped throughout the Roman world and was believed to have been a part of the worship of the god Baal centuries before. It may have been the place of the

Old Testament Baalgad. ***"And the land of the Giblites, and all Lebanon, toward the sunrising, from Baalgad under mount Hermon unto the entering into Hamath." Joshua 13:5***

★*"By the way" is used in Mark's gospel seven times in two chapters.* **(Mark 8:27, 9:33-34, 10:17, 32, 46, 52)** *This depicts the steady movement of Jesus and His disciples. Things are recorded as they happened "on the journey" or "along the road" as they were walking. Jesus is moving quickly because the window of time is closing in when He must go down the Jordan Valley, through Jericho, and make His climb up to Jerusalem for His passion.*

"Whom do men say that I am?" – Up until this time, the disciple's eyes have been opened to Jesus the Messiah, but their image of Him is still out of focus, like the blind man who saw *men as trees walking.* They are about to feel a second touch from the Master. While the spiritual lessons that Jesus is about to give may include a warning about different gods of the Roman world, such as *Pan,* Jesus and His disciples were on the *outskirts* of Caesarea Philippi when He asked them this question. The disciples answer the first question of Jesus by saying that other men say that He is *John the Baptist, Elijah, or one of the prophets.* Their image was still not clear, so Jesus asked them the question in a different way.

"But whom say ye that I am?" – The quivering voice of Simon Peter said, *"Thou art the Christ." "Christ"* comes from the Greek word *"Christos"* meaning, *"the anointed one."* But Peter really said, *"Thou art the Mashiach, or Messiah."* The following reminds us of the real reason why we have the New Testament:

> *He first findeth his own brother Simon, and saith unto him, We have found the Messias, which is, being interpreted, the Christ.*
>
> John 1:41

> *But these are written, that ye might believe that Jesus is the Christ, the Son of God; and that believing ye might have life through his name.*
>
> John 20:31

> *Whosoever believeth that Jesus is the Christ is born of God: and every one that loveth him that begat loveth him also that is begotten of him.*
>
> I John 5:1

Jesus employs the disciples to conceal the *messianic secret* until His mission can be accomplished.

Jesus Teaches About the Suffering Messiah

> **Mark 8:31-33** – *And he began to teach them, that the Son of man must suffer many things, and be rejected of the elders, and of the chief priests, and scribes, and be killed, and after three days rise again. And he spake that saying openly. And Peter took him, and began to rebuke him. But when he had turned about*

and looked on his disciples, he rebuked Peter, saying, Get thee behind me, Satan: for thou savourest not the things that be of God, but the things that be of men.

Jesus did not teach them here in a parable, He made it clear. He would not be the political and military figure that people had imagined. It is very hard for us today to imagine anything else but Jesus dying on a cross, but to those first disciples of Jesus they had never considered such a thought. There was not one, but *two* comings of the Messiah of Israel, and the first coming He would be the *Suffering Messiah* of Isaiah:

Who hath believed our report? and to whom is the arm of the LORD revealed? For he shall grow up before him as a tender plant, and as a root out of a dry ground: he hath no form nor comeliness; and when we shall see him, there is no beauty that we should desire him. He is despised and rejected of men; a man of sorrows, and acquainted with grief: and we hid as it were our faces from him; he was despised, and we esteemed him not. Surely he hath borne our griefs, and carried our sorrows: yet we did esteem him stricken, smitten of God, and afflicted. But he was wounded for our transgressions, he was bruised for our iniquities: the chastisement of our peace was upon him; and with his stripes we are healed. All we like sheep have gone astray; we have turned every one to his own way; and the LORD *hath laid on him the iniquity of us all. He was oppressed, and he was afflicted, yet he opened not his mouth: he is brought as a lamb to the slaughter, and as a sheep before her shearers is dumb, so he openeth not his mouth.*

Isaiah 53:1-7

The God of heaven was going to use the unbelief of *the elders, the chief priests, and scribes* to fulfill the Hebrew scripture. Would the confrontations that Jesus had in the Galilee with the Pharisees make more sense now?

"Get thee behind me Satan" – Notice that Mark does not mention the change of Peter's name like **John 1:42,** or the blessing pronounced upon Peter like in **Matthew 16:17.** Peter was dictating to Mark what to write down, and he did not want to exalt himself. The thought of Jesus being killed by the corrupt religious leaders is more than his flesh can handle. The devil starts to speak through Peter trying to discourage Jesus from going to the cross. When we get in the flesh, we leave ourselves open for the devil to use us.

Underneath all of the beautiful teachings and profound miracles of our Lord, Satan was there all the time trying to divert His attention away from doing the Father's will. Here he even speaks through one of Jesus' choicest disciples. Try to imagine these fishermen from Galilee taking the message of the suffering Messiah into the Roman world for the very first time. Think of Peter telling Mark about this experience and how Jesus transformed him from being a Galilean fisherman to being the spiritual leader of the disciples. Jesus would break down the paradigms in the minds of Peter and the disciples in such a way they could never imagine—through the cross and the resurrection!

The Value of Life and the Value of a Soul

> **Mark 8:34-38 -** *And when he had called the people unto him with his disciples also, he said unto them, Whosoever will come after me, let him deny himself, and take up his cross, and follow me. For whosoever will save his life shall lose it; but whosoever shall lose his life for my sake and the gospel's, the same shall save it. For what shall it profit a man, if he shall gain the whole world, and lose his own soul? Or what shall a man give in exchange for his soul? Whosoever therefore shall be ashamed of me and of my words in this adulterous and sinful generation; of him also shall the Son of man be ashamed, when he cometh in the glory of his Father with the holy angels.*

As Jesus would have to carry a crossbar to the site of His own crucifixion, everyone who decides to follow Him must endure persecution as well. A true disciple of Jesus may not be crucified as Jesus, but he will have to be committed to going through hardships and possibly death itself. This idea that being a Christian is supposed to be filled with health and wealth is not biblically founded. Jesus uses the Hebrew double paradox that *whosoever shall save his life shall lose it and whosoever shall lose his life shall save it.* In simple words, if we live our lives seeking our own dreams and successes, we will never find out what life is really all about. But if we give up our goals in life in order to follow Christ, we will find the true meaning of life.

"For what shall it profit a man, if he shall gain the whole world, and lose his own soul?" - Mark uses the Greek word for *soul* as *"psuche,"* but since the words of Jesus would have been Hebrew/Aramaic, He would have used the word *"nephesh."* The reason this is important to note is that Jesus is the *Creator,* and this connects us to the beginning:

> *And the* Lord *God formed man of the dust of the ground, and breathed into his nostrils the breath of life; and man became a living soul* (nephesh).
>
> Genesis 2:7

God did not place the soul into man like the placing of a letter into an envelope. Man became a *living soul!* There is an eternity in man! The world may look enticing, but it vanishes away. Man's soul will live forever! The disciples of Jesus would leave Israel and see a very beautiful Roman world with all of the theatres, shrines, and statues to gods and goddesses *(Like the god Pan).* But they needed to focus on the souls of the people they were going to preach to. Rome would eventually fall and cultures would come and go, but the soul of man would live forever, either in heaven or hell. The souls who believed their message of Christ are still alive in heaven today. The souls who rejected their message of Christ are still in torment today.

"Whosoever therefore shall be ashamed of me and of my words in this adulterous and sinful generation; of him also shall the Son of man be ashamed, when he cometh in the glory of his Father with the holy angels" - If the generation that the disciples would have preached to were *an adulterous and sinful generation*, how much more sinful is the generation in which we live today? These disciples would be filled with the power of the Holy Spirit on the Day of Pentecost in **Acts 2** and find the courage to never be *ashamed* of Christ. Peter would preach unashamedly in Jerusalem, and thousands would be converted. While Mark was writing these words, Peter was preaching the gospel in the Roman world unashamedly. By the time Peter suffered martyrdom under the evil hand of Nero in 64AD, this gospel of Mark would have already been circulated to countless thousands.

"when he cometh in the glory of his Father with the holy angels" -The second coming of the Messiah in His vengeance and power to destroy the unbelieving and the wicked and establishing the Messianic Kingdom is expressed in several different terms in the sacred scripture. A few of them follow:

"the great and terrible day of the Lord" – **Acts 2:20, 2 Thess. 2:3**

"the end of the world"- **Jere. 4:27, Matt. 24:29**

"in the last times"- **Isa. 2:2, Acts 2:17, I Tim.4:1, 2 Peter 3:3**

"new heaven and a new earth"- **Isa. 65:17, 2 Peter 3:13**

"coming in the clouds"- **Rev. 1:7**

"in glory with the angels"- **Matt. 24:30**

"judging the twelve tribes of Israel"- **Matt. 19:28**

Notice here also that Jesus has the authority to judge the living and the dead. **(Acts10:42)** At the appointed time, Jesus will reward those with eternal life who were not ashamed of Him and punish those who were ashamed of him. To think that Jesus might be *ashamed* of us? What a disturbing thought!

CHAPTER NINE

Jesus the Messiah is Transfigured

Mark 9:1-3 - *And he said unto them, Verily I say unto you, That there be some of them that stand here, which shall not taste of death, till they have seen the kingdom of God come with power. And after six days Jesus taketh with him Peter, and James, and John, and leadeth them up into an high mountain apart by themselves: and he was transfigured before them. And his raiment became shining, exceeding white as snow; so as no fuller on earth can white them.*

The kingdom of God had started in the hearts of all those who embraced Jesus as the Son of God, and one day the kingdom of God will come in a physical, earthly kingdom. The disciples anticipated this physical kingdom, and their hearts were sinking after Jesus had told them about His passion. So now three of the disciples are about to get a *foretaste* of the glory that is to come. This would not be a vision; they would actually see the Master be transfigured before them.

Jesus had a special mission for *Peter, James, and John,* and they were about to *see* the Messiah glorified before them. *Peter* would be given the keys to the kingdom and be the leader of the apostles. His preaching would open the door of the kingdom to many Jews on the Day of Pentecost and officially open the door to the Gentiles in **Acts 10**. *James* would become the first disciple of Jesus to face martyrdom in **Acts 12:1-2**. *John* would be the only disciple to live to be an old man and be given the book of the *Revelation of Jesus Christ* to complete the canonization of the scripture.

"leadeth them up into an high mountain" – This is believed to have been one of the high mountains ＊ in the Mount Hermon region about 40 miles north of the Sea of Galilee. Mount Hermon stands over 9,200 feet above sea level, and snow is on the top year round. Jesus is about to reveal in glorious splendor, His *Heavenly Person,* before He takes His disciples down to the lowest point on planet earth, just north of the Dead Sea.

＊ *Today, there are two Catholic churches on top of Mount Tabor in the Jezreel Valley that commemorate this event. Mount Tabor is only about 1,800 feet above sea level. However, Jesus and His disciples were in the region of Caesarea Philippi, just below Mount Hermon when the transfiguration occurred. The majority of historians, as well as many Catholic scholars, believe that Mount Hermon is the actual place.*

"he was transfigured before them. And his raiment became shining, exceeding white as snow; so as no fuller on earth can white them" – These disciples saw Jesus as the King clothed in power and great glory! Everything Jesus had done up to this point was only a taste of who He really was. While the disciples had seen miracles that no one had ever seen, the glory of the Messiah had been concealed. As we think about the previous chapters, we need to remember words like: *"Do you still not see?" Do you have eyes but cannot see?" "Who do men say that I am?"* The eyes of the disciples were open to what Jesus had been saying. All of the miracles were leading up to this moment! Jesus is more than just a *Prophet*! Jesus is more than *Israel's Messiah*! Jesus is more than the *anointed King* from David's throne! Jesus is the *Lord God Almighty*! Hallelujah!

> **Mark 9:4-6 - *And there appeared unto them Elias with Moses: and they were talking with Jesus. And Peter answered and said to Jesus, Master, it is good for us to be here: and let us make three tabernacles; one for thee, and one for Moses, and one for Elias. For he wist not what to say; for they were sore afraid.***

Elijah and Moses not only represented the *Prophets* and the *Law*, they also symbolized the *living and the dead* who believe in Jesus! Elijah never died; he ascended to heaven:

> *And it came to pass, as they still went on, and talked, that, behold, there appeared a chariot of fire, and horses of fire, and parted them both asunder; and Elijah went up by a whirlwind into heaven.*
>
> 2 Kings 2:11

The Apostle Paul would later give these Elijah-like experiences when he talked about the catching away of the true believers:

> *In a moment, in the twinkling of an eye, at the last trump: for the trumpet shall sound, and the dead shall be raised incorruptible, and we shall be changed.*
>
> I Corinthians 15:52

> *Then we which are alive and remain shall be caught up together with them in the clouds, to meet the Lord in the air: and so shall we ever be with the Lord.*
>
> I Thess.4:17

Moses died on Mount Nebo, and God buried him. Although he died physically, he enjoyed the presence of the Lord all through the centuries. Now he is standing with Jesus on top of another mountain in the Promised Land.

> *And Moses went up from the plains of Moab unto the mountain of Nebo, to the top of Pisgah, that is over against Jericho. And the LORD shewed him all the land of Gilead, unto Dan, And all Naphtali, and the land of Ephraim, and Manasseh, and all the land of Judah, unto the utmost sea, And the south, and the plain of the valley of Jericho, the city of palm trees, unto Zoar. And the LORD said unto him, This*

*is the land which I sware unto Abraham, unto
Isaac, and unto Jacob, saying, I will give it
unto thy seed: I have caused thee to see it with
thine eyes, but thou shalt not go over thither.
So Moses the servant of the LORD died there in
the land of Moab, according to the word of the
LORD. And he buried him in a valley in the
land of Moab, over against Bethpeor: but no
man knoweth of his sepulchre unto this day.
And Moses was an hundred and twenty years
old when he died: his eye was not dim, nor his
natural force abated.*

Deuteronomy 34:1-7

We have a promise from our Lord that all believers who
do not live to see His second coming will go to be *with
Him*. Note these comforting words:

*Jesus said unto her, I am the resurrection, and
the life: he that believeth in me, though he were
dead, yet shall he live.*

John 11:25

*For to this end Christ both died, and rose, and
revived, that he might be Lord both of the dead
and living.*

Romans 14:9

Moses and Elijah appearing with Jesus the Messiah on
the Mount of Transfiguration as *"two men"* **(Luke 9:30)**

may have more profound connections to Christ than most people have thought. Think about the *two men* in these two passages when Jesus is resurrected and at His ascension:

> *And it came to pass, as they were much perplexed thereabout, behold, <u>two men</u> stood by them in shining garments.*
>
> Luke 24:4

> *And while they looked stedfastly toward heaven as he went up, behold, <u>two men</u> stood by them in white apparel.*
>
> Acts 1:10

"let us make three tabernacles" – Imagine Peter telling this event to Mark and saying, *"I didn't know what to say, we were terrified!"* But Peter, being a Jew, thought the most fitting thing to do would be to quickly build three *sukkot*, or tabernacles. After all, Moses, who gave Israel the law was there:

> *Also in the fifteenth day of the seventh month, when ye have gathered in the fruit of the land, ye shall keep a feast unto the LORD seven days: on the first day shall be a sabbath, and on the eighth day shall be a sabbath. And ye shall take you on the first day the boughs of goodly trees, branches of palm trees, and the boughs of thick trees, and willows of the brook; and ye shall rejoice before the LORD your God seven days.*

And ye shall keep it a feast unto the LORD seven days in the year. It shall be a statute for ever in your generations: ye shall celebrate it in the seventh month. Ye shall dwell in booths seven days; all that are Israelites born shall dwell in booths: That your generations may know that I made the children of Israel to dwell in booths, when I brought them out of the land of Egypt: I am the LORD your God.

Leviticus 23:39-43

Mark 9:7 - *And there was a cloud that overshadowed them: and a voice came out of the cloud, saying, This is my beloved Son: hear him.*

There seems to be a parallel here of the *pillar of a cloud* that followed the children of Israel in the wilderness. The symbol of the presence of the God of Israel had now been made manifest in the Person of Jesus the Messiah.

And the LORD went before them by day in a pillar of a cloud, to lead them the way; and by night in a pillar of fire, to give them light; to go by day and night.

Exodus 13:21

The Heavenly Father spoke in an audible voice out of the *cloud* to *Peter, James, and John,* very similar to the way He spoke at the baptism of Jesus. **(Mark 1:11)** The difference being that the Father spoke to Jesus at the baptism, and here He speaks to the disciples. It is easy for us to see a picture of the Triune Godhead in this passage. The *Father* speaks, the *Holy Spirit* covers them in the cloud, and the *Son of God* is transfigured.

The time had arrived for the people of Israel to listen to their Messiah. He was greater than *Moses* or the *Prophets*. All of the Jewish feasts, the festivals, the offerings, the sacrifices, all found their fulfillment in Him. God promised Moses that there would come a *Prophet* like unto him that the people would listen to:

> **The LORD thy God will raise up unto thee a Prophet from the midst of thee, of thy brethren, like unto me; unto him ye shall hearken.**
>
> Deuteronomy 18:15

The writer of the book of Hebrews makes this powerful truth more clear when he was writing to Jewish believers who were thinking about going back into Judaism because of being persecuted.

> **God, who at sundry times and in divers manners spake in time past unto the fathers by the prophets, Hath in these last days spoken unto us by his Son, whom he hath appointed heir of all things, by whom also he made the worlds.**
>
> Hebrews 1:1-2

The Messianic Secret

> **Mark 9:8-10 -** *And suddenly, when they had looked round about, they saw no man any more, save Jesus only with themselves. And as they came down from the mountain, he charged them that they should tell no man what things they had seen, till the Son of man were risen from the dead. And they kept that saying with themselves, questioning one with another what the rising from the dead should mean.*

What a place to be! All alone with Jesus! These three disciples were so highly favored to be on a mountain with the Son of God. They *looked around* and didn't see *Moses or Elijah*, only Jesus! As they were walking down the mountain together, Jesus told them again *not to tell anyone* what they had seen. In Mark's gospel this *messianic secret* seems to be more involved than just large crowds or the mindset of the Zealots. *Yeshua* seems to be intentionally concealing His identity. Let us reflect on the message of *not telling anyone* once more:

* *Demons* - Mark 1:34
* *Leper* - Mark 1:44
* *Demons* - Mark 3:12
* *The Decapolis crowd* - Mark 7:36
* *The blind man* - Mark 8:26

* *The disciples* - Mark 8:30
* *Peter, James, and John* - Mark 9:9

It seems to be all about the *passion of the Messiah*. His ultimate mission was to suffer death and then rise again! If His identity had been understood, then He would not have suffered and died on the cross. If He had not suffered and died on the cross, He would not have risen! If He had not risen, salvation would not have been accomplished! Note that Jesus commissions them to proclaim His identity after He had risen from the dead!

The disciples still do not comprehend *what the rising from the dead* actually means. Was Jesus talking about rising up the Davidic monarchy? Was Jesus talking about the general resurrection of all of the righteous? No! Jesus was talking about His personal death on the cross, His burial, and His bodily resurrection! This would be the life-changing message these disciples would take into the Roman world. We are reminded of these words:

> *But we speak the wisdom of God in a mystery, even the hidden wisdom, which God ordained before the world unto our glory: Which none of the princes of this world knew: for had they known it, they would not have crucified the Lord of glory.*
>
> I Corinthians 2:7-8

The Coming of Elijah?

Mark 9:11-13 - *And they asked him, saying, Why say the scribes that Elias must first come? And he answered and told them, Elias verily cometh first, and restoreth all things; and how it is written of the Son of man, that he must suffer many things, and be set at nought. But I say unto you, That Elias is indeed come, and they have done unto him whatsoever they listed, as it is written of him.*

The disciples bringing up the subject of *Elijah coming* is understandable since Elijah has just appeared on the mountain with Jesus. Why did the *scribes* say that Elijah would come before the Messiah? There was a mysterious prophecy that dated back to about 400 years before Jesus came:

Behold, I will send you Elijah the prophet before the coming of the great and dreadful day of the Lord: *And he shall turn the heart of the fathers to the children, and the heart of the children to their fathers, lest I come and smite the earth with a curse.*

Malachi 4:5-6

The cryptic saying of our Lord about *Elijah has already come* proves that He is agreeing with the prophecy of Malachi, but perhaps not entirely in the way the scribes interpreted it. The prophecy may have a *two-fold meaning* that concerns the *first and second coming of Israel's Messiah.* While this has been a problematic passage for centuries, this is not uncommon in the Hebrew prophecies to wrestle with the interpretation. So if we cannot wrap our little minds around all of the hidden truths that are found in this passage, we shouldn't be surprised.

The *scribes,* like the disciples, only believed in <u>one</u> coming of the Messiah, and that the Old Testament prophet *Elijah* would come down from heaven to announce that judgment was coming. But Jesus tells the disciples that the Son of man must suffer first, and that *Elijah* has already come and announced His coming, speaking about John the Baptist. John the Baptist was in the *spirit of Elijah,* and he cleared the way for Jesus' earthly ministry. The answer to this seemingly double-talk may be found as we carefully study the scripture. Notice these verses:

> **And he shall go before him in the spirit and power of Elias, to turn the hearts of the fathers to the children, and the disobedient to the wisdom of the just; to make ready a people prepared for the Lord.**
>
> Luke 1:17

This is a clear fulfillment of Malachi's prophecy and connects to what Jesus told His disciples about John the Baptist. The future fulfillment of Elijah coming before the second coming of the Messiah may be found in the two *anointed ones* of **Zechariah** and one of the two *witnesses* in **Revelation**:

Then answered I, and said unto him, What are these <u>two olive trees</u> upon the right side of the candlestick and upon the left side thereof? And I answered again, and said unto him, What be these two olive branches which through the two golden pipes empty the golden oil out of themselves? And he answered me and said, Knowest thou not what these be? And I said, No, my lord. Then said he, These are the <u>two anointed ones</u>, that stand by the LORD *of the whole earth.*

Zechariah 4:11-14 *(Zechariah may be referring to Zerubbabel and Joshua, but this passage is also eschatological that could connect us to the two witnesses of Revelation)*

And I will give power unto my two witnesses, and they shall prophesy a thousand two hundred and threescore days, clothed in sackcloth.

Revelation 11:3 *(These two witnesses are commonly thought to be Moses and Elijah, while a few believe it is Enoch and Elijah)*

The Powerless Disciples and the Mighty Christ

Mark 9:14-29 - *And when he came to his disciples, he saw a great multitude about them, and the scribes questioning with them. And straightway all the people, when they beheld him, were greatly amazed, and running to him saluted him. And he asked the scribes, What question ye with them? And one of the multitude answered and said, Master, I have* *brought unto thee my son, which hath a dumb spirit; And wheresoever he taketh him, he teareth him: and he foameth, and gnasheth with his teeth, and pineth away: and I spake to thy disciples that they should cast him out; and they could not. He answereth him, and saith, O faithless generation, how long shall I be with you? how long shall I suffer you? bring him unto me. And they brought him unto him: and when he saw him, straightway the spirit tare him; and he fell on the ground, and wallowed foaming. And he asked his father, How long is it ago since this came unto him? And he said, Of a child. And ofttimes it hath cast him into the fire, and into the waters, to destroy him: but if thou canst do any thing, have compassion on us, and help us. Jesus said unto him, If thou canst believe, all things are possible to him that believeth. And straightway the father of the child cried out, and said with tears, Lord, I believe; help thou mine unbelief. When Jesus saw that the people came running together, he rebuked the foul spirit, saying unto him, Thou dumb and deaf spirit, I charge thee, come out of him, and enter no more into him. And the spirit cried, and rent him sore, and came out of him: and he was as one dead; insomuch that many said, He is dead. But Jesus took him by the hand, and lifted him up;*

> *and he arose. And when he was come into the house, his disciples asked him privately, Why could not we cast him out? And he said unto them, This kind can come forth by nothing, but by prayer and fasting.*

This strange passage has troubled this author for years trying to understand *why* the disciples of Jesus could not cast the demon out of this young boy. Jesus had already commissioned the disciples and given them power over the unclean spirits in **Mark 6:7**. Was it the carnal spirit of the multitude? Was it the unbelief and religious spirit of the scribes? Did the disciples not have enough faith? Or was this particular level of demonic activity so strong that it took the mighty Christ to cast him out? When we consider that this is where Jesus deliberately brought His disciples for *Peter's great confession,* to first teach the disciples about *His death and resurrection, and* where *He was transfigured,* then there must be something powerful about this location. There is a real tendency to try and overspiritualize every little detail of this mysterious passage, but let's try to keep things in context and place the points in three categories:

1) *The common truths*
2) *The uncommon beliefs*
3) *The spiritual lessons*

The Common Truths

* ★ *The powerless disciples* – For some unknown reason, they had lost their power.
* ★ *The multitude* – There is no help from the multitude gathered around.
* ★ *The scribes* – The scribes were questioning the disciples about Jesus.
* ★ *The father* – The *honest* father knew his son had a demonic spirit and had brought his son to the disciples of Jesus for help. He was *honest* when he cried out and told Jesus, *"I believe, help thou mine unbelief."*
* ★ *The young boy* – Probably a teenage boy who had been demonic possessed from childhood. The demon was throwing the boy into the fire and into the water trying to kill him.
* ★ *The demon* – When the evil spirit *saw* Jesus, he began to torment the boy even more. The demon knew who Jesus was.
* ★ *The Mighty Christ* – Jesus spoke directly to the dumb and deaf spirit and commanded it to come out of the boy. The spirit was so strong that it even cried out and left the boy looking as one dead. Jesus took the boy by the hand and lifted him up.

The Uncommon Beliefs

* *Gateway to Hell* – This was a cave behind the temple to the god *Pan* where child sacrifices were thrown. Strong demonic activity!

* *Temple of Pan* – This pagan god was worshipped in Greek mythology. It is where we get the name *"panic."* The Romans named it *Faunus*. A large rock cliff contained numerous niches of statues. A very evil place!

* *Temple to Caesar* – There was a Temple in Caesarea Philippi where they worshipped *Caesar* as god! A plethora of gods were worshipped in this region.

* *Selene* – She was the goddess of the *moon*. This is where we get the idea of people being *moonstruck or crazy*, or *"lunatic,"* like the condition that was given to this young boy in **Matt. 17:15**. It was believed in Greek mythology that *Selene* had a sexual relationship with the god, *Pan*.

* *Nymphs* – In mythology, these women-like beings liked to hang around mountains and rivers, attracted to certain locations. This was the beginning of the Jordan River where three springs, *Snir, Dan, and Banias* met.

* *Nephilim* – These were the giants that were born out of the fallen angels having relations with the daughters of men in **Genesis 6:4**. This happened on *Mount Hermon*, close to where this miracle took

place. This was considered to be such an evil act that demons still resided in this region.

* ***Tribe of Dan*** – The tribe of *Dan* committed terrible idolatry under *Rehoboam* in 930BC, not far from this location. It became known as the place where sorcery and heresies originated.

The Spiritual Lessons

* *We need a stronger faith living in a demonic world*
* *We need to see the importance of prayer and fasting*
* *We should never trust in our religious traditions*
* *We should never be influenced by the multitudes*
* *We should never trust in our own power*
* *The disciples would soon face all of the pagan deities, and they would need to place their trust completely in the power of Christ*
* *Only the Mighty Christ can defeat Satan!*

Jesus Back in Galilee

Mark 9:30-32 – *And they departed thence, and passed through Galilee; and he would not that any man should know it. For he taught his disciples, and said unto them, The Son of man is delivered into the hands of men, and they shall kill him; and after that he is killed, he shall rise the third day. But they understood not that saying, and were afraid to ask him.*

Jesus and His disciples have made the walk back down from Caesarea Philippi to the Sea of Galilee. Being back in the familiar home of the disciples, Jesus now tells them the second time about His pending death and resurrection. While Jesus knew about His cross before the foundation of the world, the disciples still did not understand. To say they *were afraid* seems like an understatement. Little did the disciples know that the day was coming soon when they would proclaim the gospel of Christ in the power of the Holy Spirit to the known world!

Jesus Back Home in Capernaum

> **Mark 9:33-37 -** *And he came to Capernaum: and being in the house he asked them, What was it that ye disputed among yourselves by the way? But they held their peace: for by the way they had disputed among themselves, who should be the greatest. And he sat down, and called the twelve, and saith unto them, If any man desire to be first, the same shall be last of all, and servant of all. And he took a child, and set him in the midst of them: and when he had taken him in his arms, he said unto them, Whosoever shall receive one of such children in my name, receiveth me: and whosoever shall receive me, receiveth not me, but him that sent me.*

Maybe the special election of Peter, James, and John, and

the transfiguration caused a division among the disciples about who should be the greatest? These uneducated disciples were of the common sort, and they had to deal with jealousy and pride like everyone else. All of those carnal attitudes would vanish away once they received the Holy Spirit. The *all-knowing* Christ perceived what the disciples were discussing. He proceeded to tell them that greatness in God's eyes is measured by *humility and service*. These disciples would be the pillars of the early church, so they would have to lead by example. There was no place in God's kingdom for worldly honor and attention.

"And he took a child, * and set him in the midst of them" – Placing a child in the arms of Jesus is one of the most moving scenes in the gospels. This is the first of two accounts that Mark writes about Jesus touching a child. This author believes that this child felt heavenly love and compassion like never before when Jesus placed *him* in His arms, and later became a great follower of Christ in the first century. Try to imagine if you had been the mother or the father of this little child.

Not only were the disciples to be humble *like a child*, Jesus was saying that they should *receive* little children *in his name*. Contrary to what some denominations teach, Jesus is not saying there is some magical formula by saying a specific name, like the English *"JESUS"* or the Hebrew *"YESHUA"* or the Greek *"IESOUS"* or the Latin *"IESVS."* *In the name of* is a Hebrew idiom that stands for everything Jesus claimed to be and everything He did, and in His authority. They must receive little children as *receiving Jesus*, and by doing so they would be *receiving the Father in heaven who sent Jesus.* This should change the way that all of us who claim to be followers of Jesus must think toward little children, as well as other brothers and sisters. Jesus came into this world as a babe in a manger in order to show the world how we are to live. As *humble servants* we are to show the world what true humility is all about. It's more than just living a certain way, it's about how we *receive* others.

Jesus was showing that He was authentic, trustworthy, and had nothing to hide. He came to bring truth to the world! A child was noted in ancient times for always telling the latest news running from house to house in the little Jewish villages. The time was soon approaching when the disciples would not keep the messianic secret to themselves anymore.

Jesus Rebukes the Disciples

> **Mark 9:38-41 - *And John answered him, saying, Master, we saw one casting out devils in thy name, and he followeth not us: and we forbad him, because he followeth not us. But Jesus said, Forbid him not: for there is no man which shall do a miracle in my name, that can lightly speak evil of me. For he that is not against us is on our part. For whosoever shall give you a cup of water to drink in my name, because ye belong to Christ, verily I say unto you, he shall not lose his reward.***

It's noteworthy how many times we encounter Jesus casting out demons, as well as His disciples casting out demons. In this case, we have someone who is casting out demons in the name of Jesus who is not a part of the inner circle of the disciples. In our modern church world, people fail to see that demonic possession is a reality. People are filled with Satan just like believers are filled with Jesus. We need to be strong in the Lord and recognize our enemy at work in the lives of our family and friends, and call it what it is. Here the apostle John sees someone who is performing exorcisms in the name of the Lord who was not a part of their group. John and the other disciples rebuked the man. But Jesus surprised the disciples and told them to *not* rebuke the man. This man was not speaking evil against Jesus, as the Pharisees did in **Matt. 12.**

While Jesus and the disciples were the leaders, they were to be inclusive when it came to God's kingdom. There should not be a spirit of competition with other believers as long as they do not speak evil against Jesus. The kingdom of God is much broader than we might realize. We might not always agree with others on every little doctrine, but as long as they believe that Jesus is the Messiah, the Son of God, we are on the same team. Shooting down our own soldiers is a work of the devil lurking in the shadows of the body of Christ.

"For whosoever shall give you a cup of water to drink in my name, because ye belong to Christ, verily I say unto you, he shall not lose his reward" - Notice the contrast between casting out demons and *giving a cup of cold water.* Our Lord

is not impressed with the level of ministry we might have, or how large our church may be. It is the motive and the compassion in which we serve Him. Everyone has been given a different gift and a different measure of faith. A small country church is just as important to God as the large mega church. We should not be prideful about our ministries or our college degrees, but realize that we should be honored just to have a small part in His eternal work. When someone gave one of Jesus' disciples a *cup of cold water* because he believed in Jesus, his deed would be remembered. Sometimes this author wonders just how few disciples there really are in the world who are serving Jesus out of a pure heart of love!

Jesus, Hyperboles, and Hell Fire

> **Mark 9:42-48 -** *And whosoever shall offend one of these little ones that believe in me, it is better for him that a millstone were hanged about his neck, and he were cast into the sea. And if thy hand offend thee, cut it off: it is better for thee to enter into life maimed, than having two hands to go into hell, into the fire that never shall be quenched: Where their worm dieth not, and the fire is not quenched. And if thy foot offend thee, cut it off: it is better for thee to enter halt into life, than having two feet to be cast into hell, ★ into the fire that never shall be quenched: Where their worm*

dieth not, and the fire is not quenched. And if thine eye offend thee, pluck it out: it is better for thee to enter into the kingdom of God with one eye, than having two eyes to be cast into hell fire: Where their worm dieth not, and the fire is not quenched.

The style of teaching that Christ did is valid proof that there is a Hebrew thought behind the Greek text. The heart of our Lord is so tender toward children and how we should treat each other, that when He gives warnings about *offending His little ones,* He gives several drastic illustrations, called Hebrew *hyperboles*:

"Millstone were hanged about his neck, and he were cast into the sea" – These smaller millstones were used for grinding wheat and barley into flour, and the larger ones for grinding the oil out of olives. Even the smallest millstone weighed over 100 pounds. Where Jesus said these words was close to the shore of the Sea of Galilee. Jesus has just previously said that giving a cup of cold water in His name would be remembered, and now He says that causing others to sin will result in the most severe punishment. The Eternal God is keeping a record!

"If thy hand, foot, or eye offend thee, cut it off or pluck it out" – Jesus is not talking about body mutilation. That would not go far enough in controlling sin. Sin is a matter of the heart more so than a limb or an organ. The disciples needed to know that serving in the kingdom wasn't just about being rewarded one day, but it was a life of sacrifice

here and now. Sin not only hinders our relationship with the Holy Father, but it can hinder others from coming to faith in Christ. This is serious business!

"Where their worm dieth not, and the fire is not quenched" - Jesus is using a passage of scripture from **Isaiah 66:24**, *"And they shall go forth, and look upon the carcases of the men that have transgressed against me: for their worm shall not die, neither shall their fire be quenched; and they shall be an abhorring unto all flesh"*.

Evidently one of the horrible things about hell will be that everyone will have his own *worm*. He will always be able to remember his own sins, especially rejecting Jesus as his personal Savior! The person that dies without Christ will suffer in the fires of hell as long as the righteous person will enjoy the bliss of heaven, forever!

★ The Greek word Gehennah comes from the Hebrew words Gey-Hinnom. Jesus used this word 11 times in the gospels. This valley just south of Jerusalem was a place of cultic worship in the Old Testament. The gods of Molech and Baal were worshipped by sacrificing children. It's interesting that Jesus has been talking about little children and now refers to a horrible place where children were sacrificed. **(Jere.7:30-32, 19:1-6, 32:35)** *In Jesus' time the valley served as a garbage dump where refuse burned continually.*

Salt and Sacrifice

> **Mark 9:49-50 -** *For every one shall be salted with fire, and every sacrifice shall be salted with salt. Salt is good: but if the salt have lost*

his saltness, wherewith will ye season it? Have salt in yourselves, and have peace one with another.

Jesus is referring to a passage about sacrifices in the Torah:

And every oblation of thy meat offering shalt thou season with salt; neither shalt thou suffer the salt of the covenant of thy God to be lacking from thy meat offering: with all thine offerings thou shalt offer salt.

Leviticus 2:13

As the sacrifices required *salt*, a servant in God's kingdom also requires sacrifice and suffering. As we are purified by the Holy Spirit, our living sacrifice becomes acceptable to God. The *salt* also symbolizes seasoning, and followers of Jesus need to be well seasoned. After the disciples had been arguing about who would be the greatest, they rebuked someone who was casting out demons in Jesus' name. At that moment they had lost their seasoning. Their lives would need the indwelling power of the Holy Spirit to keep them from offending others and from the spirit of competition. God's children are supposed to be the preservative that keep our communities from decay!

CHAPTER TEN

Jesus and the Law of Divorce

Mark 10:1-12 - *And he arose from thence, and cometh into the coasts of Judaea by the farther side of Jordan: and the people resort unto him again; and, as he was wont, he taught them again. And the Pharisees came to him, and asked him, Is it lawful for a man to put away his wife? tempting him. And he answered and said unto them, What did Moses command you? And they said, Moses suffered to write a bill of divorcement, and to put her away. And Jesus answered and said unto them, For the hardness of your heart he wrote you this precept. But from the beginning of the creation God made them male and female. For this cause shall a man leave his father and mother, and cleave to his wife; And they twain shall be one flesh: so then they are no more twain, but one flesh. What therefore God hath joined* *together, let not man put asunder. And in the house his disciples asked him again of the same matter. And he saith unto them, Whosoever shall put away his wife, and marry another, committeth adultery against her. And if a woman shall put away her husband, and be married to another, she committeth adultery.*

Jesus has left the Galilee, and the location is south to the *farther side of Jordan,* or to the land of *Perea.* ★ The Pharisees have tried many different times to trap the Messiah in His words, and this time they are using the much-debated subject of *divorce.* ★ Notice they are *tempting him.* The religious Jews were abusing the Law of Moses concerning *divorce.* They had misunderstood what God intended from the beginning. They had added their own selfish reasons for obtaining a *divorce* from their wives. This is the passage they were abusing:

When a man hath taken a wife, and married her, and it come to pass that she find no favour in his eyes, because he hath found some uncleanness in her: then let him write her a bill of divorcement, and give it in her hand, and send her out of his house. And when she is departed out of his house, she may go and be another man's wife.

Deuteronomy 24:1-2

God's intent was for man to live with one woman until death separated them. When sin entered into the world, He allowed *divorce* under certain situations. But because the Pharisees are using this subject trying to trap Jesus, He tells them that *divorce* was only allowed because of the *hardness of their hearts*, as a result of sin coming into the world. God never designed the law of *divorce* for men to take advantage of their wives or wives to take advantage of their husbands. It was to protect the innocent when there was unfaithfulness. The original meaning of getting a *divorce* was *to cut the marriage ties* and to dissolve the marriage. So when a *writing of divorcement* was given, the persons involved were allowed to remarry under the Jewish law. As strange as it may sound to many religious people today, *divorce* <u>was</u> allowed in the Bible for these reasons:

* ★ *When Israel married pagan wives* (Ezra 9:10-11)
* ★ *God divorced Israel for spiritual idolatry* (Jeremiah 3:8)
* ★ *Sexual immorality* (Matt.5:32, 19:9)
* ★ *Abandonment by an unbeliever* (I Corinthians 7:15)

To fully understand all that Jesus said about *divorce* and *remarriage,* one needs to study **Matthew 19:1-12**. If a man decided to be castrated or if he had the gift of celibacy, then there would be no need for remarriage. These cases sound extreme but were more common in ancient times.

"And in the house his disciples asked him again of the same matter. And he saith unto them, Whosoever shall put away his wife, and marry another, committeth adultery

against her. And if a woman shall put away her husband, and be married to another, she committeth adultery" – Notice that the questions and answers were perplexing to the disciples, so they *asked Jesus again in the house.* If a woman were given a *writing of divorcement* in Jesus' time without the husband having sufficient biblical reasons, *(like the Pharisees were doing)* then both parties would be committing adultery if they remarried. We must keep our thoughts within the context, and remember that Jesus was not condemning divorced people or going against His own law, but was dealing with the Pharisees who were abusing the law of *divorce.*

Since women were considered second-class in the Roman world, Mark's writing would have been a warning to the Jewish and Gentile believers in Rome to take marriage seriously. The church was made up of families, and godly marriages would help to build a strong church. While Simon Peter was one of the primary leaders in the early church and dictated to Mark what to write down, it would not be but a few years until Peter and *his wife* would both face martyrdom in Rome.

*Perea, also known in the four gospels as the "land beyond Jordan" would later be called Transjordan in the writings of Jerome. It was a territory that was ruled by Herod the Great and after his death was bequeathed to Herod Antipas along with Galilee. Perea was on the east side of the Jordan River, stretching from about one third of the way down from the Sea of Galilee to about one third of the way southeast of the Dead Sea. This chapter in Mark's gospel

started the "Perean Ministry of Jesus" before entering into Jericho on His final journey to Jerusalem.

*In our world today the Jews and the Gentiles are very liberal when it comes to divorce. One reason is because people do not marry the person that God intended for them to marry. God is not joining people together in most cases. Divorce causes psychological effects on children such as anxiety, depression, and leaves scars that sometimes never go away. The family unit has been broken down in our evil world, and there is very little commitment among husbands or wives. When a believer in Christ is seeking a husband or a wife, he or she needs to be sure of marrying another believer. There is no promise in the Bible from God that a marriage will be blessed when a believer marries an unbeliever. Even when there are two believers, they need to be counseled about the responsibilities and commitments they are making to each other. Forgiveness for adultery and fornication and broken marriages are certainly available at the cross of Jesus. But we need to be reminded that marriage was designed by God to be "one man for one woman" for a lifelong union!

Jesus Blesses Little Children

> **Mark 10:13-16 - *And they brought young children to him, that he should touch them: and his disciples rebuked those that brought them. But when Jesus saw it, he was much displeased, and said unto them, Suffer the little children to come unto me, and forbid them not: for of such is the kingdom of God. Verily***

I say unto you, Whosoever shall not receive the kingdom of God as a little child, he shall not enter therein. And he took them up in his arms, put his hands upon them, and blessed them.

Children are the fruits of marriage, and they are the ones who suffer from divorce the most. Jesus takes the opportunity once again to teach His disciples the importance of being childlike in their trust in God. Here Jesus embraces the little children and pronounces a Jewish blessing upon them. We do not know the prayer of Jesus verbatim, but there was a Jewish prayer for boys and another for girls. Jesus' prayer may have been something along these lines:

"May God make you like Ephraim and Manasseh"
"May God make you like Sarah, Rebecca, Rachel, and Leah."
"May God bless you and protect you. May God's face shine toward you and give you favor. May God look favorably upon you and grant you peace."

The Good Master Meets a *"good"* man

Mark 10:17-22 - *And when he was gone forth into the way, there came one running, and kneeled to him, and asked him, Good Master, what shall I do that I may inherit eternal life? And Jesus said unto him, Why callest thou me good? there is none good but one, that*

183

is, God. Thou knowest the commandments, Do not commit adultery, Do not kill, Do not steal, Do not bear false witness, Defraud not, Honour thy father and mother. And he answered and said unto him, Master, all these have I observed from my youth. Then Jesus beholding him loved him, and said unto him, One thing thou lackest: go thy way, sell whatsoever thou hast, and give to the poor, and thou shalt have treasure in heaven: and come, take up the cross, and follow me. And he was sad at that saying, and went away grieved: for he had great possessions.

This episode in the ministry of the Messiah is so important that it is recorded in *Matthew, Mark, and Luke.* This man had seen the crowds following Jesus, and maybe he had asked rabbis before the same question. But he was not expecting what he was about to hear from the *Great Rabbi!*

One of the dangers over the years in evangelism is that we try to give one formula of salvation for everybody. But here Jesus didn't tell the man to say a prayer. Jesus didn't tell him that he had to believe the gospel. Jesus didn't tell him that he had to be baptized or join a church. Each individual person has different vices, and he or she needs to be handled in a little different way. We would be wise to remember this, and try not to place everyone in the same spiritual box. This man wanted eternal life, but he had never talked to *The Eternal Life* before! This man thought that eternal life could just be tacked on to everything else in his life. He had possessed more than the average person ever possesses in one life, and he thought that eternal life could also be possessed by human efforts. The overall truth of this story lies in the fact that this *rich man* was throwing the word *"good"* around, and he thought that Jesus was *"Good."* Just imagine that! Let's list a few of this young man's noble achievements:

> ***He came running to Jesus***
> ***He knelt down before Jesus***
> ***He called Jesus "Good Master"***
> ***He was concerned about eternal life***
> ***He was wealthy***
> ***He had been a moral person***

Jesus began by telling this young man that no one is *good,* ★ *but God.* This man thought that he had kept the commandments, but in reality he had broken them all ★ and didn't know it. He had a god in his life—money! He did not love the Lord with all of his heart because his money was in the way. Jesus knew how to put His finger on the man's problem. Here is a noble young man who would be considered *good* by most church standards today, but our Lord was telling him that he needed to repent! There was a god in his life, and he must give it up and follow Him. We could list this young man's condemnation in this order:

Pride – He could not humble himself because of his high status in life.

Possessions – He thought more of his possessions than eternal life.

Price – He was not willing to pay the price.

> *★"The LORD looked down from heaven upon the children of men, to see if there were any that did understand, and seek God. They are all gone aside, they are all together become filthy: there is none that doeth good, no, not one."*
>
> Psalm 14:2-3

> *★"For whosoever shall keep the whole law, and yet offend in one point, he is guilty of all."*
>
> James 2:10

Jesus Warns Against Riches

> **Mark 10:23-27 –** *And Jesus looked round about, and saith unto his disciples, How hardly shall they that have riches enter into the kingdom of God! And the disciples were astonished at his words. But Jesus answereth again, and saith unto them, Children, how hard is it for them that trust in riches to enter into the kingdom of God! It is easier for a camel to go through the eye of a needle, than for a rich man to enter into the kingdom of God. And they were astonished out of measure,*

saying among themselves, Who then can be
saved? And Jesus looking upon them saith,
With men it is impossible, but not with God:
for with God all things are possible.

This is one of the many hard sayings of Jesus that has also been misinterpreted over the centuries. Jesus was using an adage of a Hebrew *hyperbole* ★ in a way that was often used in Jewish literature.

★*They do not show a man a palm tree of gold, nor an elephant going through the eye of a needle.*

Berakhot 55b

Jesus was using the meeting with the man who could not give up his possessions to show His disciples that people who have riches will have a very difficult time entering into God's kingdom. This was revolutionary because the disciples had always been told that the more wealth one had, the more he was favored by God. While prosperity can be a blessing from the Lord to enable people to promote God's kingdom throughout the world, most of the time it becomes a major obstacle in their spiritual life, and even prevents many from going to heaven when life is over.

Just like it is *impossible* for a *camel to go through the eye of a sewing needle*, it is impossible for anyone to achieve goodness or salvation apart from a miracle of the Lord. Most of us today who live in the western world have a higher than average income than the wealthy people had when Jesus walked the earth. This is a warning to all of us! Beware of the prosperity gospel that has taken countless people down the road to spiritual destruction. Know what the Bible really has to say about wealth and that even the wicked may prosper. ⋆ Jesus was born in poverty, lived in obscurity, and had very little worldly possessions. He did this to show us the importance of eternal things.

⋆Truly God is good to Israel, even to such as are of a clean heart. But as for me, my feet were almost gone; my steps had well nigh slipped. For I was envious at the foolish, when I saw the prosperity of the wicked. For there are no bands in their death: but their strength is firm. They are not in trouble as other men; neither are they plagued like other men. Therefore pride compasseth them about as a chain; violence covereth them as a garment. Their eyes stand out with fatness: they have more than heart could wish. They are corrupt, and speak wickedly concerning oppression: they speak loftily. They set their mouth against the heavens, and their tongue walketh through the earth. Therefore his people return hither: and waters of a full cup are wrung out to them. And they say, How doth God know? and is there knowledge in the most High? Behold, these are the ungodly, who prosper in the world; they increase in riches. Verily I have cleansed my heart in vain, and washed my hands in innocency. For all the day long have I been

plagued, and chastened every morning. If I say, I will speak thus; behold, I should offend against the generation of thy children. When I thought to know this, it was too painful for me; Until I went into the sanctuary of God; then understood I their end. Surely thou didst set them in slippery places: thou castedst them down into destruction. How are they brought into desolation, as in a moment! they are utterly consumed with terrors. As a dream when one awaketh; so, O Lord, when thou awakest, thou shalt despise their image. Thus my heart was grieved, and I was pricked in my reins. So foolish was I, and ignorant: I was as a beast before thee. Nevertheless I am continually with thee: thou hast holden me by my right hand. Thou shalt guide me with thy counsel, and afterward receive me to glory. Whom have I in heaven but thee? and there is none upon earth that I desire beside thee. My flesh and my heart faileth: but God is the strength of my heart, and my portion for ever. For, lo, they that are far from thee shall perish: thou hast destroyed all them that go a whoring from thee. But it is good for me to draw near to God: I have put my trust in the Lord GOD, that I may declare all thy works.

Psalm 73

Jesus and Rewards in the Age to Come

> **Mark 10:28-31 -** *Then Peter began to say unto him, Lo, we have left all, and have followed thee. And Jesus answered and said, Verily I say unto you, There is no man that hath left house, or brethren, or sisters, or father, or mother, or wife, or children, or lands, for my sake, and the gospel's, But he shall receive an hundredfold now in this time, houses, and brethren, and sisters, and mothers, and children, and lands, with persecutions; and in the world to come eternal life. But many that are first shall be last; and the last first.*

Peter is agreeing with what Jesus has just said, but now he is reminding Jesus, *as though Jesus didn't know*, that they had left their fishing business and their families back in Capernaum to follow Him. These words of our Lord are very harsh, and most believers do not have strong enough faith to apply what Jesus is saying. Jesus knew what the future held for these disciples, and He knew that their faith would be put to the test. Jesus wanted Peter to know a few important truths about God's kingdom:

* *Just because Peter was one of the first ones chosen didn't necessarily mean that he would be rewarded the most. Some that were chosen later might be rewarded even more.*

* *Sacrifice in God's service must be done for Jesus' sake and the gospel's sake, not just to look pious or religious.*
* *In the present age, or "olam hazeh" there will be times when the wives or husbands or children will not follow Christ, so the disciples of Christ will have to leave them and stay true to the Lord's calling. They will receive a hundredfold in this life, maybe not in exactly the same way, but with Christian brothers and sisters and sweet fellowship with the saints. But that did not mean they would not suffer persecutions.*
* *But in the age to come, or "olam habah" the rewards would be much greater than anything in this life, they would receive eternal life.*

Jesus' Final Prediction About His Passion

Mark 10:32-34 - *And they were in the way going up to Jerusalem; and Jesus went before them: and they were amazed; and as they followed, they were afraid. And he took again the twelve, and began to tell them what things should happen unto him, Saying, Behold, we go up to Jerusalem; and the Son of man shall be delivered unto the chief priests, and unto the scribes; and they shall condemn him to death, and shall deliver him to the Gentiles: And they shall mock him, and shall scourge him, and shall spit upon him, and shall kill him: and the third day he shall rise again.*

Jesus and His disciples have left the other side of Jordan and are going toward the ancient city of Jericho on their way to Jerusalem. ★ Imagine Jesus leading the way and the disciples following behind. They knew what Jesus had told them twice before about His pending death in Jerusalem, and now He is deliberately walking in that direction! They *were afraid* in a way they never had been before! In this final prediction, Jesus is telling His disciples more specific details about what is going to happen in Jerusalem:

* *Delivered to the chief priests*
* *Delivered unto the scribes*
* *He shall be condemned to death*
* *Delivered to the Gentiles (Romans)*
* *He shall be mocked*
* *They shall scourge Him*
* *They shall spit upon Him*
* *They shall kill Him*
* *And the third day He shall rise again*

★From where Jesus and His disciples were, one can see the Judean mountains behind the city of Jericho looking east. From over 1,200 feet <u>below</u> sea level they knew that the journey would be hard and long going, some 2,500 feet <u>above</u> sea level to Jerusalem. We know that this was in the springtime and that patches of green grass were on the mountains, and the Jordan River was swelling with water from the winter rain. The past three years had been filled with life-changing moments with the Master, and they had no way of knowing what they would encounter in Jerusalem. All

of these moments help us understand what Jesus was teaching His disciples. Our lives are filled with seasons of joy and happiness, but because of sin, physical death hangs in the shadows.

The Desire of James and John

> **Mark 10:35-40 -** *And James and John, the sons of Zebedee, come unto him, saying, Master, we would that thou shouldest do for us whatsoever we shall desire. And he said unto them, What would ye that I should do for you? They said unto him, Grant unto us that we may sit, one on thy right hand, and the other on thy left hand, in thy glory. But Jesus said unto them, Ye know not what ye ask: can ye drink of the cup that I drink of? and be baptized with the baptism that I am baptized with? And they said unto him, We can. And Jesus said unto them, Ye shall indeed drink of the cup that I drink of; and with the baptism that I am baptized withal shall ye be baptized: But to sit on my right hand and on my left hand is not mine to give; but it shall be given to them for whom it is prepared.*

"What would ye that I should do for you"- Jesus asked the same question to the blind man in Jericho. **(Mark 10:51)** Mark may have been showing to his readers in Rome the contrast between Jesus asking this question to

193

the rich young ruler, and the ruler asking Jesus; *"What must I do to inherit eternal life."* It's not what we can do, but it is what Jesus can do for us!

Jesus knew what their desire was, but He wanted to hear it from them, just as He wants us to bring our requests to Him in prayer. It's helpful here to remember that *James and John* saw Jesus at the Mount of Transfiguration, **(Mark 9:2)** and they knew that Jesus would be in *His glory* one day. Just as they saw Moses and Elijah standing beside Jesus, they too wanted to be near Jesus. What a thought! The Bible records for us that *James and John* suffered greatly for the kingdom of God:

> *Now about that time Herod the king stretched forth his hands to vex certain of the church. And he killed James the brother of John with the sword.*
>
> Acts 12:1-2

> *I John, who also am your brother, and companion in tribulation, and in the kingdom and patience of Jesus Christ, was in the isle that is called Patmos, for the word of God, and for the testimony of Jesus Christ.*
>
> Revelation 1:9

It is also recorded that the 12 apostles will have their names written on the foundations of the New Jerusalem:

And the wall of the city had twelve foundations, and in them the names of the twelve apostles of the Lamb.

Revelation 21:14

"the baptism that I am baptized with" **-** These strange words carry so much weight that it is difficult to quickly pass over their meaning. Because so much confusion and division have occurred over the centuries about the word *baptism,* ★ let's spend a little time explaining how the word is used in translations and where it may have begun. The Greek word *baptizo* may come from the Latin *immersio,* but it probably originated from the Hebrew word *tabal,* which means *"to dip or plunge."* The word *baptizo* is used in the Greek Septuagint translation when Naaman was *dipped,* (Hebrew *tabal*), seven times in the Jordan River. **(2 Kings 5:14)** Here our Lord may have spoken the word *tabal* to be identified with His pending trial and suffering. This author thinks this is the word Jesus may have originally used, because *tabal* was also the Hebrew word that was used when being connected with *dip* and *sacrifice* in places like **Leviticus 4:6, 9:9, 14:6**. This would have connected Jesus' death on the cross by fulfilling the sacrifices in the Torah. Jesus had already been *water baptized,* so He uses the Jewish term again, but this time to be identified with His suffering. *Baptism* was a Jewish way to be *identified* with someone or with some thing. Here are a few thoughts about interpreting the translated word *baptism or immersion* in the New Testament:

Before entering into the Temple or a synagogue, the Jews were immersed in a ritual bath called a mikveh, ★ to be identified with ritual cleansing.

During the ministry of John the Baptist, baptism was a means of being identified with true repentance. (Matthew 3:11)

Jesus was water baptized to be identified with His death, burial, and resurrection as the Lamb of God for the sins of His people. (Mark 1:9-11)

Jesus never water baptized anyone. (John 4:1-2)

Jesus uses the word baptism here to be identified with His trial and suffering that awaited Him in Jerusalem. (Mark 10:38-39)

Jesus would baptize His followers with the Holy Spirit. (Matthew 3:11, I Corinthians 12:13)

Water baptism is used to be identified with Jesus. (Acts 2:38, Romans 6:3-4)

The apostle Paul made it clear that water baptism was not his primary mission, but he was to preach the gospel. (I Corinthians 1:13-17)

*Immersion is the true meaning of the word baptism in the New Testament, but water baptism was never intended to be the <u>means</u> of salvation. There were other modes of baptism practiced among the first believers, but only when there was a scarcity of water, such as sprinkling. In later centuries many believers would focus so much on the water baptism and lose sight of the finished work of Christ on the cross. Those who believe in water baptism for salvation have a difficult time explaining the other reasons why the word is used in the New Testament. There are those who only fixate water to the word baptize.

*While it is not specifically stated in the Old Testament about how and where to place a ritual bath, the sprinklings and washings gave way to the strong Jewish tradition of ceremonial washings in collected pools of water. Ruins from hundreds of ritual baths have been found in Israel from the Second Temple period. **(516BC-70AD)** Over 60 ritual baths have been found below the Southern Steps in Jerusalem where the Jews would enter into the Temple compound. Ritual baths have been discovered close to synagogues in many places like Magdala and Gamla. Ritual baths have been found in Jewish homes in places such as Sepphoris in Galilee. There were strict Jewish regulations of clean, natural water that had to be used from springs or rainwater. If vessels were used to bring water to the ritual bath, they had to be clean vessels such as stone, not metal. This helps us to understand the extreme care and effort that went into ritual baths in Jesus' time.

Jesus and True Leadership

> **Mark 10:41-45 -** *And when the ten heard it, they began to be much displeased with James and John. But Jesus called them to him, and saith unto them, Ye know that they which are accounted to rule over the Gentiles exercise lordship over them; and their great ones exercise authority upon them. But so shall it not be among you: but whosoever will be great among you, shall be your minister: And whosoever of you will be the chiefest, shall be servant of all. For even the Son of man came not to be ministered unto, but to minister, and to give his life a ransom for many.*

The ambition of James and John led Jesus to clarify the true nature of being a leader. The disciples were not to be in competition with each other or to be like the sons of Herod ★ who always desired to be ruling over a territory or ruling over people.

★Herod the king died in 1BC and left Israel to his three sons, Archelaus, Antipas, and Philip. **(Matthew 2:1, 2:22, Luke 3:1)**

Jesus was the true model of being a leader in God's kingdom. He showed the disciples the importance of being humble, meek, and compassionate to all. He was the very *King of Heaven,* and He chose to live a life of poverty and rejected worldly pomp and splendor. He was the *Suffering Servant* that Isaiah wrote about:

Behold, my servant shall deal prudently, he shall be exalted and extolled, and be very high. As many were astonied at thee; his visage was so marred more than any man, and his form more than the sons of men: So shall he sprinkle many nations; the kings shall shut their mouths at him: for that which had not been told them shall they see; and that which they had not heard shall they consider. Who hath believed our report? and to whom is the arm of the LORD revealed? For he shall grow up before him as a tender plant, and as a root out of a dry ground: he hath no form nor comeliness; and when we shall see him, there is no beauty that we should desire him. He is despised and rejected of men; a man of sorrows, and acquainted with grief: and we hid as it were our faces from him; he was despised, and we esteemed him not. Surely he hath borne our griefs, and carried our sorrows: yet we did esteem him stricken, smitten of God, and afflicted. But he was wounded for our transgressions, he was bruised for our iniquities: the chastisement of our peace was upon him; and with his stripes we are healed. All we like sheep have gone astray; we have turned every one to his own way; and the

Lord hath laid on him the iniquity of us all. He was oppressed, and he was afflicted, yet he opened not his mouth: he is brought as a lamb to the slaughter, and as a sheep before her shearers is dumb, so he openeth not his mouth. He was taken from prison and from judgment: and who shall declare his generation? for he was cut off out of the land of the living: for the transgression of my people was he stricken. And he made his grave with the wicked, and with the rich in his death; because he had done no violence, neither was any deceit in his mouth. Yet it pleased the Lord to bruise him; he hath put him to grief: when thou shalt make his soul an offering for sin, he shall see his seed, he shall prolong his days, and the pleasure of the Lord shall prosper in his hand. He shall see of the travail of his soul, and shall be satisfied: by his knowledge shall my righteous servant justify many; for he shall bear their iniquities. Therefore will I divide him a portion with the great, and he shall divide the spoil with the strong; because he hath poured out his soul unto death: and he was numbered with the transgressors; and he bare the sin of many, and made intercession for the transgressors. Isaiah 52:13-15; 53:1-12

If the disciples wanted to be great in God's kingdom, they too had to be a *servant*. Greatness in God's kingdom does not work the same way that it does in earthly kingdoms. The greatest in God's kingdom will be the one who was the best *servant*.

"For even the Son of man came not to be ministered unto, but to minister, and to give his life a ransom for many" – The word *many* is an Hebrew idiom for *all*. Jesus gave His life for all!

> ***And he is the propitiation for our sins: and not for ours only, but also for the sins of the whole world.***
>
> I John 2:2

The word *ransom* carries with it the need that humanity has for a *Redeemer*. Notice the wording in this section of the Torah:

> ***And if a sojourner or stranger wax rich by thee, and thy brother that dwelleth by him wax poor, and sell himself unto the stranger or sojourner by thee, or to the stock of the stranger's family: After that he is sold he may be redeemed again; one of his brethren may redeem him: Either his uncle, or his uncle's son, may redeem him, or any that is nigh of kin unto him of his family may redeem him; or if he be able, he may redeem himself.***
>
> Leviticus 25:47-49

This also connects Jesus the Messiah to the God of the Old Testament who is Israel's *Redeemer*:

> *Fear not, thou worm Jacob, and ye men of Israel; I will help thee, saith the LORD, and thy redeemer, the Holy One of Israel.*
>
> Isaiah 41:14

> *For thy Maker is thine husband; the LORD of hosts is his name; and thy Redeemer the Holy One of Israel; The God of the whole earth shall he be called.*
>
> Isaiah 54:5

Jesus Gives Sight to Blind Bartimaeus

> **Mark 10:46-52** - *And they came to Jericho: and as he went out of Jericho with his disciples and a great number of people, blind Bartimaeus, the son of Timaeus, sat by the highway side begging. And when he heard that it was Jesus of Nazareth, he began to cry out, and say, Jesus, thou son of David, have mercy on me. And many charged him that he should hold his peace: but he cried the more a great deal, Thou son of David, have mercy on me. And Jesus stood still, and commanded him to be called. And they call the blind man, saying unto him, Be of good comfort, rise; he calleth thee. And he, casting away his garment, rose, and came*

to Jesus. And Jesus answered and said unto him, What wilt thou that I should do unto thee? The blind man said unto him, Lord, that I might receive my sight. And Jesus said unto him, Go thy way; thy faith hath made thee whole. And immediately he received his sight, and followed Jesus in the way.

This is one of the last miracles (healing Malchus' ear) recorded in Mark's gospel before the resurrection of Jesus the Messiah. The wording in Mark's account has been one of this writer's personal favorite miracles of Christ for many years. Jesus giving sight to the blind was truly a *messianic miracle* showing that He was the long-awaited Messiah of Israel:

> *Then the eyes of the blind shall be opened, and the ears of the deaf shall be unstopped.*
>
> Isaiah 35:5

> *Since the world began was it not heard that any man opened the eyes of one that was born blind.*
>
> John 9:32

Jesus and His disciples had been on the other side of the Jordan River, and now they make their way westward to the ancient city of Jericho. This would be the last city they would see before starting the arduous climb up the Judean mountains into Jerusalem, some 18 miles away. Jericho was about 1,300 feet below sea level, and Jerusalem was over 2,500 feet above sea level. Jesus and His disciples were being followed by a large number of people, and the streets of Jericho were filled with noise as the carpenter from Nazareth was passing by. As they were leaving Jericho, a blind man was sitting on the side of the main road begging. Mark's account gives us the blind man's name:

"Bartimaeus, the son of Timaeus" - This is one of the examples of why it is important to study the Hebrew background of the ministry of Jesus. The Greek rendering here means, *"highly prized or honored,"* while the Hebrew meaning is *"ceremonially or ritually unclean."* The name comes from two Hebrew words—*"bar" "timaeus" = "son" "unclean."* The Hebrew word for *unclean* comes from the word *"tame"* pronounced *taw may*, and it is used countless times throughout the Old Testament for people, places, animals, or anything that was *unclean. (Study unclean in Leviticus)* This blind man not only was considered religiously *unclean*, but he may have been the son of a man who was also blind. He was not allowed to worship in the synagogue, and the local people looked at him with infamy because it was the custom that some sin had caused him to be blind.

"Jesus of Nazareth,.... Thou Son of David" - When the blind man heard that it was *Jesus of Nazareth*, He believed that Jesus was the *Son of David*, the Messiah of Israel! Wow! Those were powerful words coming from a man who could not see. The religious leaders could see Jesus with their eyes, but did not know who He was. His cry caused Jesus to *stand still!* Try to imagine the joy that must have been in the heart of Bartimaeus when he heard that Jesus had called for him. *He cast aside his garment and came to Jesus.*

"Lord, that I might receive my sight" – The trembling request of a blind man on the road leaving Jericho touched the heart of the Lord, who created man. Jesus had created man to enjoy everything beautiful that He had made. This poor man couldn't see creation, but he knew the One who created everything! *His faith in Jesus made him whole.* Not only did Jesus give him his eyesight, He placed the man who had an *unclean* name back in the Jewish community with a *clean* standing. Hallelujah!

"And immediately he received his sight, and followed Jesus in the way" – This author believes that this man used his new found vision to follow Jesus all the way into Jerusalem. What expressions must have been on his face! What a glow of grace the people must have seen coming from his eyes! He knew who Jesus was, and he was allowed to follow Him!

Mark seems to be giving his readers a powerful contrast within just a few verses between a rich man who had great possessions and a poor blind man who had nothing. To those early believers who were living under the pride of Rome, this would have been a powerful spiritual lesson:

* *A rich man who would not give up his possessions to follow Jesus, and a blind man who owned nothing was rich in faith.*
* *A rich man walks away from Jesus, and a blind man was restored and started walking with Jesus.*

* *A rich man had a good reputation, while the blind man had a bad reputation.*
* *A rich man thought he could earn his eternal life, and the blind man knew that only Jesus could provide what he needed.*
* *A rich man walked away sadly, while the blind man found joy.*
* *A rich man could not let go of his wealth, while the blind man threw away his cloak and came to Jesus.*
* *Jesus told the rich man to "go and sell everything you have," but to the blind man Jesus said, "thy faith hath made thee whole."*

CHAPTER ELEVEN

Jesus the Messiah Fulfills Zechariah 9:9

Mark 11:1-7 – *And when they came nigh to Jerusalem, unto Bethphage and Bethany, at the mount of Olives, he sendeth forth two of his disciples, And saith unto them, Go your way into the village over against you: and as soon as ye be entered into it, ye shall find a colt tied, whereon never man sat; loose him, and bring him. And if any man say unto you, Why do ye this? say ye that the Lord hath need of him; and straightway he will send him hither. And they went their way, and found the colt tied by the door without in a place where two ways met; and they loose him. And certain of them that stood there said unto them, What do ye, loosing the colt? And they said unto them even as Jesus had commanded: and they let them go. And they brought the colt to Jesus, and cast their garments on him; and he sat upon him.*

After climbing up the Judean mountains from Jericho, Jesus and His disciples ascend to the top of the Mount of Olives. This was during the feast of Passover, and thousands of pilgrims were rushing to see the awesome view of the holy city Jerusalem. About two miles east of Jerusalem was the village of *Bethphage* ★ on the summit of the Mount of Olives, and *Bethany* was just over the mountain on the eastern slope. *Bethphage* means *"house of unripe figs,"* and *Bethany* means *"house of poverty."*

★The Church in Bethphage today is a Franciscan church that was built in 1883, over a twelfth century Crusader church. Underneath the Crusader ruins was discovered a Byzantine shrine from the fourth century. Every year the Palm Sunday services begin at this church where Jesus started His journey down the Mount of Olives.

The fact that Jesus knew where the *colt* was and that the *colt* had never been sat upon showed His power over the animal world. This was a major prophecy fulfilled that was written some 500 years before showing the humility of the Messiah. He came to Israel riding a donkey offering peace:

> **Rejoice greatly, O daughter of Zion; shout, O daughter of Jerusalem: behold, thy King cometh unto thee: he is just, and having salvation; lowly, and riding upon an ass, and upon a colt the foal of an ass.**
>
> Zechariah 9:9

But we should also notice that within the prophecy of Zechariah, the very next verse talks about when the King will come cutting off the chariot and the horse to establish His earthly kingdom:

> *And I will cut off the chariot from Ephraim,*
> *and the horse from Jerusalem, and the battle*
> *bow shall be cut off: and he shall speak peace*
> *unto the heathen: and his dominion shall be*
> *from sea even to sea, and from the river even*
> *to the ends of the earth.*
>
> Zechariah 9:10

There is also a hidden prophecy in the dying blessing of Jacob that is often forgotten:

> *The sceptre shall not depart from Judah, nor*
> *a lawgiver from between his feet, until Shiloh*
> *come; and unto him shall the gathering of the*
> *people be. Binding his foal unto the vine, and*
> *his ass's colt unto the choice vine; he washed*
> *his garments in wine, and his clothes in the*
> *blood of grapes.*
>
> Genesis 49:10-11

Shiloh, pronounced *Shee-lo*, is an epithet of Israel's Messiah. The scepter departed Israel in 6AD when capital punishment was given into the hands of Rome. Jesus was born before the scepter departed, 2BC, and the common people have been gathering to see and hear Him for the last three years. In the dying blessing of Jacob, the coming of the Messiah would be connected not only to a donkey, but to a *colt*.

The Messiah's Triumphal Entry into Jerusalem

> **Mark 11:8-11** - *And many spread their garments in the way: and others cut down branches off the trees, and strawed them in the way. And they that went before, and they that followed, cried, saying, Hosanna; Blessed is he that cometh in the name of the Lord: Blessed be the kingdom of our father David, that cometh in the name of the Lord: Hosanna in the highest. And Jesus entered into Jerusalem, and into the temple: and when he had looked round about upon all things, and now the eventide was come, he went out unto Bethany with the twelve.*

This *triumphal entry of Jesus* recalls the procession of king Solomon into Jerusalem some 1,000 years before and that a *greater than Solomon* had arrived:

> *And king David said, Call me Zadok the priest, and Nathan the prophet, and Benaiah the son of Jehoiada. And they came before the king. The king also said unto them, Take with you the servants of your lord, and cause Solomon my son to ride upon mine own mule, and bring him down to Gihon: And let Zadok the priest*

and Nathan the prophet anoint him there king over Israel: and blow ye with the trumpet, and say, God save king Solomon. Then ye shall come up after him, that he may come and sit upon my throne; for he shall be king in my stead: and I have appointed him to be ruler over Israel and over Judah. And Benaiah the son of Jehoiada answered the king, and said, Amen: the LORD God of my lord the king say so too. As the LORD hath been with my lord the king, even so be he with Solomon, and make his throne greater than the throne of my lord king David. So Zadok the priest, and Nathan the prophet, and Benaiah the son of Jehoiada, and the Cherethites, and the Pelethites, went down, and caused Solomon to ride upon king David's mule, and brought him to Gihon. And Zadok the priest took an horn of oil out of the tabernacle, and anointed Solomon. And they blew the trumpet; and all the people said, God save king Solomon. And all the people came up after him, and the people piped with pipes, and rejoiced with great joy, so that the earth rent with the sound of them.

I Kings 1:32-40

The date is believed to have been the first week of April in the year 32AD. The relevance of Jesus coming into Jerusalem during the Passover feast surrounds the traditional chant of pilgrims who came into Jerusalem from **Psalm 118**. The solemn and joyous tones of **Psalm 118** form the background music for the dramatic events that lead up to the crucifixion of the Messiah. Jesus will even quote from this Psalm a little later. Notice the wording of just a few of the verses:

> *The stone which the builders refused is become the head stone of the corner. This is the LORD's doing; it is marvellous in our eyes. This is the day which the LORD hath made; we will rejoice and be glad in it. Save now, I beseech thee, O LORD: O LORD, I beseech thee, send now prosperity. Blessed be he that cometh in the name of the LORD: we have blessed you out of the house of the LORD. God is the LORD, which hath shewed us light: bind the sacrifice with cords, even unto the horns of the altar. Thou art my God, and I will praise thee: thou art my God, I will exalt thee. O give thanks unto the LORD; for he is good: for his mercy endureth for ever.*
>
> Psalm 118:22-29

Our Lord went into Jerusalem and even went into the Temple and *looked around*. As we will find out, He didn't like what He saw. It was getting late, so He walked back up the Mount of Olives with His disciples to the village of Bethany for the night.

The Messiah and the Fig Tree

> **Mark 11:12-14 -** *And on the morrow, when they were come from Bethany, he was hungry: And seeing a fig tree afar off having leaves, he came, if haply he might find any thing thereon: and when he came to it, he found nothing but leaves; for the time of figs was not yet. And Jesus answered and said unto it, No man eat fruit of thee hereafter for ever. And his disciples heard it.*

This has been a problematic passage for some Christian Jews over the years. Why would Jesus the Jewish Messiah curse a *fig tree*? Notice this warning in the Torah:

> *When thou shalt besiege a city a long time, in making war against it to take it, thou shalt not destroy the trees thereof by forcing an axe against them: for thou mayest eat of them, and thou shalt not cut them down (for the tree of the field is man's life) to employ them in the siege: Only the trees which thou knowest that they be not trees for meat, thou shalt destroy and cut them down; and thou shalt build bulwarks against the city that maketh war with thee, until it be subdued.*
>
> Deuteronomy 20:19-20

But the setting, the time of the year, and the spiritual meaning are totally different. Jesus is not making war in

Jerusalem. He is offering peace. He came into Jerusalem looking for spiritual fruit and just like the *fig tree*, there was no fruit. One of the key phrases in this passage is *for the time of figs was not yet.* As the *fig tree* was not ready to bear fruit, Israel was not yet ready to receive its Messiah. Jesus found only the *leaves* of outward religion. Jesus was saying that the time of the physical kingdom to be set up in Jerusalem was not yet. He uses the *fig tree* as a harbinger of Messianic events. Jesus uses the *fig tree* as a symbol of Israel to teach a powerful lesson to His followers. **(Study Jeremiah 24)**

The Messiah Purifies the Temple

> **Mark 11:15-19 -** *So they came to Jerusalem. Then Jesus went into the temple and began to drive out those who bought and sold in the temple, and overturned the tables of the money changers and the seats of those who sold doves. And He would not allow anyone to carry wares through the temple. Then He taught, saying to them, Is it not written, My house shall be called a house of prayer for all nations? But you have made it a den of thieves. And the scribes and chief priests heard it and sought how they might destroy Him; for they feared Him, because all the people were astonished at His teaching. When evening had come, He went out of the city.*

It was prophesied that the Messiah would *come to his Temple*:

> *Behold, I will send my messenger, and he shall prepare the way before me: and the* LORD, *whom ye seek, shall suddenly come to his temple, even the messenger of the covenant, whom ye delight in: behold, he shall come, saith the* LORD *of hosts. But who may abide the day of his coming? and who shall stand when he appeareth? for he is like a refiner's fire, and like fullers' soap: And he shall sit as a refiner and purifier of silver: and he shall purify the sons of Levi, and purge them as gold and silver, that they may offer unto the* LORD *an offering in righteousness. Then shall the offering of Judah and Jerusalem be pleasant unto the* LORD, *as in the days of old, and as in former years.*
>
> Malachi 3:1-4

Animals were sold in the outer court as a service to Passover pilgrims who traveled to the city to offer a sacrifice. But when Jesus came into the Temple, the merchants were in the inner court and were using the Temple to exploit their own financial gain. It was *what* they were doing and *where* they were doing it. The expulsion of the merchants recalls the vision of the prophet Zechariah during the messianic age:

Yea, every pot in Jerusalem and in Judah shall be holiness unto the LORD *of hosts: and all they that sacrifice shall come and take of them, and seethe therein: and in that day there shall be no more the Canaanite in the house of the* LORD *of hosts.*

Zechariah 14:21

When Jesus saw the religious establishment taking advantage of the foreigners who were coming into the Temple, He quotes from these verses:

Even them will I bring to my holy mountain, and make them joyful in my house of prayer: their burnt offerings and their sacrifices shall be accepted upon mine altar; for mine house shall be called an house of prayer for all people.

Isaiah 56:7

Is this house, which is called by my name, become a den of robbers in your eyes? Behold, even I have seen it, saith the LORD.

Jeremiah 7:11

Jesus and Moving Mountains

Mark 11:20-26 - And in the morning, as they passed by, they saw the fig tree dried up from the roots. And Peter calling to remembrance saith unto him, Master, behold, the fig tree which

216

thou cursedst is withered away. And Jesus answering saith unto them, Have faith in God. For verily I say unto you, That whosoever shall say unto this mountain, ★ Be thou removed, and be thou cast into the sea; and shall not doubt in his heart, but shall believe that those things which he saith shall come to pass; he shall have whatsoever he saith. Therefore I say unto you, What things soever ye desire, when ye pray, believe that ye receive them, and ye shall have them. And when ye stand praying, forgive, if ye have ought against any: that your Father also which is in heaven may forgive you your trespasses. But if ye do not forgive, neither will your Father which is in heaven forgive your trespasses.

★ *It's interesting that Jesus was standing on the Mount of Olives when He said these words. A twofold lesson: The spiritual lesson of having the faith to remove the spiritual mountains in our lives to the prophetic lesson that one day the Mount of Olives will move when Jesus returns.* **"And his feet shall stand in that day upon the mount of Olives, which is before Jerusalem on the east, and the mount of Olives shall cleave in the midst thereof toward the east and toward the west, and there shall be a very great valley; and half of the mountain shall remove toward the north, and half of it toward the south."** Zechariah 14:4.

The amazement of the disciples over the miracle of the

withered fig tree gives rise to Jesus teaching an important lesson about faith and prayer. First of all we are to have the faith *that God gives to us* and *not doubt*. We must *believe* that God hears us when we trust in the blood of His Son Jesus who has opened up the way. **(Hebrews 10:19-22)** Secondly, we must believe that we will *receive* an answer to our prayer. It may not be the exact answer that we desire, but God loves His children and He knows what is best. He will answer our prayers! Finally Jesus reminds them that harboring unforgiveness is a hindrance to our prayers. God deals with us as we deal with those around us. Four valuable lessons we can gather from these verses:

* *Have faith in God and not doubt*
* *Believe that we will receive what we ask for*
* *Forgive others as we pray*
* *The Father forgives us when we forgive others*

Jesus and the Baptism of John

Mark 11:27-33 - *And they come again to Jerusalem: and as he was walking in the temple, there come to him the chief priests, and the scribes, and the elders, And say unto him, By what authority doest thou these things? and who gave thee this authority to do these things? And Jesus answered and said unto them, I will also ask of you one question, and answer me, and I will tell you by what authority I* *do these things. The baptism of John, was it from heaven, or of men? answer me. And they reasoned with themselves, saying, If we shall say, From heaven; he will say, Why then did ye not believe him? But if we shall say, Of men; they feared the people: for all men counted John, that he was a prophet indeed. And they answered and said unto Jesus, We cannot tell. And Jesus answering saith unto them, Neither do I tell you by what authority I do these things.*

The *chief priests, scribes, and elders* want to know who gives Jesus the authority to cleanse the Temple? The Sadducees are in control of the Temple, so how could a carpenter from Nazareth come into their holy place and overthrow the tables of the moneychangers? Jesus answers them by giving them a question, *"The baptism of John, was it from heaven, or of men? Answer me."*

The religious interrogators reasoned among themselves that if they denied that John's baptism was from heaven, then they would lose favor with the people, because the people honored John and knew that he was a powerful prophet. If they say that John's baptism was from heaven, then they are condemning themselves for not believing in John's message. Jesus knew that they could not give an answer. The point is that the God of Israel who commissioned John the Baptist's ministry is the same authority that sent Jesus to Israel. The God of Abraham, Isaac, and Jacob, who they were claiming to worship in the Temple, was walking in their midst in human flesh! What a thought!

CHAPTER TWELVE

Jesus and the Parable of the Householder

Mark 12:1-9 - *And he began to speak unto them by parables. A certain man planted a vineyard, and set an hedge about it, and digged a place for the winefat, and built a tower, and let it out to husbandmen, and went into a far country. And at the season he sent to the husbandmen a servant, that he might receive from the husbandmen of the fruit of the vineyard. And they caught him, and beat him, and sent him away empty. And again he sent unto them another servant; and at him they cast stones, and wounded him in the head, and sent him away shamefully handled. And again he sent another; and him they killed, and many others; beating some, and killing some. Having yet therefore one son, his wellbeloved, he sent him also last unto them, saying, They will reverence my son. But those husbandmen said* *among themselves, This is the heir; come, let us kill him, and the inheritance shall be ours. And they took him, and killed him, and cast him out of the vineyard. What shall therefore the lord of the vineyard do? he will come and destroy the husbandmen, and will give the vineyard unto others.*

Sometimes we read this parable very haphazardly, or we seem to skip over it entirely. This is one of the most important parables that Jesus ever gave that was directly given to the Judean religious leaders. This parable has been used over the centuries by Replacement Theologians *(those who teach that the church has replaced Israel)* to show that God is through with Israel, and the promises now belong to the Church. In order to understand this important parable of our Lord, let's break it down as follows:

Owner of the vineyard = **God of Israel**

Vineyard = **Israel**

Husbandmen = **Religious leaders**

Fruit of the vineyard = **True righteousness**

Servants sent = **Prophets**

Son sent = **Jesus the Messiah**

Destroy the husbandmen = **Roman invasion in 70AD**

New husbandmen = **New Jewish community who believed in Jesus**

Jesus also seems to be given a parable that parallels a parable from the prophet Isaiah. Israel is compared to a vineyard in that God had done everything possible for them to bring forth grapes, but instead they brought forth wild grapes. Notice the comparison:

> *Now will I sing to my wellbeloved a song of my beloved touching his vineyard. My wellbeloved hath a vineyard in a very fruitful hill: And he fenced it, and gathered out the stones thereof, and planted it with the choicest vine, and built a tower in the midst of it, and also made a winepress therein: and he looked that it should bring forth grapes, and it brought forth wild grapes. And now, O inhabitants of Jerusalem, and men of Judah, judge, I pray you, betwixt me and my vineyard. What could have been done more to my vineyard, that I have not done in it? wherefore, when I looked that it should bring forth grapes, brought it forth wild grapes? And now go to; I will tell you what I will do to my vineyard: I will take away the hedge thereof, and it shall be eaten up; and break down the wall thereof, and it shall be trodden down: And I will lay it waste: it shall not be pruned, nor digged; but there shall come up briers and thorns: I will also command the clouds that they rain no rain upon it. For the vineyard of the LORD of hosts is the house*

of Israel, and the men of Judah his pleasant plant: and he looked for judgment, but behold oppression; for righteousness, but behold a cry.

Isaiah 5:1-7

Jesus Quotes from Psalm 118

Mark 12:10-12 - *And have ye not read this scripture; The stone which the builders rejected is become the head of the corner: This was the Lord's doing, and it is marvellous in our eyes? And they sought to lay hold on him, but feared the people: for they knew that he had spoken the parable against them: and they left him, and went their way.*

Jesus is quoting from **Psalm 118:22-23**, a psalm that was chanted by the Passover pilgrims flocking to Jerusalem. While the religious leaders would reject their Messiah *(stone),* ★ His work would be called *marvelous in the eyes* of those who believed in Him—Jews and Gentiles. This passage is so important in understanding this parable of Jesus, and it is also mentioned in the writings of the Apostle Paul and the Apostle Peter:

Now therefore ye are no more strangers and foreigners, but fellowcitizens with the saints, and of the household of God; And are built upon the foundation of the apostles and prophets, Jesus Christ himself being the chief corner stone.

Ephesians 2:19-20

To whom coming, as unto a living stone, disallowed indeed of men, but chosen of God, and precious, Ye also, as lively stones, are built up a spiritual house, an holy priesthood, to offer up spiritual sacrifices, acceptable to God by Jesus Christ. Wherefore also it is contained in the scripture, Behold, I lay in Sion a chief corner stone, elect, precious: and he that believeth on him shall not be confounded. Unto you therefore which believe he is precious: but unto them which be disobedient, the stone which the builders disallowed, the same is made the head of the corner, And a stone of stumbling, and a rock of offence, even to them which stumble at the word, being disobedient: whereunto also they were appointed.

I Peter 2:4-8

★ There is also a strong connection with Jesus the Son of David being rejected to the rejection and anointing of the shepherd boy, David, by the prophet Samuel in **I Samuel 16**. *The seven sons of Jesse did not understand why God would choose the youngest to be king over Israel. The fact that Jesus was the stone thrown away and yet becomes the chief cornerstone for the new community links us to two other Old Testament passages -*

"And he shall be for a sanctuary; but for a stone of stumbling and for a rock of offence to both the houses of Israel, for a gin and for a snare to the inhabitants of Jerusalem."

Isaiah 8:14.

"Therefore thus saith the Lord God, Behold, I lay in Zion for a foundation a stone, a tried stone, a precious corner stone, a sure foundation: he that believeth shall not make haste."

Isaiah 28:16.

The Pharisees and the Herodians

Mark 12:13-17 - *And they send unto him certain of the Pharisees and of the Herodians, to catch him in his words. And when they were come, they say unto him, Master, we know that thou art true, and carest for no man: for thou regardest not the person of men, but teachest the way of God in truth: Is it lawful to give tribute to Caesar, or not? Shall we give, or shall we not give? But he, knowing their hypocrisy, said unto them, Why tempt ye me? bring me a penny, that I may see it. And they brought it. And he saith unto them, Whose is this image and superscription? And they said unto him, Caesar's. And Jesus answering said unto them, Render to Caesar the things that*

are Caesar's, and to God the things that are God's. And they marvelled at him.

The *Pharisees* were the religious fundamentalists of their day, and the *Herodians* were the secular liberals of their day. Ordinarily the two groups would have nothing at all in common, but together they were hoping to use their opposing worldview to trap *Yeshua*. They would pose a question to our Lord about the painful reminder of Roman occupation and paying the poll tax that everyone had to pay.

If Jesus said *"we should pay taxes to Caesar,"* then the Pharisees would accuse Him of being a traitor to Israel and discredit His messianic claims. If Jesus said *"we should not pay taxes to Caesar,"* then the Herodians would accuse Him of being a traitor to Rome and an enemy of Caesar. They thought for sure they had Jesus where they wanted Him.

The response that Jesus gave would challenge both the *Pharisees* and the *Herodians*. He asks to see a coin! The *Pharisees* used a *Tyrian shekel* ★ in the Temple, but the *Herodians* would have carried a Roman *denarius* ★ with Caesar's image.

★ *The Tyrian shekel was printed in Jerusalem and contained 94 percent silver, while the denarius only contained 80 percent silver. It had been originally printed in Tyre, but Herod the Great started printing them in Jerusalem to control the most important coin to religious Jews.*

★ *In Jesus' time the coin was a Roman denarius that had the image of Tiberius Caesar. (14-37AD) The inscription would have been in Latin, "Tiberius Caesar Divi" which means, "The Divine Emperor Tiberius."*

"Whose is this image and superscription? And they said unto him, Caesar's. And Jesus answering said unto them, Render to Caesar the things that are Caesar's, and to God the things that are God's. And they marvelled at him" - The coin had Caesar's image stamped on it, so it must belong to Caesar. God's image was not found on a coin, but on every human being:

> **So God created man in his own image, in the image of God created he him; male and female created he them.**
>
> Genesis 1:27

God's image was on the *Pharisees* and the *Herodians*, so they must surrender to Him! Not only did this cause them to *marvel*, but it should cause every one of us to *marvel!* Have we surrendered ourselves to God through faith in His Son, the Lord Jesus the Messiah?

Jesus and the Sadducees

> **Mark 12:18-23 - Then come unto him the Sadducees, which say there is no resurrection; and they asked him, saying, Master, Moses wrote unto us, If a man's brother die, and leave his wife behind him, and leave no children, that his brother should take his wife, and raise up seed unto his brother. Now there were seven**

brethren: and the first took a wife, and dying left no seed. And the second took her, and died, neither left he any seed: and the third likewise. And the seven had her, and left no seed: last of all the woman died also. In the resurrection therefore, when they shall rise, whose wife shall she be of them? for the seven had her to wife.

The *Sadducees* were priestly aristocrats who managed the Temple in Jerusalem. We know by history and by **Acts 23:8** that they did not believe in a resurrection, and they only believed in the Torah, or the first five books of the Bible. So they set out to give Jesus a very hypothetical question about the resurrection as a mockery and trying to prove there is no resurrection. But like the *Pharisees and Herodians*, they didn't know the Person they were talking to. They refer to the Levirate law where if a brother died childless, it required his living brother to marry the widow and to have children so the family name would carry on:

If brethren dwell together, and one of them die, and have no child, the wife of the dead shall not marry without unto a stranger: her husband's brother shall go in unto her, and take her to him to wife, and perform the duty of an husband's brother unto her. And it shall be, that the firstborn which she beareth shall succeed in the name of his brother which is dead, that his name be not put out of Israel.

Deuteronomy 25:5-6

Maybe the *Sadducees* had used this story many times to pull out at dinner parties or social gatherings to tease the Pharisees. So they ask Jesus that if *seven* brothers had the woman as a wife and they died without leaving any children, which man would be her husband in the resurrection? We can just imagine the chuckles that were going on after they asked Jesus the question. They are trying to point out how ridiculous it is to believe in a resurrection. But Jesus shows how ignorant they really are!

The Ignorance of the Sadducees

Mark 12:24-27 - *And Jesus answering said unto them, Do ye not therefore err, because ye know not the scriptures, neither the power of God? For when they shall rise from the dead, they neither marry, nor are given in marriage; but are as the angels which are in heaven. And as touching the dead, that they rise: have ye not read in the book of Moses, how in the bush God spake unto him, saying, I am the God of Abraham, and the God of Isaac, and the God of Jacob? He is not the God of the dead, but the God of the living: ye therefore do greatly err.*

Jesus makes two very important points:

* *They do not know the scriptures*
* *They do not know the power of God*

The Sadducees believed that if it wasn't found in the books of Moses, then it was not true. Jesus said they were ignorant of the scriptures because of their narrow-minded interpretations, like the Pharisees not leaving any room for other ways of handling the scriptures. They did not allow for God's power to resurrect the dead. The Pharisees taught that if God had the power to make man, then He certainly could remake man. *

* Jewish rabbis taught that if glassware could be created by the breath of a human, melted down and then remade, then how much more could the breath of Almighty God create a human being, and after he dies physically, be remade by the breath of God.

Jesus lets them know that in the resurrection there will be no need of procreation. Marriage will not be necessary in heaven. Jesus is not saying that people will *be* angels, but we will be *like* the angels in that sense. Things will be purified in the resurrected state.

Jesus reminds them of Moses and the burning bush where God spoke to Moses and said, **"I am the God of Abraham, and the God of Isaac, and the God of Jacob."** Jesus ended His answer to their ridiculous question by saying, **"He is not the God of the dead, but the God of the living."** What is so powerful about Jesus' answer is that the Sadducees had probably just prayed the Jewish liturgy prayer of *Amidah* ✱ that morning that includes, *"Blessed are you Lord our God of our Fathers, the God of Abraham, the God of Isaac, and the God of Jacob, God Most High."* Jesus took a portion from not only their daily prayers, but from the *five books of Moses* to show that Abraham, Isaac, and Jacob, were still living and God was still their God! Hallelujah!

✱ *The Jewish Amidah is the central prayer that religious Jews recite three times every day. It is also called the standing prayer, or the Shemoneh Esreh.*

Jesus and the First and Second Commandments

> **Mark 12:28-31 - *And one of the scribes came, and having heard them reasoning together, and perceiving that he had answered them well, asked him, Which is the first commandment of all? And Jesus answered him, The first of all the commandments is, Hear, O Israel; The Lord our God is one Lord: And thou shalt love the Lord thy God with all thy heart, and with all thy soul, and with all thy mind, and with all thy strength: this is the first commandment. And the second is like, namely this, Thou shalt love thy neighbour as thyself. There is none other commandment greater than these.***

There was a *scribe*, doubtless a Pharisee, that was listening to the conversation between Jesus and the Sadducees. Understandably, the scribe was intrigued with the wisdom of our Lord. So he decides to pose a legitimate question to Jesus without an ulterior motive. ***"What is the first commandment?"***

Jesus responded immediately with the words from the *Shema*, which means *"hear"* from **Deuteronomy 6:4–5**. The motivation for keeping the other commandments is *loving God*. How does anyone prove that they love God? Is it just some affectionate feeling that we generate in our minds? We demonstrate our love for God by obeying His commandments. The apostle John would later write these words:

> **For this is the love of God, that we keep his commandments: and his commandments are not grievous.**
>
> I John 5:3

Jesus gave the second greatest commandment by quoting from **Leviticus 19:18.** Because the first commandment and the second commandment both start with the words ***"and you shall love,"*** they compliment each other and shed light on each other. There was a style of Jewish teaching called *G'zerah Shevah* that was a methodology to *decree* two different contexts that were considered *equal*. So Jesus combines **Deuteronomy 6:4–5** to **Leviticus 19:18.**

This thought of *loving one's neighbor* fulfilling the law is reflected in the epistles of Paul and James:

> **For this, Thou shalt not commit adultery, Thou shalt not kill, Thou shalt not steal, Thou shalt**

not bear false witness, Thou shalt not covet; and if there be any other commandment, it is briefly comprehended in this saying, namely, Thou shalt love thy neighbour as thyself. Love worketh no ill to his neighbour: therefore love is the fulfilling of the law.

Romans 13:9-10

For all the law is fulfilled in one word, even in this; Thou shalt love thy neighbour as thyself.

Galatians 5:14

If ye fulfil the royal law according to the scripture, Thou shalt love thy neighbour as thyself, ye do well.

James 2:8

Not Far From the Kingdom of God

Mark 12:32-34 - *And the scribe said unto him, Well, Master, thou hast said the truth: for there is one God; and there is none other but he: And to love him with all the heart, and with all the understanding, and with all the soul, and with all the strength, and to love his neighbour as himself, is more than all whole burnt offerings and sacrifices. And when Jesus saw that he answered discreetly, he said unto him, Thou art not far from the kingdom of*

God. And no man after that durst ask him any question.

The scribe answers Jesus back with what sounds like a redundant statement, and then he mentions *burnt offerings and sacrifices*. One of the primary reasons why God imposed the sacrificial system of killing animals upon Israel was to eradicate their tendency to drift off into idolatry like they did when they worshipped the golden calf. **(Exodus 32)** The other reason was to show the seriousness of their sins by death and the shedding of blood. God's number one requirement was for them to simply love Him with all of their heart and to love each other as they loved themselves.

But Jesus wanted this scribe to know that just reciting the *Shema* or knowing the scriptures was not enough. The very God of Moses was standing in front of him, and he was close to becoming a part of God's kingdom, but not yet. There are many people in our world that may be nice moral people and may even be religious. But to become a member of God's kingdom, we must acknowledge the truth that we have not loved God with all of our heart, and we have not loved our neighbor as ourselves. We must repent and embrace the sacrifice that Jesus made upon the cross and be washed from our sins in His sinless blood! There are many who are not far from the kingdom of God!

The Lord Said To My Lord

> **Mark 12:35-37** - *And Jesus answered and said, while he taught in the temple, How say the scribes that Christ is the son of David?* ★ *For David himself said by the Holy Ghost, The* LORD *said to my Lord, Sit thou on my right hand, till I make thine enemies thy footstool. David therefore himself calleth him Lord; and whence is he then his son? And the common people heard him gladly.*

★ *This is a profound affirmation from Christ our Lord that God kept His covenant that He made with king David in* **2 Samuel 7:12-16**. *The promise of the Redeemer that the Seed of the Woman would bruise the head of the serpent was given in* **Genesis 3:15**. *The Seed of the Woman would come through the Seed of Abraham, Isaac, and Jacob.* **Genesis 12:1-3**. *The Seed of the Woman would also come through the tribe of Judah in* **Genesis 49:10**. *The Seed of the Woman would come through king David,* **"I have made a covenant with my chosen, I have sworn unto David my servant." Psalm 89:3**. *(The first king of Israel was Saul who was from the tribe of Benjamin) The very first verse in the New Testament* (or Covenant) *is* **The book of the generation of Jesus Christ, <u>the son of David</u>, the son of Abraham." Matthew 1:1**.

The scribes knew well the passage that Jesus was quoting, but the original wording helps to explain:

> *The LORD* (Yehovah) *said unto my Lord*
> (Adonai, or Messiah), *Sit thou at my right*
> *hand, until I make thine enemies thy footstool.*
> Psalm 110:1

The problem was that they knew that the Messiah of Israel would be the *Son of David* **(2 Samuel 7:12-14, Luke 1:32, Rom.1:3),** but they did not know that *David's Son* would also be his *Lord.* Through the inspiration of the *Holy Ghost,* David wrote these messianic words that the scribes had never unraveled. Jesus is the *Son of David* in His humanity and yet, Jesus as the divine *Son of God* is David's *Lord.* While it still may sound somewhat confusing to us, notice that **the common people heard him gladly.** This author has wondered many times how many of the *common people* knew just who Jesus was, while most of the religious establishment did not. Our Lord seems to place more faith within the hearts of the common people. **(James 2:5)**

Jesus Warns the Common People

> **Mark 12:38-40 -** *And he said unto them in his doctrine, Beware of the scribes, which love to go in long clothing, and love salutations in the marketplaces, And the chief seats in the synagogues, and the uppermost rooms at feasts: Which devour widows' houses, and for a pretence make long prayers: these shall receive greater damnation.*

There is nothing that causes our Lord any more remorse than religious hypocrisy. We cannot overemphasize the fact that when Jesus walked this earth, His heart was filled with love for all, but His heart was filled with anger toward the religious leaders who were misleading the common people. They were supposed to be leading the common people to their Messiah instead of trying to look pious on the outside. Notice the strong points of condemnation that Jesus gives:

* *The scribes love to go in long clothing*
* *The scribes love to be recognized in the marketplaces*
* *The scribes loved the chief seats in the synagogues*
* *The scribes loved the uppermost rooms at the religious feasts*
* *The scribes devoured widow's houses with pretension prayers*
* *The scribes for a pretense make long prayers*
* *The scribes would receive the greater damnation*

Jesus and the Widow's Mite

Mark 12:41-44 - *And Jesus sat over against the treasury, and beheld how the people cast money into the treasury: and many that were rich cast in much. And there came a certain poor widow, and she threw in two mites, * which make a farthing. And he called unto him his disciples, and saith unto them, Verily*

I say unto you, That this poor widow hath cast more in, than all they which have cast into the treasury: For all they did cast in of their abundance; but she of her want did cast in all that she had, even all her living.

Jesus has just given the *pretext* by stating that the scribes *devour widow's houses*. Then Mark gives us the account of Jesus watching people casting their money into the treasury. While He was watching intently, there was a *poor widow who cast in two mites* which was the smallest currency in Jesus' time. Not only were the scribes misleading the widows by praying long, pretentious prayers in their *houses*, they were telling them that they had to give money to the Temple for which they really didn't have to give. They didn't have paper money in Jesus' time, so they cast their coins into the Temple treasury. The hypocrites cast in many coins in order to make the *trumpet sound*, which Jesus condemned. **(Matthew 6:2)** There were 13 trumpet-shaped boxes along the outer wall of the Women's Court where people would cast in their coins. The Spirit of the God of Israel was not in the Temple that Herod had built, and the *widow's two mites* were not being used for the right purposes. Sound familiar? She was doing what the scribes were telling her to do. But her heart was right! This is what Jesus saw and wanted His disciples to remember. What a lesson!

* *There were about six major denominations of coins in Jesus' time that were used in everyday Jewish life. The smallest coin was*

a lepton, which was worth 1/64 of one denarius, a daily wage. The word "lepton" means "small" and was printed out of bronze. The word "mite" and "farthing" are old English words from the 1611 KJV translation.

CHAPTER THIRTEEN

Jesus Answers the Disciple's Questions (The Olivet Discourse)

> **Mark 13:1-4** - *And as he went out of the temple, one of his disciples saith unto him, Master, see what manner of stones and what buildings are here! And Jesus answering said unto him, Seest thou these great buildings? there shall not be left one stone upon another, that shall not be thrown down. And as he sat upon the mount of Olives over against the temple, Peter and James and John and Andrew asked him privately, Tell us, when shall these things be? and what shall be the sign when all these things shall be fulfilled?*

Mark 13 parallels **Matthew 24** and remain the most complex and difficult chapters in the four gospels. Entire books have been written about the events in this one chapter. Before this author tries to throw a grain of sand of commentary on this chapter, a brief introduction is much needed. There is no way that the finite mind of any human can fathom the infinite mind of Almighty God. The questions that the disciples asked Jesus seemed to cause Him to see not only the future events unfold during the first century, but the next 2,000 years, the great tribulation period, and His second coming. Because of the establishment of the Catholic Church and the Protestant Reformation, many theologians have tried to interpret these verses many different ways. During the Catholic Reformation which started with the Council of Trent (1545-1563AD) in northern Italy, was the belief called *Preterism*, which stated that all of the words of Jesus in this chapter were all fulfilled when the Temple was destroyed in 70AD. On the other hand, while this author holds to a *dispensational* theology, there are *hyper-dispensationalists* who seem to focus too much on the church age without considering the events of Israel's history and overspiritualize many of the events that Jesus foretold that will happen in the future. But some of the confusion can be resolved when we see more clearly the questions that the disciples were asking Jesus. Notice Matthew's rendering of the three questions:

> *And as he sat upon the mount of Olives, the disciples came unto him privately, saying, Tell us, when shall these things be? and what shall be the sign of thy coming, and of the end of the world?*
>
> Matthew 24:3

The disciples wanted to know three things:

★ *When will the Temple be destroyed?*
★ *When will the end of the world come?*
★ *When will Jesus return?*

While it is very difficult to simplify such a comprehensive chapter, we will attempt to group the subjects together.

When will the Temple be destroyed? – They were sitting on the Mount of Olives east of Jerusalem where the view of the Temple was breathtaking. The Temple in Jesus' time was built by *Herod the Great* ★ starting from around 18-19BC and was not completed until 64AD under the Roman procurator, *Lucceius Albinus.* The Temple that Jesus and the disciples saw contained massive columns, colonnades, grand stairways, gates and courtyards, shining marble, copper, silver, and gold-adorned buildings that spread for more than 170,000 square yards. Some of the stones were over 40 feet long and weighed over 100 tons. Scholars are still baffled over how Herod was able to bring them to their location and fit them so perfectly without needing mortar. With the natural senses the Temple looked indestructible.

★ *While Herod was a wicked evil puppet of Rome, he was one of the greatest architect designers the world has ever seen. Among his greatest achievements, in addition to the Temple in Jerusalem, were building the spectacular seaport of Caesarea Maritima, the fortresses of the Herodium in Bethlehem, and the Masada in the Judean Desert.*

When Jesus said that *not one stone will be left upon another,* He was referring to the Temple compound proper, not the retaining walls ★ that surrounded the Temple compound. The Temple in Jerusalem was destroyed by the Roman invasion in 70AD. ★ The destruction of the Temple caused the biblical Sadducees and Pharisees to vanish off the pages of history. The valuable personal records of the Jews concerning the 12 tribes of Israel were also burned.

★ *The Western Wall, as it has come to be called, was part of the retaining wall that was holding up the Temple compound and still remains as the most holy religious Jewish site. There are 45 stone courses, 28 above the ground level and 17 beneath. The first seven visible stone courses above the ground and the lower 17 stone courses were placed there by Herod the Great. Because the religious Jews do not believe their Messiah has ever arrived, they believe the Spirit of the God of Israel remains on the Temple Mount. They offer their prayers to the closest part of the Temple that was not destroyed. It became a place of prayer by Suleiman the Magnificent in the 1500's and has been recognized by the religious Jews more and more over the last 150 years.*

★ *Flavius Josephus, in his Wars of the Jews, records that over one million people were killed, mostly Jews, and over 97,000 were taken as slaves. The Romans attacked during the time of the Passover, so the population would have been much greater than normal. When the Romans set fire to the Temple, the gold melted down into the cracks of the stones. The invading army led by Titus toppled over the stones in order to get the gold. It is interesting that Titus would not accept the normal wreath of victory because he looked at the invasion of Jerusalem as merely an instrument of divine wrath.*

When will the end of the world come?" – This is where Jesus begins to weave together the *birth pains of the course of the ages to come* and *the great tribulation* that will come upon Israel before He returns. He combines many of the events that will happen during the lifetime of the apostles during the first century, along with many of the events during the church age down through the centuries. History has proven the words of our Lord to be true, and we are still seeing the fulfillment of His predictions today. Instead of trying to overspiritualize each point that is rather self-explanatory, it is better read together in order to better feel what the disciples must have felt as Jesus spoke these words. The temptation is to tear down every verse and phrase and attempt to read modern-day events into them. With only a few comments, let's try not to disrupt the God-given flow of the context:

(The Course of This Age)

> **Mark 13:5-13 -** *And Jesus answering them began to say, Take heed lest any man deceive you: For many shall come in my name, saying, I am Christ; and shall deceive many. And when ye shall hear of wars and rumours of wars, be ye not troubled: for such things must needs be; but the end shall not be yet. For nation shall rise against nation, and kingdom against kingdom:*

and there shall be <u>earthquakes</u> * in divers places, and there shall be famines and troubles: these are the beginnings of sorrows. But take heed to yourselves: for they shall deliver you up to councils; and in the synagogues ye shall be beaten: and ye shall be brought before rulers and kings for my sake, for a testimony against them. <u>And the gospel must first be published among all nations</u>. * But when they shall lead you, and deliver you up, take no thought beforehand what ye shall speak, neither do ye premeditate: but whatsoever shall be given you in that hour, that speak ye: for it is not ye that speak, but the Holy Ghost. Now the brother shall betray the brother to death, and the father the son; and children shall rise up against their parents, and shall cause them to be put to death. And ye shall be hated of all men for my name's sake: but he that shall endure unto the end, the same shall be saved.

* *Many Jewish rabbis believe that the signs of blood moons in recent years are a clear warning that we will see earthquakes intensify.*

* *There is no possible way that the gospel could be preached into the world during the first century. Printing presses were not invented until hundreds of years later. But today through the means of modern technology, the world is internationally connected. There are over 1,800 satellites in space that have the capability* *of spreading the gospel into the hearts of millions at one time. With the touch pad of a cellphone, the world can hear the gospel in seconds.*

(The Great Tribulation of Israel)

> **Mark 13:14-23 - *But when ye shall see the abomination of desolation, spoken of by Daniel the prophet, standing where it ought not, (let him that readeth understand,) then let them that be in Judaea flee to the mountains: And let him that is on the housetop not go down into the house, neither enter therein, to take any thing out of his house: And let him that is in the field not turn back again for to take up his garment. But woe to them that are with child, and to them that give suck in those days! And pray ye that your flight be not in the winter. For in those days shall be affliction, such as was not from the beginning of the creation which God created unto this time, neither shall be. And except that the Lord had shortened those days, no flesh should be saved: but for the elect's sake, whom he hath chosen, he hath shortened the days. And then if any man shall say to you, Lo, here is Christ; or, lo, he is there; believe him not: For false Christs and false prophets shall rise, and shall shew signs and wonders, to seduce, if it were possible, even the elect.***

> *But take ye heed: behold, I have foretold you*
> *all things.*

"The Abomination of Desolation" - This is a vital point that Jesus makes alluding to the book of **Daniel 9:25-27, 11:31, 12:11**. Jesus looks ahead in time and sees events that will repeat what was written in the words of the prophet Daniel. One of the most detestable events of the *great tribulation* of Israel will parallel what took place more than a century and a half before Jesus walked the earth. What the *Antichrist* will perform in the *Third Temple* during the tribulation period will mirror what happened during other devastating moments in Jewish history, ★ past and future for the disciples of Jesus.

The wicked Seleucid ruler *Antiochus Epiphanes* (175-164BC) profaned the Temple and tried to put an end to the religious Jews observing the Torah. He set up an idol of Zeus in the Temple and sacrificed swine on the altar of the Lord. This brought about the Maccabean Revolt (167-160BC). Notice the Jewish history recorded:

> *Now the fifteenth day of the month Casleu, in*
> *the hundred forty and fifth year, they set up the*
> *abomination of desolation upon the altar, and builded*
> *idol altars throughout the cities of Juda on every side;*
> *And burnt incense at the doors of their houses, and*
> *in the streets. And when they had rent in pieces the*
> *books of the law which they found, they burnt them*
> *with fire. And whosoever was found with any the*

book of the testament, or if any committed to the law, the king's commandment was, that they should put him to death. Thus did they by their authority unto the Israelites every month, to as many as were found in the cities. Now the five and twentieth day of the month they did sacrifice upon the idol altar, which was upon the altar of God. At which time according to the commandment they put to death certain women, that had caused their children to be circumcised. And they hanged the infants about their necks, and rifled their houses, and slew them that had circumcised them. Howbeit many in Israel were fully resolved and confirmed in themselves not to eat any unclean thing. Wherefore the rather to die, that they might not be defiled with meats, and that they might not profane the holy covenant: so then they died. And there was very great wrath upon Israel.

I Maccabees 1:54–64

* *An attempt was made by the Roman Emperor Caligula in 41AD to defile the Temple in Jerusalem, but his death prevented it. The Temple Mount was desecrated once again by the Roman Emperor Hadrian around 135AD. He built a temple to Jupiter and expelled all Jews from Jerusalem. As a form of mockery, he rebuilt and renamed Jerusalem Aelia Capitolina, which combines his Roman family name to Jerusalem being the capital of Jupiter. Jerusalem remained Aelia Capitolina until 638AD. Hadrian also renamed Israel, Palaestina, from the enemy of Israel, the Philistines,* *to disconnect the Jews from the land. Much of the Israeli-Palestine conflict today sprang from the hateful work of Hadrian.*

The *abomination of desolation* is such a bizarre and dramatic event concerning end-time prophecy and Israel, we need to connect the scriptures together to see the importance:

> *Know therefore and understand, that from the going forth of the commandment to restore and to build Jerusalem unto the Messiah the Prince shall be seven weeks, and threescore and two weeks: the street shall be built again, and the wall, even in troublous times. And after threescore and two weeks shall Messiah be cut off, but not for himself: and the people of the prince that shall come shall destroy the city and the sanctuary; and the end thereof shall be with a flood, and unto the end of the war desolations are determined. And he shall confirm the covenant with many for one week: and in the midst of the week he shall cause the sacrifice and the oblation to cease, and for the overspreading of abominations he shall make it desolate, even until the consummation, and that determined shall be poured upon the desolate.*
>
> Daniel 9:25-27

> *But when ye shall see the abomination of desolation, spoken of by Daniel the prophet,*

standing where it ought not, (let him that readeth understand,) then let them that be in Judaea flee to the mountains.

Mark 13:14

Let no man deceive you by any means: for that day shall not come, except there come a falling away first, and that man of sin be revealed, the son of perdition; Who opposeth and exalteth himself above all that is called God, or that is worshipped; so that he as God sitteth in the temple of God, shewing himself that he is God.

2 Thessalonians 2:3-4

And deceiveth them that dwell on the earth by the means of those miracles which he had power to do in the sight of the beast; saying to them that dwell on the earth, that they should make an image to the beast, which had the wound by a sword, and did live. And he had power to give life unto the image of the beast, that the image of the beast should both speak, and cause that as many as would not worship the image of the beast should be killed.

Revelation 13:14-15

Notice that Jesus' words in **Mark 13:19** about the *great tribulation* of Israel are very similar to the words of Daniel. *"For in those days shall be a time of affliction, such as was*

251

not from the beginning of the creation which God created unto this time, neither shall be."

And at that time shall Michael stand up, the great prince which standeth for the children of thy people: and there shall be a time of trouble, such as never was since there was a nation even to that same time: and at that time thy people shall be delivered, every one that shall be found written the book.

Daniel 12:1

The Second Coming of the Lord Jesus Christ

Mark 13:24-27 - *But in those days, after that tribulation, the sun shall be darkened, and the moon shall not give her light, And the stars of heaven shall fall, and the powers that are in heaven shall be shaken. And then shall they see the Son of man coming in the clouds with great power and glory. And then shall he send his angels, and shall gather together his elect from the four winds, from the uttermost part of the earth to the uttermost part of heaven.*

There are several obvious but important truths that Jesus is teaching His disciples from the Mount of Olives:

* *He will come twice* (the disciples only understood one coming)
* *He will return after the great tribulation*
* *He will return in the form of the Son of man* (Daniel 7:13)
* *He will return as the Sovereign Ruler of the universe*

It's interesting that Jesus is using the cosmic disturbance language in the manner the prophets of old used when referring to divine judgment against pagan kingdoms. Here Jesus is using them as a sign just prior to His return to judge the world:

> *Behold, the day of the LORD cometh, cruel both with wrath and fierce anger, to lay the land desolate: and he shall destroy the sinners thereof out of it. For the stars of heaven and the constellations thereof shall not give their light: the sun shall be darkened in his going forth, and the moon shall not cause her light to shine.*
>
> Isaiah 13:9-10

> *And all the host of heaven shall be dissolved, and the heavens shall be rolled together as a scroll: and all their host shall fall down, as the leaf falleth off from the vine, and as a falling fig from the fig tree.*
>
> Isaiah 34:4

> *And when I shall put thee out, I will cover the heaven, and make the stars thereof dark; I will cover the sun with a cloud, and the moon shall not give her light. All the bright lights of heaven will I make dark over thee, and set darkness upon thy land, saith the Lord GOD.*
>
> Ezekiel 32:7-8

The earth shall quake before them; the heavens shall tremble: the sun and the moon shall be dark, and the stars shall withdraw their shining.

Joel 2:10

The sun shall be turned into darkness, and the moon into blood, before the great and terrible day of the LORD come.

Joel 2:31

And it shall come to pass in that day, saith the Lord GOD, that I will cause the sun to go down at noon, and I will darken the earth in the clear day.

Amos 8:9

Regardless of what the scoffers may say, **2 Peter 3:3–10**, Jesus the Lord will return. World history is swiftly moving toward a final conclusion that God has ordained in His Word. It is part of God's plan! Make no mistake about it, Jesus is coming back! Here are a few reasons why:

* *There are close to 500 promises, direct and indirect, in the Old Testament that demand the Second Coming*
* *The teaching of Christ Himself demands the Second Coming*
* *The Holy Spirit demands the Second Coming in the New Testament*
* *The promise for the Church demands the Second Coming*

* *The corruption of the world demands the Second Coming*
* *The future of Israel demands the Second Coming*
* *The destruction of Satan demands the Second Coming*
* *The hope of the saints demands the Second Coming*

Jesus and the Parable of the Fig Tree

> **Mark 13:28-33 -** *Now learn a parable of the fig tree; When her branch is yet tender, and putteth forth leaves, ye know that summer is near: So ye in like manner, when ye shall see these things come to pass, know that it is nigh, even at the doors. Verily I say unto you, that this generation shall not pass, till all these things be done. Heaven and earth shall pass away: but my words shall not pass away. But of that day and that hour knoweth no man, no, not the angels which are in heaven, neither the Son, but the Father. Take ye heed, watch and pray: for ye know not when the time is.*

The *fig tree*, or the Hebrew *te'enah*, is indigenous to Israel and holds a distinct importance throughout the Old Testament. Here are a few examples:

* *Adam and Eve covered their nakedness with fig leaves* (Gen.3:7)
* *The fig tree was one of the God-given blessings of the Promised Land* (Deut.8:8-10)

255

* *The fig tree was a sign of blessing for when Israel was living in prosperity* (I Kings 4:25)
* *The fig tree was a place to rest while meditating upon God's Word* (John 1:48)

The fig tree being a symbol for Israel is undeniable. Note the following:

> *I found Israel like grapes in the wilderness; I saw your fathers as the firstripe in the fig tree at her first time: but they went to Baalpeor, and separated themselves unto that shame; and their abominations were according as they loved.*
>
> Hosea 9:10

> *Thus saith the LORD, the God of Israel; Like these good figs, so will I acknowledge them that are carried away captive of Judah, whom I have sent out of this place into the land of the Chaldeans for their good.*
>
> Jeremiah 24:5

Jesus cursed the *fig tree* just a few hours back as a sign that Israel was not bringing forth biblical fruit.

> *And on the morrow, when they were come from Bethany, he was hungry: And seeing a fig tree afar off having leaves, he came, if haply he might find any thing thereon: and when he*

came to it, he found nothing but leaves; for the time of figs was not yet. And Jesus answered and said unto it, No man eat fruit of thee hereafter for ever. And his disciples heard it.

Mark 11:12-14

Here Jesus uses the *fig tree* as a symbol of Israel's future restoration as a major sign just before His return. Although many scholars and historians refuse to accept the restoration of Israel, God's Word makes it very clear. A careful study of passages like **Romans 9-11,** states clearly that God used the unbelief of the people of Israel to give the Gentiles an opportunity to hear the gospel. After this *dispensation of the Gentiles,* God will turn again to Israel and fulfill His promises of the kingdom of David being restored. It may be difficult to understand, but we are seeing signs of the fig tree starting to blossom once again. Here are a few examples:

* *Israel re-born as a nation in 1948*
* *The Hebrew language as the mother tongue* (Zephaniah 3:9)
* *The regathering of the Jews* (Over 7 million in Israel – *2019 population*)
* *The Six-Day War in 1967* (Israel regaining control of Jerusalem)
* *The desert blossoming like a rose* (Isaiah 35:1)
* *The former and latter rainfall* (Joel 2:23)
* *The wealth and prosperity of Israel*

- ★ *The jealousy of the surrounding nations for Israel's natural resources*
- ★ *The fight between Islam and Israel over the Temple Mount*
- ★ *The move of the US Embassy to Jerusalem in 2018*
- ★ *The Temple Institute in Jerusalem preparing for the Third Temple*
- ★ *The invading armies from the north* (Ezekiel 38-39)
- ★ *Vultures are back in the land of Israel* (Rev.19:17-18)
- ★ *Israel regaining sovereignty over the Golan Heights*

"Verily I say unto you, that this generation shall not pass, till all these things be done" - Two possible interpretations here:

1) *The generation that sees the fig tree start to blossom again will not pass away until all things are fulfilled.*
2) *The word "generation" or the Hebrew dowr, can also mean posterity, and the Jewish nation will certainly not cease to exist until the words of Jesus are fulfilled.*

"Heaven and earth shall pass away: but my words shall not pass away. But of that day and that hour knoweth no man, no, not the angels which are in heaven, neither the Son, but the Father. Take ye heed, watch and pray: for ye know not when the time is" - The Hebrew idiom *heaven and earth* means everything. It's like saying *young and old* to refer to everyone. When Jesus of Nazareth walked this earth as a man, He humbled Himself not to know the time of His

return. But *now* as the *glorified Christ*, seated in heaven, He certainly knows!

Jesus Goes on a Far Journey and Commands to Watch

> **Mark 13:34-37 -** *For the Son of Man is as a man taking a far journey, who left his house, and gave authority to his servants, and to every man his work, and commanded the porter to watch. Watch ye therefore: for ye know not when the master of the house cometh, at even, or at midnight, or at the cockcrowing, or in the morning: Lest coming suddenly he find you sleeping. And what I say unto you I say unto all, Watch.*

Let's review the subjects in the parable that Jesus gives to better understand:

* *Master of the household* = Jesus
* *The house* = The work of God's kingdom
* *The servants* = The disciples and all who work for the kingdom
* *The return of the Master* = The Second Coming of Christ
* *The servant found sleeping* * = The servants who turned away from the kingdom work
* *Lesson* = All servants are to stay busy and to watch

    ★ *There was a Jewish custom that when the captain of the Temple guards made his nightly rounds and found any watchmen sleeping, he would awaken him by lighting his garments on fire.*

Alfred Edersheim, *Middoth 1.2*

Mark was again writing to a Roman audience, and he uses the Roman custom of dividing the night into four shifts: *evening-midnight-rooster crowing-morning.* Since the earth has many different time clocks, the Second Coming of the Lord Jesus the Christ will be known and seen by the whole world! What a thought!

CHAPTER FOURTEEN

Chief Priests Plot to Kill Jesus

> **Mark 14:1-2 -** *After two days was the feast of the passover, and of unleavened bread: and the chief priests and the scribes sought how they might take him by craft, and put him to death. But they said, Not on the feast day, lest there be an uproar of the people.* *

While the paschal lambs were being inspected and prepared for the sin sacrifices for the nation of Israel, the *Lamb of God* was also being inspected to be the supreme sacrifice for the sins of the whole world. What a strange dichotomy we find here! The *chief priests and scribes* were in position as the godly leaders of the nation, and yet they were trying to find a way to kill the *sinless Messiah* of Israel. Their inspections of Jesus were through the eyes of sin, hate, and unbelief. Of course this was all in the foreknowledge of God sending Jesus into the world at just the right time. But in the natural sense, this shows how blind and how evil religion can be. Here we read that during the two most sacred feasts of the Jewish year, *Passover and Unleavened Bread,* ★ they were plotting how they could trap their Messiah and *put him to death.*

★ *The population of Jerusalem was between 40,000 and 50,000 during Jesus' time, but during the three major feasts, the crowds could reach several hundred thousand. There were three major feasts that were required of Jewish males to attend, and two of them were in the spring. The religious leaders had to think of a way to trap Jesus without stirring up the crowds. They didn't want to incite a Jewish revolt and bring Rome's attention to Jerusalem.* **" Three times in a year shall all thy males appear before the LORD thy God in the place which he shall choose; in the feast of unleavened bread, and in the feast of weeks, and in the feast of tabernacles: and they shall not appear before the LORD empty.**

Deuteronomy 16:16

★ *While these two Jewish feasts are mentioned together, the feast of Passover only lasted for 24 hours, while the feast of Unleavened Bread lasted for seven days.* **"In the fourteenth day of the first month at even is the LORD's passover. And on the fifteenth day of the same month is the feast of unleavened bread unto the LORD: seven days ye must eat unleavened bread. In the first day ye shall have an holy convocation: ye shall do no servile work therein. But ye shall offer an offering made by fire unto the LORD seven days: in the seventh day is an holy convocation: ye shall do no servile work therein."**

Leviticus 23:5–8

Jesus the Messiah Being Anointed in Bethany

> **Mark 14:3-9** - *And being in Bethany in the house of Simon the leper, as he sat at meat, there came a woman having an alabaster box of ointment of spikenard very precious; and she brake the box, and poured it on his head. And there were some that had indignation within themselves, and said, Why was this waste of the ointment made? For it might have been sold for more than three hundred pence, and have been given to the poor. And they murmured against her. And Jesus said, Let her alone; why trouble ye her? she hath wrought a good work on me. For ye have the poor with you always, and whensoever ye will ye may do them good: but me ye have not always. She hath done what she could: she is come aforehand to anoint my body to the burying. Verily I say unto you, Wheresoever this gospel shall be preached throughout the whole world, this also that she hath done shall be spoken of for a memorial of her.*

Scholars have debated over the *location* of this anointing of our Lord by the woman. Was it in the house of *Simon the leper*, as Mark and Matthew record, or was it in the house of Mary, Martha, and Lazarus, as **John 12** records? After doing more research, this author thinks that it is very possible that there were two different settings. There were three different meals eaten over the course of the Sabbath that week, each one with a high level of sanctity and joy. Mark and Matthew do not mention the woman's name, while John clearly states it was Mary, the sister of Lazarus. **(John 11:1-2)** The anointing in Mark is *two days* before Passover, and the anointing in John is *six days* before Passover. We cannot be dogmatic, but this seems to solve the problem.

"alabaster box of spikenard very precious"- There is much more to this anointing than we have been told. First of all, this was *pure nard*; that came from the roots of a blooming *Valerian* flower that grew on the Himalayan mountain range in India, over 16,000 feet high. It was well known to be the most luxurious essential oil in the eastern world. The cost of the *spikenard* was more than *300 denarius*. This would be thousands of dollars in today's world. It was most likely everything this woman had in the world as far as value. It had an amber color, and the fragrance was so strong that it would cling to the hair and skin for a long time. This fragrance would have stayed on the body of the Lord Jesus for days, and very likely through His passion week. What a thought! The offering up Jesus as the Lamb of God was a sweet aroma to the Heavenly Father.

Spikenard was used in the Temple in Jerusalem as part of the *ketoret,* or the specialized incense offering. While the hypocritical priests were offering this expensive fragrance in the Temple, this woman was offering her best with a heart of true faith in Jesus as her Messiah. It is also mentioned in the **Song of Solomon 1:12, 4:13-14,** as a symbol of pure love between the bride and the bridegroom. The *spikenard* symbolized the very best, and this woman was showing that her love for Jesus was pure and genuine. We are reminded of the passage where they were to give the Lord their very best:

> *Out of all your gifts ye shall offer every heave*
> *offering of the* LORD, *of all the* <u>best</u> *thereof,*
> *even the hallowed part thereof out of it*
> Numbers 18:29

"For ye have the poor with you always, and whensoever ye will ye may do them good" – The parallel Old Testament passage would be **Deuteronomy 15:11**: *"For the poor shall never cease out of the land: therefore I command thee, saying, Thou shalt open thine hand wide unto thy brother, to thy poor, and to thy needy, in thy land."* Jesus wasn't being insensitive concerning the poor, for His ministry was marked by His deep love for the poor. He was telling His disciples that His inestimable time with them was very short.

"She hath done what she could: she is come aforehand to anoint my body to the burying. Verily I say unto you, Wheresoever this gospel shall be preached throughout the whole world, this also that she hath done shall be spoken of for a memorial of her" – While the chief priests and scribes were plotting to kill Jesus, this woman was anointing him for His impending death and burial. Executed criminals

were not given special treatment before they were killed, but Jesus would be crucified and falsely accused as a blasphemer and enemy of Rome. He was the long-awaited Messiah of Israel, and this woman knew it! Again, think of this fragrance staying on the body of Jesus throughout His trial, His betrayal, His beatings, and possibly while He was on the cross. Maybe the sweet fragrance on His body and hair would be a reminder to Jesus of the people who truly loved him.

This woman's act of love resulted in a lasting legacy. Not only did her anointing put into motion the betrayal and death of the Messiah of Israel, her deed would be recorded in the golden pages of God's Word, and we are still reading about it to this day. Wow!

Jesus the Messiah Betrayed by Judas Iscariot

> **Mark 14:10-11 - *And Judas Iscariot, one of the twelve, went unto the chief priests, to betray him unto them. And when they heard it, they were glad, and promised to give him money. And he sought how he might conveniently betray him.***

Mark places the anointing of the expensive ointment by the woman between the unbelief of the chief priests and the betrayal of one of the 12 disciples. Interesting! Maybe Judas thought that Jesus would deliver them from the Romans and be the conquering Messiah that he had longed for?

When he heard Jesus talk about His burial, then possibly he felt like his past three years of following Jesus were wasted. Whatever the motive, the betrayal of Jesus from one of His own disciples holds one of the darkest moments in the history of the world.

We know from the other gospel accounts that Judas betrayed Jesus for 30 pieces of silver. We need to contrast that to the extravagant price of the spikenard of the woman. While Mark's account is brief concerning Judas, his betrayal was foretold centuries before:

> *Yea, mine own familiar friend, in whom I trusted, <u>which did eat of my bread</u>, hath lifted up his heel against me.*
>
> Psalm 41:9

> *And I said unto them, If ye think good, give me my price; and if not, forbear. So they weighed for my price thirty pieces of silver. And the* LORD *said unto me, Cast it unto the potter: a goodly price that I was prised at of them. And I took the thirty pieces of silver, and cast them to the potter in the house of the* LORD.
>
> Zechariah 11:12-13

Jesus the *"Passover Lamb"* Prepares the Passover

> **Mark 14:12-16 –** *And the first day of unleavened bread, when they killed the passover, his disciples said unto him, Where wilt thou that we go and*

> *prepare that thou mayest eat the passover? And he sendeth forth two of his disciples, and saith unto them, Go ye into the city, and there shall meet you a man bearing a pitcher of water: follow him. And wheresoever he shall go in, say ye to the goodman of the house, The Master saith, Where is the guestchamber, where I shall eat the passover with my disciples? And he will shew you a large upper room furnished and prepared: there make ready for us. And his disciples went forth, and came into the city, and found as he had said unto them: and they made ready the passover.*

There are many *uncommon* points of interests in this passage:

* *when they killed the passover* – A foreshadow that *Jesus the Passover* would be killed. **(I Corinthians 5:7)**
* *eat the passover* – It is not known if there was a lamb to eat at this particular Passover meal. But the true *Lamb of God* was sitting at the table. (Notice Mark 14:17-22)
* *man bearing a pitcher* – Very unusual for a man to be carrying water, as this was a job normally for the women. **(Gen.24:11, Exodus 2:16, John 4:7)** Men carried water only in the *Essene* ★ community. (Some scholars believe that Mark carried the pitcher?)

* ***the goodman of the house*** – The *goodman of the house* <u>must</u> have known the *Master* was Jesus.
* ***the disciples found as he had said*** – Jesus *knew* everything beforehand.

* *The Essenes were another sect within Judaism during the time of Jesus. They lived in various towns and had a celibate community just north of the Dead Sea, called Qumran. They practiced poverty, daily immersion, and asceticism. Several thousand are recorded in the writings of Pliny the Elder* (Natural History, 79AD) *and Flavius Josephus* (The Jewish War, 75AD). *They saw the corrupt leadership in the Temple in Jerusalem and separated themselves from the Pharisees and Sadducees. They are credited with writing the Dead Sea Scrolls that were discovered in the mountains in 1946-48.*

The Passover Lamb Eats with His Betrayer

Mark 14:17-21 – *And in the evening he cometh with the twelve. And as they sat and did eat, Jesus said, Verily I say unto you, One of you which eateth with me shall betray me.¹⁹ And they began to be sorrowful, and to say unto him one by one, Is it I? and another said, Is it I? And he answered and said unto them, It is one of the twelve, that dippeth with me in the dish. The Son of man indeed goeth, as it is written of him: but woe to that man by whom the Son*

of man is betrayed! good were it for that man
if he had never been born.

Notice here that the disciple that would *betray* the Son of God would *eat with him.* Notice the wording earlier in Mark's gospel:

And Judas Iscariot, which also betrayed him.
Mark 3:19

This is also a direct connection to the prophecy in **Psalm 41:9.** The custom in Jesus' time was to place several different dishes on the table that contained the bitter herbs, and there evidently was a dish close to Jesus and Judas. Judas must have been seated on one side of Jesus, and we know that the beloved John was on the other side. **(John 13:23)** For Jesus to take a piece of morsel and dip it in the *same* dish as Judas was an act of honor and love. Was Jesus giving Judas one last chance to turn from his dastardly deed? The darkness that was in the heart of Judas Iscariot is emphasized with these points:

* *Judas allowed Satan to enter into him*
* *Judas betrayed the very Son of God*
* *Judas was eating the last Passover with the Lord Himself*
* *Judas fulfilled a negative Old Testament prophecy*
* *Judas was filled with the greed for money*
* *Judas was even condemned by the Lord Himself*
* *Judas would be remembered for his evil deed by the first church*

* *Judas would be remembered throughout history for his betrayal*
* *Judas ended his own life*

Jesus Eats the Matzah *(Afikomen)*

> **Mark 14:22 - *And as they did eat, Jesus took bread, and blessed, and brake it, and gave to them, and said, Take, eat: this is my body.***

First of all, notice that Mark uses the same language here— *bread, blessed, brake, gave*—as when Jesus fed the multitude in **Mark 6:41**. During the first and second Temple period, the *matzah* bread was a symbolic substitute for the *passover lamb*. It came to be called the *afikomen, "that which comes."* Jesus may very well have been connecting the *afikomen* to Himself as the Messiah *who would come.* Jesus seems to be superimposing symbolism on top of symbolism. The last bread to be eaten at the *Seder* supper was symbolic of the *passover lamb,* and Jesus is <u>the</u> Passover Lamb! We cannot be certain about *all* of the customs of Jesus' time, but the disciples ate the *matzah* bread that symbolized the body of Jesus. ***"Take, eat: this is my body."*** Jesus had been hidden, but now He is being revealed to His disciples. Although we cannot see Jesus now, He lives within us as we *by faith* eat of His flesh.

Jesus and the Blood of the New Covenant

> **Mark 14:23-25** - *And he took the cup, and when he had given thanks, he gave it to them: and they all drank of it. And he said unto them, This is my blood of the new testament, which is shed for many. Verily I say unto you, I will drink no more of the fruit of the vine, until that day that I drink it new in the kingdom of God.*

The wine symbolizes the blood of the Messiah that was also to be internalized like the bread. That had to *drink* it! When Jesus said *"This is my blood of the new testament, which is shed for __many__,"* it was another way of saying His blood was shed for *everyone* who would receive Him. We cannot overemphasize the importance of the blood of Jesus. All of the blood sacrifices in the Old Covenant would find their fulfillment in the sinless blood of Christ. Notice carefully how the prophecy was given to the prophet *Jeremiah*:

> *Behold, the days come, saith the* LORD, *that I will make a new covenant with the house of Israel, and with the house of Judah: Not according to the covenant that I made with their fathers in the day that I took them by the hand to bring them out of the land of Egypt; which my covenant they brake, although I was*

an husband unto them, saith the LORD: *But this shall be the covenant that I will make with the house of Israel; After those days, saith the* LORD, *I will put my law in their inward parts, and write it in their hearts; and will be their God, and they shall be my people. And they shall teach no more every man his neighbour, and every man his brother, saying, Know the* LORD: *for they shall all know me, from the least of them unto the greatest of them, saith the* LORD: *for I will forgive their iniquity, and I will remember their sin no more.*

Jeremiah 31:31–34

It would take the blood of the Messiah to bring in the New Covenant. The water of baptism is only a symbol; it is faith in the blood of Jesus that justifies the believer:

Much more then, being now justified by his blood, we shall be saved from wrath through him.

Romans 5:9

There is no forgiveness of sins apart from the sinless blood of the Messiah. Observe the writer to the Jewish Christians in the book of Hebrews:

And almost all things are by the law purged with blood; and without shedding of blood is no remission.

Hebrews 9:22

"Verily I say unto you, I will drink no more of the fruit of the vine, until that day that I drink it new in the kingdom of God" **-** There are hundreds of verses in the Old Testament that speak about the future kingdom being restored to Israel. Here Jesus the Messiah affirms those prophecies. The disciples were fellowshipping with their Lord Messiah one last time before His death on the cross. But He promises them that they will have fellowship with Him once again in the coming kingdom. It is also prophesied that there will be an abundance of *wine* in the Messianic Kingdom. Notice the prophet Isaiah:

> *And in this mountain shall the* LORD *of hosts make unto all people a feast of fat things, a feast of wines on the lees, of fat things full of marrow, of wines on the lees well refined.*
>
> Isaiah 25:6

Prophecies, Promises, & Peter

> **Mark 14:26-31** - *And when they had sung an hymn, they went out into the mount of Olives. And Jesus saith unto them, All ye shall be offended because of me this night: for it is written, I will smite the shepherd, and the sheep shall be scattered. But after that I am risen, I will go before you into Galilee. But Peter said unto him, Although all shall be offended, yet will not I. And Jesus saith unto*

him, Verily I say unto thee, That this day, even in this night, before the cock crow twice, thou shalt deny me thrice. But he spake the more vehemently, If I should die with thee, I will not deny thee in any wise. Likewise also said they all.

Leaving the Upper Room, the disciples and Jesus started singing one of the *Hallel,* or praise Psalm that was such an integral part of the Passover celebration. **(Psalms 115–118)** Imagine the voice of Jesus singing the traditional, Jewish melodies of the early first century, words like these:

Open to me the gates of righteousness: I will go into them, and I will praise the LORD: This gate of the LORD, into which the righteous shall enter. I will praise thee: for thou hast heard me, and art become my salvation. The stone which the builders refused is become the head stone of the corner. This is the LORD's doing; it is marvellous in our eyes. This is the day which the LORD hath made; we will rejoice and be glad in it. Save now, I beseech thee, O LORD: O LORD, I beseech thee, send now prosperity. Blessed be he that cometh in the name of the LORD: we have blessed you out of the house of the LORD.

Psalm 118:19-26

Jesus states that one of the prophecies in *Zechariah*, that was written almost 500 years before, was referring to His impending death on the cross. The prophecy pointed to His immediate followers being scattered as *sheep* and the Messiah being the smitten *Shepherd*:

> *Awake, O sword, against my shepherd, and against the man that is my fellow, saith the LORD of hosts: smite the shepherd, and the sheep shall be scattered: and I will turn mine hand upon the little ones.*
>
> Zechariah 13:7

"But after that I am risen, I will go before you into Galilee" – Jesus first called His disciples about 80 miles north of Jerusalem in Galilee to be His disciples. Now Jesus is telling them that He is going to die, but He will rise again and meet them where He initially called them. Jesus wanted them to see Him alive in the home they loved and where they had special memories of being with Him for more than three years. The gospel they would take to the known world would also be filled with their personal experiences they had with Jesus the risen Lord. Their message would not be complete without experiencing the risen Jesus back in Galilee, away from the religious and political strife in Jerusalem.

"And Jesus saith unto him, Verily I say unto thee, That this day, even in this night, before the cock crow twice, thou shalt deny me thrice" – Some have debated if the *cock*

crow was a certain time of the morning, or was it a real rooster? While there was a period of time called the *cock crowing* between 12:00–3:00 a.m., **(Mark 13:35)** this author believes Jesus was referring to a real rooster that *crowed twice.* Jesus knew when the rooster would crow, and that it would crow two different times throughout the three denials of Peter. Roosters can crow anytime during the night, as well as daybreak. Maybe our Divine Lord caused the rooster to crow to fulfill what He had told Peter? Either way, Jesus knew that Peter would deny him when He called him along the shores of the Galilee. But Jesus also knew that Peter, along with the other disciples, would give their lives for His sake. A rooster symbolized a *new morning*, and this would certainly be a new morning of grace and forgiveness for Simon Peter and the disciples. We should never judge anyone by the bad chapters in their lives. The Lord works through the bad and the good to make us what we need to be for His kingdom!

The Anointed One on the Mount of Anointing

> **Mark 14:32-42 - *And they came to a place which was named Gethsemane: and he saith to his disciples, Sit ye here, while I shall pray. And he taketh with him Peter and James and John, and began to be sore amazed, and to be very heavy; And saith unto them, My soul is exceeding sorrowful unto death: tarry ye here, and watch. And he went forward a little, and***

fell on the ground, and prayed that, if it were possible, the hour might pass from him. And he said, Abba, Father, all things are possible unto thee; take away this cup from me: nevertheless not what I will, but what thou wilt. And he cometh, and findeth them sleeping, and saith unto Peter, Simon, sleepest thou? couldest not thou watch one hour? Watch ye and pray, lest ye enter into temptation. The spirit truly is ready, but the flesh is weak. And again he went away, and prayed, and spake the same words. And when he returned, he found them asleep again, (for their eyes were heavy,) neither wist they what to answer him. And he cometh the third time, and saith unto them, Sleep on now, and take your rest: it is enough, the hour is come; behold, the Son of man is betrayed into the hands of sinners. Rise up, let us go; lo, he that betrayeth me is at hand.

Near the foot of the Mount of Olives were thousands of olive trees, just above the *Kidron Valley,* where apparently the Master and His disciples pitched their camp during the feast of *Unleavened Bread.* The Messiah of Israel being on the Mount of Olives in the midst of an olive tree grove holds much significance:

★ **Gethsemane =** gat shemen *(place of the olive press)*

* ***Mount of Olives*** = Har hamashicah *(the mount of the anointing)*
* ***Jesus the Messiah*** = Yeshua Ha Mashiach *(Jesus the Anointed One)*
* ***Messiah's Mountain of Return*** = *"And his feet shall stand in that day upon the Mount of Olives, which is before Jerusalem on the east, and the Mount of Olives shall cleave in the midst thereof toward the east and toward the west, and there shall be a very great valley; and half of the mountain shall remove toward the north, and half of it toward the south."*

Zechariah 14:4

"Peter and James and John"- These three disciples were with Jesus at the raising of *Jairus'* daughter in **Mark 5**, and the *Mount of Transfiguration* in **Mark 9**.

"My soul is exceeding sorrowful unto death"- Jesus wasn't afraid of death itself, it was the fact that He was going to become sin on the cross. The sinless Christ would become sin, so sinful man could be imputed perfect righteousness. What a thought!

> ***For he hath made him to be sin for us, who knew no sin; that we might be made the righteousness of God in him.***
>
> 2 Corinthians 5:21

While the *Eternal Godhead* was inseparable, the incomprehensible pressure of all of the sin of mankind would be pressed upon the Son. Try to imagine all of the sins from the first man, Adam, being pressed upon the *Man Christ Jesus,* much like an olive press has to put extreme amounts of pressure on the olives to squeeze out the olive oil.

"And he went forward a little, and fell on the ground, ★ ***and prayed that, if it were possible, the hour might pass from him. And he said, Abba, Father, all things are possible unto thee; take away this cup from me: nevertheless not what I will, but what thou wilt"*** – Notice the similarities of Jesus' words here and His words in **Mark 10:38**, *"But Jesus said unto them, Ye know not what ye ask: can ye drink of the cup that I drink of? and be baptized with the baptism that I am baptized with?"* We see and feel the humanity of Jesus as He prays to the Father and as He surrenders to the Father's will. If there were any other way for mankind to be reconciled to a Holy God, Jesus would not have had to die on the cross. Sinful man cannot keep the perfect laws of God. Sinful man cannot perform enough religious deeds or live morally enough to get to God. Church ordinances with good intentions could never bring sinful man to God. The holy justice of the universe had to be met, and Jesus the *God-Man* was the only way that God could be just and still justify the sinner at the same time.

Notice the words *take away this cup from me.* All of the punishment for man's sin would be placed upon the sinless Messiah. Because of God's eternal love for the world, His wrath would be poured out on Jesus so man could have everlasting life. This imagery of the *cup* is used in some of the prophecies concerning the wrath of the Lord:

Awake, awake, stand up, O Jerusalem, which hast drunk at the hand of the LORD *the cup of his fury; thou hast drunken the dregs of the cup of trembling, and wrung them out.*

Isaiah 51:17

★ *A Roman Catholic Basilica, The Church of all Nations, stands today over the place where Jesus knelt and prayed. It was built in 1924 over the ruins of a Crusader Chapel from 1345AD that stood over a Byzantine Church from the fourth century. It is most likely the place where some of the first century Jewish believers worshipped. It is one of the most sacred churches in the Holy Land. The church has beautiful mosaic paintings on the wall that depict Jesus praying and the band of soldiers coming to arrest Jesus, with Judas leading the way.*

The Arrest of Jesus the Messiah

Mark 14:43-46 – *And immediately, while he yet spake, cometh Judas, one of the twelve, and with him a great multitude with swords and staves, from the chief priests and the scribes and the elders. And he that betrayed him had given them a token, saying, Whomsoever I shall kiss, that same is he; take him, and lead him away safely. And as soon as he was come, he goeth straightway to him, and saith, Master, master; and kissed him. And they laid their hands on him, and took him.*

The betrayal by Judas Iscariot set in motion these five history-changing events in the life and ministry of Jesus the Messiah:

* *Arrest*
* *Trial*
* *Crucifixion*
* *Burial*
* *Resurrection*

The torches of the soldiers cast a dark shadow in the Garden of Gethsemane while one of the darkest moments in the history of the world was taking place. When the eyes of Jesus pierced the eyes of Judas, it was something that Judas would never get over. He would commit suicide even before the death of Jesus on the cross. Judas sealed his reputation for the centuries with a *kiss*. Normally a *kiss* in Bible times was a sign of love and affection:

> *Thou gavest me no kiss: but this woman since the time I came in hath not ceased to kiss my feet.*
> Luke 7:45

> *Salute one another with an holy kiss.*
> Romans 16:16

> *Greet ye one another with a kiss of charity. Peace be with you all that are in Christ Jesus. Amen.*
> I Peter 5:14

This verse seems to put everything into perspective:

Faithful are the wounds of a friend; but the kisses of an enemy are deceitful.

Proverbs 27:6

"Master, master" – In a favorable sense, there are only a few times in the sacred scriptures when God calls someone's name twice. It was always when God was about to perform something very important in the history of the nation of Israel, or when Jesus was teaching someone a very important lesson. Jesus also spoke the Father's name twice when He was on the cross:

* ★ *Abraham, Abraham* – Genesis 22:11
* ★ *Jacob, Jacob* – Genesis 46:2
* ★ *Moses, Moses* – Exodus 3:4
* ★ *Samuel, Samuel* – 1 Samuel 3:10
* ★ *Martha, Martha* – Luke 10:41
* ★ *Simon, Simon* – Luke 22:31
* ★ *Saul, Saul* – Acts 9:4
* ★ *Eloi, Eloi* – Mark 15:34, Matthew 27:46, Psalm 22:1

But there are at least three times in the four gospels when speaking a name twice has a message of judgment and condemnation:

* ★ *Jerusalem, Jerusalem* – Matthew 23:37; Luke 13:34
* ★ *Lord, Lord* – Matthew 7:21,22, 25:11; Luke 6:46; 13:25
* ★ *Master, master* – Mark 14:45

Peter, the Servant of the High Priest, and the Young Man

> **Mark 14:47-52 -** *And one of them that stood by drew a sword, and smote a servant of the high priest, and cut off his ear. And Jesus answered and said unto them, Are ye come out, as against a thief, with swords and with staves to take me? I was daily with you in the temple teaching, and ye took me not: but the scriptures must be fulfilled. And they all forsook him, and fled. And there followed him a certain young man, having a linen cloth cast about his naked body; and the young men laid hold on him: And he left the linen cloth, and fled from them naked.*

When studying the four gospels together, we know that this disciple who drew the sword was *Simon Peter* in **John 18:10**. We know that the servant's name was *Malchus,* ★ also in **John 18:10**. It is also recorded in **Luke 22:51** that Jesus healed the servant's ear.

★ *The name Malchus means "king," and he was a servant of the high priest. Maybe he was in line to one day be a priest, but he would need to have a body without any deformities in order to serve in the Temple. There is no mention of Malchus in church history, so we cannot be certain of what happened to him. But one would like to think that he became of a member of the believing community in the first century. There are only a handful of names* mentioned in the life and ministry of Christ, and they all were significant either in a negative or positive way. So we are left with the question, "Did Malchus become a follower of Jesus, or did he turn away from the Savior who healed Him in the Garden of Gethsemane?"

"a certain young man"- Most scholars agree that this *young man* was *John Mark*, the author of this gospel. If so, he chose to remain anonymous in light of the episode's embarrassing details. We know that Mark's mother had a house in Jerusalem where the early believers met to pray:

> *And when he had considered the thing, he came to the house of Mary the mother of John, whose surname was Mark; where many were gathered together praying.*
>
> Acts 12:12

Could this have been the Upper Room? Could the young Mark have followed Jesus and the disciples to the Garden of Gethsemane? If the other disciples were sleeping, who passed on to us the prayers of Jesus and the events that took place? So it seems as though we find Peter collaborating with Mark in writing this second gospel.

Jesus Before the Sanhedrin

> **Mark 14:53-65 - *And they led Jesus away to the high priest: and with him were assembled all the chief priests and the elders and the scribes. ★ And Peter followed him afar off, even***

into the palace of the high priest: and he sat with the servants, and warmed himself at the fire. And the chief priests and all the council sought for witness against Jesus to put him to death; and found none. For many bare false witness against him, but their witness agreed not together. And there arose certain, and bare false witness against him, saying, We heard him say, I will destroy this temple that is made with hands, and within three days I will build another made without hands. But neither so did their witness agree together. And the high priest stood up in the midst, and asked Jesus, saying, Answerest thou nothing? what is it which these witness against thee? But he held his peace, and answered nothing. Again the high priest asked him, and said unto him, Art thou the Christ, the Son of the Blessed? And Jesus said, I am: and ye shall see the Son of man sitting on the right hand of power, and coming in the clouds of heaven. Then the high priest rent his clothes, and saith, What need we any further witnesses? Ye have heard the blasphemy: what think ye? And they all condemned him to be guilty of death. And some began to spit on him, and to cover his face, and to buffet him, and to say unto him, Prophesy: and the servants did strike him with the palms of their hands.

Although there was a Jewish court during the second century BC, the head court, called the Sanhedrin, was mentioned in the writings of Flavius Josephus to be officially organized around 57BC. In Jesus' time there was a Great Sanhedrin of 71 members who met in the Hall of the Hewn Stones in the Temple in Jerusalem. The high priest in Jesus' time was Joseph Caiaphas (18–36AD). In 1990, an ornate ossuary was found just south of Jerusalem with the Aramaic inscription "Joseph son of Caiaphas." Since the ossuary dates back to Jesus' time, scholars do believe that these were the actual bones of the high priest.

Without going into extensive details, it seems as though the trial of Jesus was not the official *Sanhedrin*, but a kangaroo court assembled quickly in the middle of the night in order to quickly dispose of their nasty business against the sinless Jesus. When we study the Jewish order and law during the early first century, this kangaroo court violated numerous rules, a few of which follow:

* ***They were not in the Temple, but in a private meeting house***
* ***No trials could be held on feast days of an evening before a feast of Sabbath***
* ***A guilty verdict could not be declared the same day as the trial***
* ***The witnesses do not agree, and yet the trial goes on***
* ***There had to be a defense lawyer for the accused; Jesus had no one***
* ***The accused could not incriminate himself***

- ★ *Accusing Jesus of blaspheming His own Holy Name is ludicrous* (Lev.24:16)
- ★ *The high priest rent his garment which was forbidden in the Torah* (Lev.21:10)

"We heard him say, I will destroy this temple that is made with hands, and within three days I will build another made without hands" – This was a false indictment because Jesus was referring to His body, not the physical Temple in Jerusalem. They remembered the words of Jesus at the beginning of His ministry, but they misrepresented what He said:

> *Jesus answered and said unto them, Destroy this temple, and in three days I will raise it up. Then said the Jews, Forty and six years was this temple in building, and wilt thou rear it up in three days? But he spake of the temple of his body. When therefore he was risen from the dead, his disciples remembered that he had said this unto them; and they believed the scripture, and the word which Jesus had said.*
>
> John 2:19-22

"Again the high priest asked him, and said unto him, Art thou the Christ, the Son of the Blessed? And Jesus said, I am: and ye shall see the Son of man sitting on the right hand of power, and coming in the clouds of heaven"– Jesus accepts the charge that He is truly the *Messiah of Israel, the*

Son of God! Jesus goes even farther to identify Himself as the apocalyptic *Son of man* in the prophecies of Daniel, who will triumph over His enemies:

I saw in the night visions, and, behold, one like the Son of man came with the clouds of heaven, and came to the Ancient of days, and they brought him near before him.

Daniel 7:13

Even *spitting* on the precious Savior was prophesied centuries before:

I gave my back to the smiters, and my cheeks to them that plucked off the hair: I hid not my face from shame and spitting. Isaiah 50:6

Peter Denies the Lord

Mark 14:66-72 - *And as Peter was beneath in the palace, ★ there cometh one of the maids of the high priest: And when she saw Peter warming himself, she looked upon him, and said, And thou also wast with Jesus of Nazareth. But he denied, saying, I know not, neither understand I what thou sayest. And he went out into the porch; and the cock crew. And a maid saw him again, and began to say to them that stood by, This is one of them. And he denied it again. And a little after, they that stood by said again* *to Peter, Surely thou art one of them: for thou art a Galilaean, and thy speech agreeth thereto. But he began to curse and to swear, saying, I know not this man of whom ye speak. And the second time the cock crew. And Peter called to mind the word that Jesus said unto him, Before the cock crow twice, thou shalt deny me thrice. And when he thought thereon, he wept.*

* *Just south of Jerusalem the Church of Saint Peter in Gallicantu stands over what is believed to be the house of Caiaphas. Gallicantu in Latin means, "cock's crow." A dungeon and a water cistern were discovered underneath where they kept the prisoners that dates back to Jesus' time. There are also white stone steps leading up to the palace from Jesus' time. The first mention of the location being that of Caiaphas was written by Pilgrim of Bordeaux in his Holy Land itinerary in 333-334AD. The first church was built in 457AD, and the latter church was built in 1931. As is the case oftentimes, there most likely was a first century place of worship there.*

As Jesus predicted, we find here the rooster *crowing twice* and Simon Peter denying Jesus *three times*. Most people spoke two or three languages in Israel in Jesus' time. The three most common languages were *Hebrew, Greek, and Latin.* **(John 19:20)** The *Aramaic* language that was spoken by the Galileans was a close dialect of the Hebrew. There was no curse word in the religious Hebrew language, but there was in Greek and Latin. We do not know what words Peter actually used when he began to *curse and to swear*, but it definitely was not Hebrew. The Greek word that Mark uses for *curse* is, *anathematizo*, and it means, *"to invoke, or to declare a penalty."* Peter was excommunicating himself by saying *he was cursed of God.* So not only was Simon Peter denying His Lord, he was pronouncing judgment upon himself. Peter was probably saying to himself, *"How could I love Christ and be denying Him?"* This would help us understand the bitter weeping and the forsakenness that Peter must have felt:

> *"And when he thought thereon, <u>he wept</u>"*
>
> Mark 14:72

> *"Simon Peter saith unto them, <u>I go a fishing</u>"*
>
> John 21:3

Paul used a form of the same Greek word when describing anyone who did not love the Lord Jesus Christ.

> *If any man love not the Lord Jesus Christ, let him be Anathema Maranatha.*
>
> I Corinthians 16:22

The good news is that Jesus knew this would happen before He called Peter. Jesus would use Peter's denial to help sift him of his pride and arrogance. This would also be a major part in Peter's life in molding him into the man that would help change the course of the world.

CHAPTER FIFTEEN

Jesus Before Pontius Pilate

Mark 15:1-6 - *And straightway in the morning the chief priests held a consultation with the elders and scribes and the whole council, and bound Jesus, and carried him away, and delivered him to Pilate.* ⋆ *And Pilate asked him, Art thou the King of the Jews? And he answering said unto them, Thou sayest it. And the chief priests accused him of many things: but he answered nothing. And Pilate asked him again, saying, Answerest thou nothing? behold how many things they witness against thee. But Jesus yet answered nothing; so that Pilate marvelled. Now at that feast he released unto them one prisoner, whomsoever they desired.*

⋆ *The historicity of Pontius Pilate was proven again when a stone plaque was discovered in 1961 behind the Roman theater in Caesarea. The Latin inscription stated that Pontius Pilate was the Roman procurator and had dedicated a building to the*

Emperor Tiberias. Pilate served from 26-36AD *as the fifth Roman Procurator beginning with Coponius,* 6-9AD, *Ambivulus,* 9-12AD, *Rufus,* 12-15AD, *and Gratus,* 15-26AD. *His home was in Caesarea on the seacoast, but he was stationed in Jerusalem during Jewish feasts to keep down any revolts. Pilate's name is also mentioned in* **Acts 4:27,** ***"For of a truth against thy holy child Jesus, whom thou hast anointed, both Herod, and Pontius Pilate, with the Gentiles, and the people of Israel, were gathered together,"*** *and in* **I Timothy 6:13,** ***"I give thee charge in the sight of God, who quickeneth all things, and before Christ Jesus, who before Pontius Pilate witnessed a good confession."*** *Pilate's name would be forever recorded in a negative light in church history in the Nicene Creed of the First Council of Constantinople in* **381AD:**

> *I believe in one <u>God</u>, the Father Almighty*
> *Maker of heaven and earth, and of all things visible*
> *and invisible: And in one Lord <u>Jesus Christ</u>,*
> *the only-begotten Son of God, begotten of the Father*
> *before all worlds;*
> *God of God, Light of Light, very God of very God;*
> *begotten, not made, being of one substance with the*
> *Father,*
> *by Whom all things were made:*
> *Who for us men and for our salvation came down*
> *from Heaven,*
> *and was incarnate by the Holy Ghost of the Virgin*
> *Mary, and was made man:*

And was crucified also for us under <u>Pontius Pilate</u>;
he suffered and was buried:
And the third day he rose again according to the
Scriptures:
And ascended into Heaven, and sitteth on the right
hand of the Father:
And he shall come again, with glory, to judge both
the quick and the dead:
Whose Kingdom will have no end: And I believe in
the <u>Holy Ghost</u> the Lord, and Giver of Life,
Who proceedeth from the Father and the Son
Who with the Father and the Son together is
worshipped and glorified,
Who spake by the Prophets.
And I believe in One Holy, Catholic, and Apostolic
Church,
I acknowledge one Baptism for the remission of sins.
And I look for the Resurrection of the Dead:
And the Life of the world to come. Amen.

It is believed that Jesus spent the night in the house of Caiaphas. Because of the thousands who were coming into Jerusalem for the Passover, the *chief priests, with the elders and scribes*, wanted to take Jesus to Pilate *early in the morning*. The religious leaders did not want to give the *Galilean Zealots* time to start a revolt. There is also some historical evidence that Roman affairs began at the earliest hour of the day. So the timing was absolutely crucial, but little did the Romans and the religious leaders know that God's timing was also crucial as well, for *the hour had come*. Capital punishment had been taken out of the hands of Israel in 6AD, when *Herod Archelaus* (**Matt.2:22**) was deposed and replaced by the first Roman Procurator *Coponius*. Israel was under the boot of Rome, and God would use *Pontius Pilate* to help fulfill the Hebrew scripture.

"But Jesus yet answered nothing" – Other than a few short statements, Jesus remained silent throughout the trial and when He stood before Pilate. This was fulfilling the prophecy of Isaiah:

> *He was oppressed, and he was afflicted, yet he opened not his mouth: he is brought as a lamb to the slaughter, and as a sheep before her shearers is dumb, so he openeth not his mouth.*
>
> Isaiah 53:7

Barabbas Released

Mark 15:7-15 – *And there was one named Barabbas, which lay bound with them that had made insurrection with him, who had committed murder in the insurrection. And the multitude crying aloud began to desire him to do as he had ever done unto them. But Pilate answered them, saying, Will ye that I release unto you the King of the Jews? For he knew that the chief priests had delivered him for envy. But the chief priests moved the people,*

★ that he should rather release Barabbas unto them. And Pilate answered and said again unto them, What will ye then that I shall do unto him whom ye call the King of the Jews? And they cried out again, Crucify him. Then Pilate said unto them, Why, what evil hath he done? And they cried out the more exceedingly, Crucify him. And so Pilate, willing to content the people, released Barabbas unto them, and delivered Jesus, when he had scourged him, to be crucified.

★ This was not the same crowd that had welcomed Jesus as the King riding the donkey into Jerusalem. **(Mark 11:9-10)** *This crowd was a lynch mob that the chief priests and elders had organized. From the trial to the releasing of Barabbas, the innocent Jesus knew that this was the reason He had come into the world. When sinful man thinks that he is ruling the affairs, the Almighty God is overruling to accomplish His sovereign will!*

The name *Barabbas* in Aramaic means *"son of the father"* which gives the tragic irony of the guilty *Barabbas* being released and the innocent Jesus *"the Son of the Father,"* the *"King of the Jews"* taking His place. Notice that Pilate detected the *envy* of the religious leaders of Jesus, but he lacked the integrity to release Jesus and crumbled beneath the pressure of the Jerusalem mob.

Jesus Crowned with a Crown of Thorns

> **Mark 15:16-20** - *And the soldiers led him away into the hall, called Praetorium; and they call together the whole band. And they clothed him with purple, and platted a crown of thorns, ★ and put it about his head, And began to salute him, Hail, King of the Jews! And they smote him on the head with a reed, and did spit upon him, and bowing their knees worshipped him. And when they had mocked him, they took off the purple from him, and put his own clothes on him, and led him out to crucify him.*

★ *There is a strong tradition that the thorns came from the Ziziphus tree, later known as the Ziziphus spina-christi. This species of tree still exists in Israel today and lives to be over 2,000 years old.*

The *Praetorium* was a large building built by *Herod the Great* within the old city of Jerusalem. *Praetor* comes from the Latin word for *leader*. The *whole band* was a military cohort of up to 600 soldiers.

The mockery of Jesus is surrounded with paradox and irony. Unknowingly they were *bowing their knees* to the real royal *King of the Jews!* Jesus would wear a *crown of thorns* that symbolized the curse that sin had brought into the world:

Thorns also and thistles shall it bring forth to thee; and thou shalt eat the herb of the field.

Genesis 3:18

In contrast, these passages of scripture come to mind when Jesus returns:

Wherefore God also hath highly exalted him, and given him a name which is above every name: That at the name of Jesus every knee should bow, of things in heaven, and things in earth, and things under the earth; And that every tongue should confess that Jesus Christ is Lord, to the glory of God the Father.

Philippians 2:9–11

And I saw heaven opened, and behold a white horse; and he that sat upon him was called Faithful and True, and in righteousness he doth judge and make war. His eyes were as a flame of fire, and on his head were many crowns; and he had a name written, that no man knew, but he himself. And he was clothed with a vesture dipped in blood: and his name is called The Word of God. And the armies which were in heaven followed him upon white horses, clothed in fine linen, white and clean. And out of his mouth goeth a sharp sword, that with it he should smite the nations: and he shall rule them with a rod of iron: and he treadeth the winepress of the fierceness and wrath of Almighty God. And he hath on his vesture and on his thigh a name written, KING OF KINGS, AND LORD OF LORDS.

Revelation 19:11-16

Simon of Cyrene and His Two Boys

Mark 15:21 – *And they compel one Simon a Cyrenian, who passed by, coming out of the country, the father of Alexander and Rufus, to bear his cross.*

The Romans had the power to recruit Jews for temporary service to assist in their criminal acts. The severe *scourging* left Jesus so weak that He was unable to carry the estimated *100 pound* crossbeam upon His shoulders and where His precious hands would be tied. According to Roman customs, the criminals were to carry their own cross through the city as a way of showing the people that Rome was in charge and to discourage anyone who might be thinking about starting a revolt. But after a short distance, Jesus could not go any further. Rome wanted Jesus to stay alive until He was crucified. They *compel* a pilgrim from the country of *Cyrene* ★ *named Simon* to carry the crossbeam for Jesus. There was a large group of Jews who lived in northern Africa, and evidently *Simon* had come to Jerusalem to keep the Passover feast. But when he left his homeland to come to Jerusalem, *Simon* had no idea that he was going to be one of the most blessed men to ever live. He may not have known just who Jesus was or even why He was being sentenced, but his name would be written in the pages of God's Holy Word!

Mark mentions to his readers in Rome that *Simon* was the father of *Alexander* ★ *and Rufus*. Only Mark records their names. Why? It is believed that *Simon of Cyrene* took up his own cross and followed Jesus in the first century. His family also became believers and was well known among the believers in Rome. It is also believed that his sons became leaders among the early Jewish believers. Could it be that *Rufus* was in the congregation at Rome?

> **Salute Rufus chosen in the Lord, and his mother and mine.**   Romans 16:13

★ *Cyrene was about 800 miles from Jerusalem, just across the Mediterranean Sea from Rome, in northern Africa. Simon must have traveled for weeks and went to great expense to come to the Passover. It is also commonly believed that Simon was a black man. But since there were over 100,000 Grecian Jews living in Cyrene, we cannot be absolutely certain.*

★ *In 1941 a first-century tomb was found in the Kidron Valley just east of Jerusalem. The tomb had not been opened since the first century and dates back to Jesus' time. One of the ossuaries had the inscription written twice, "Alexander son of Simon." Now archaeologists believe that the ossuary contained the bones of Simon and his son, Alexander. While they cannot be sure that this is* the same person, normally ossuaries were used only for the people who were well known or who played a significant role in Judaism or Christianity.

Jesus the Messiah Crucified at 9:00 A.M.

> **Mark 15:22-26 - *And they bring him unto the place Golgotha, * which is, being interpreted, The place of a skull. And they gave him to drink wine mingled with myrrh: but he received it not. And when they had crucified him, they parted his garments, casting lots upon them, what every man should take. And it was the third hour, and they crucified him. And the superscription of his accusation was written over, THE KING OF THE JEWS.***

* We know that Golgotha was outside the walls of the city of Jerusalem. There are two possible locations that were outside the walls in Jesus' time: The Church of the Holy Sepulcher that stands on the west side, and Gordon's Calvary on the north side. Most scholars believe the Holy Sepulcher is the correct location, but Gordon's Calvary feels more like the real spot. There are also three possible reasons the place was called Golgotha: 1) Because it may have been littered with skulls of men who had been executed 2) Because it was on a hill that had the shadows of the face of a skull 3) Because the hill was barren, smooth, and round like the top of a skull.

"And they gave him to drink wine mingled with myrrh: but he received it not" - This was to numb the nerves of the one being crucified, but Jesus refused. Observe these words that were written by king Solomon:

> *Give strong drink unto him that is ready to perish, and wine unto those that be of heavy hearts. Let him drink, and forget his poverty, and remember his misery no more.*
>
> Proverbs 31:6-7

Crucifixion was adopted by the Romans from the earlier practice invented by the Persians. It would not have been a beautiful cross that stood high up on a hill that we have seen in Christian art. Archaeologists tell us that it was the custom to nail the crossbeam to the upright stump of an olive tree. Jesus was crucified upon a *tree*, not a square timbered cross. It was the Roman custom to crucify criminals on the side of a busy thoroughfare so the crowd could see that Rome was in control. It is very important that we see the connection to the Old Testament prophecies:

> *And if a man have committed a sin worthy of death, and he be to be put to death, and thou hang him on a tree: His body shall not remain all night upon the tree, but thou shalt in any wise bury him that day; (for he that is hanged is accursed of God;) that thy land be not defiled, which the LORD thy God giveth thee for an inheritance.*
>
> Deuteronomy 21:22-23 (Galatians 3:13)

And the LORD *said unto Moses, Make thee a fiery serpent, and set it upon a pole: and it shall come to pass, that every one that is bitten, when he looketh upon it, shall live. And Moses made a serpent of brass, and put it upon a pole, and it came to pass, that if a serpent had bitten any man, when he beheld the serpent of brass, he lived.*

Numbers 21:8-9 (John 3:14)

For dogs have compassed me: the assembly of the wicked have inclosed me: they pierced my hands and my feet.

Psalms 22:16

He is despised and rejected of men; a man of sorrows, and acquainted with grief: and we hid as it were our faces from him; he was despised, and we esteemed him not. Surely he hath borne our griefs, and carried our sorrows: yet we did esteem him stricken, smitten of God, and afflicted. But he was wounded for our transgressions, he was bruised for our iniquities: the chastisement of our peace was upon him; and with his stripes we are healed. All we like sheep have gone astray; we have turned every one to his own way; and the LORD *hath laid on him the iniquity of us all. He was oppressed, and he was afflicted, yet he opened not his mouth: he is brought as a lamb to the slaughter, and as a sheep before her shearers is dumb, so he openeth not his mouth.*

Isaiah 53:3-7

And I will pour upon the house of David, and upon the inhabitants of Jerusalem, the spirit of grace and of supplications: and they shall look upon me whom they have pierced, and they shall mourn for him, as one mourneth for his only son, and shall be in bitterness for him, as one that is in bitterness for his firstborn.

Zechariah 12:10

And one shall say unto him, What are these wounds in thine hands? Then he shall answer, Those with which I was wounded in the house of my friends. Awake, O sword, against my shepherd, and against the man that is my fellow, saith the LORD of hosts: smite the shepherd, and the sheep shall be scattered: and I will turn mine hand upon the little ones.

Zechariah 13:6-7

It's interesting that Simon Peter, who had dictated to Mark what to write down in this gospel, described the cross of Jesus as a *tree*:

And we are witnesses of all things which he did both in the land of the Jews, and in Jerusalem;

304

whom they slew and hanged on a tree. Acts 10:39

Who his own self bare our sins in his own body on the tree, that we, being dead to sins, should live unto righteousness: by whose stripes ye were healed.

I Peter 2:24

"they parted his garments, casting lots upon them" – Notice the accuracy of the prophecy written by David:

They part my garments among them, and cast lots upon my vesture.

Psalm 22:18

"And it was the third hour, and they crucified him" – The apostle John, writing over 50 years later, used the Roman clock ★ and says that Jesus was facing Pilate at the *sixth hour*, which was 6:00 a.m., and was crucified in the early morning. **(John 19:14)** Mark used the Roman time in some places, but here he chose to use the Jewish time of the *third hour,* which was 9:00 a.m., when writing about the crucifixion of Israel's Messiah. This is significant because at the very same time that Jesus the Messiah was being lifted up between heaven and earth for the sins of the world, the lamb of the morning sacrifice was being placed upon the altar. As the high priest lifted up his hands and pronounced the Aaronic benediction, Jesus was lifting His outstretched hands as the expression of His eternal love for humanity.

Jesus was the supreme morning sacrifice! * We can see how heinous sin must be in the eyes of a Holy God when it required such a sacrifice of His only begotten Son!

* *Roman time went from 12:00 a.m. to 12:00 p.m., and Jewish time went from 6:00 a.m. to 6:00 p.m.*

* *Since the details are sketchy and seemingly at variance, we cannot be dogmatic about the chronology. Sometimes it is just better to let the Holy Scriptures stand in tension with one another than to force a timeline to fit. But when we study all four gospels carefully, a Thursday crucifixion would help solve the problem with the three days and three nights. According to* **John 19:31***, Friday was a High Sabbath. Often on a biblical calendar we find a double Sabbath during weeks that have a Jewish feast. The "Good Friday" is actually a corrupt form of "God Friday" and originated in the fourth century Greek Church. Here is a model that might help to explain:*

Thursday = Day One and Night One
Friday = Day Two and Night Two
Saturday = Day Three and Night Three
Sunday = Day of Resurrection

"And the superscription of his accusation was written over, THE KING OF THE JEWS" - It's very interesting that this title was used by Gentiles; *The Wise Men, Pontius Pilate, and the Roman soldiers.* The Jews would normally say *King of Israel*. The title *King* is what disturbed Pilate, because this was a title that implied possible rebellion against the Roman Empire.

Jesus was Numbered with the Transgressors

> **Mark 15:27-28** - *And with him they crucify two thieves; the one on his right hand, and the other on his left. And the scripture was fulfilled, which saith, And he was numbered with the transgressors.*

This fulfilled a prophecy in Isaiah of Israel's Messiah not only dying *with* the transgressors, but also dying for their sins as well:

> *Therefore will I divide him a portion with the great, and he shall divide the spoil with the strong; because he hath poured out his soul unto death: and he was numbered with the transgressors; and he bare the sin of many, and made intercession for the transgressors.*
>
> Isaiah 53:12

Jesus the Messiah Being Mocked on the Cross (9:00 a.m.–12:00 p.m.)

> **Mark 15:29-32** - *And they that passed by railed on him, wagging their heads, and saying, Ah, thou that destroyest the temple, and buildest it in three days, Save thyself, and come down from the cross. Likewise also the chief priests mocking said among themselves with the scribes, He saved others; himself he cannot save.*

Let Christ the King of Israel descend now from the cross, that we may see and believe. And they that were crucified with him reviled him.

It was the Passover, the busiest time of the year for Jerusalem. As the dusty roads and gates of the city were being thronged with pilgrims, there were crosses alongside one of the roads where people entered. The crosses were a reminder to Israel that they were not redeemed, Rome was in charge. But little did most of the people know that the Redeemer of mankind was on one of the crosses. There were many there from the towns, villages, and hamlets throughout the countryside that did believe in Jesus as the Christ, and many of them had been *saved* by His mercy and grace. We can imagine how their hands grew limp and their stomachs must have felt as they saw their Lord being nailed to a tree. The fact that He did *not* come down from the cross is the reason we have the gospel today. The mystery of the cross is that Jesus not only allowed them to crucify Him, but He *stayed* on the cross. Aren't we glad that He did!

In the natural, it's bad enough that the world would kill the sinless Son of God, but they seemed to enjoy doing it. While the *King of Heaven* was dying on a tree, the world was acting like silly children. Four groups of people who mocked Jesus on the cross follow:

* ⋆ *The crowd that passed by*
* ⋆ *The Roman soldiers*

* *The two transgressors* (One was later saved in **Luke 23:43**)
* *The religious leaders*

Notice these two passages of scripture: one was a prophecy, while the other one was the words of Jesus that they never forgot:

> *But I am a worm, and no man; a reproach of men, and despised of the people. All they that see me laugh me to scorn: they shoot out the lip, they shake the head, saying, He trusted on the LORD that he would deliver him: let him deliver him, seeing he delighted in him.*
>
> Psalm 22:6-8

> *Jesus answered and said unto them, Destroy this temple, and in three days I will raise it up.*
>
> John 2:19

Darkness over All of the Land

> **Mark 15:33 – *And when the sixth hour was come, there was darkness * over the whole land until the ninth hour.***

* This darkness is also mentioned in the writings of Origen (Contra Celsus, ii, 33) *and Eusebius* (Chron.) *quoting the writings of the historian Phlegon of Tralles. Phlegon wrote that the darkness occurred during the reign of Tiberias Caesar in the middle*

of the day. Since the Passover was always during a full moon, it was impossible for this to be an eclipse. It was truly a supernatural sign from the heavens.

Since Jesus was suffering the judgment for the sins of the world on Passover, there was darkness that also covered the land of Egypt when God was sending warnings to Pharaoh.

> **And the LORD said unto Moses, Stretch out thine hand toward heaven, that there may be darkness over the land of Egypt, even darkness which may be felt. And Moses stretched forth his hand toward heaven; and there was a thick darkness in all the land of Egypt three days: They saw not one another, neither rose any from his place for three days: but all the children of Israel had light in their dwellings.**
>
> Exodus 10:21–23

The book of Amos was written during the eighth century BC concerning the judgment that was coming to Israel. The in-depth truths of the Hebrew language also connect us to the exact time when darkness would come while Israel's Messiah was on the cross.

> **And it shall come to pass in that day, saith the Lord GOD, that I will cause the sun to go down at noon, and I will darken the earth in the clear day.**
>
> Amos 8:9

This darkness was symbolic of the *Light of the World* entering into the domain of the kingdom of darkness to gain victory for His people.

> *Blotting out the handwriting of ordinances that was against us, which was contrary to us, and took it out of the way, nailing it to his cross; And having spoiled principalities and powers, he made a shew of them openly, triumphing over them in it.*
>
> Colossians 2:14-15

> *For this purpose the Son of God was manifested, that he might destroy the works of the devil.*
>
> I John 3:8

The darkness could also symbolize the judgment that was coming to Jerusalem in 70AD.

Jesus Cries Out at the Ninth Hour

> **Mark 15:34-37 - *And at the ninth hour Jesus cried with a loud voice, saying, Eloi, Eloi, lama sabachthani? which is, being interpreted, My God, my God, why hast thou forsaken me? And some of them that stood by, when they heard it, said, Behold, he calleth Elias. And one ran and filled a spunge full of vinegar, and put it on a reed, and gave him to drink, saying, Let alone; let us see whether Elias will come***

to take him down. And Jesus cried with a loud voice, and gave up the ghost.

While the channels and gutters of the Temple compound were filled with the blood of the sacrificial lambs, the Lamb of God was shedding the last of His sinless blood on the cross. About that time Jesus cries and fulfills another prophecy:

My God, my God, why hast thou forsaken me?
Psalm 22:1a

It has been preached over the centuries that the Father turned His back on Jesus the Son. But after further studies, this author does not believe that the Father and the Son were ever separated. How could God be separated from Himself?

To wit, that God was in Christ, reconciling the world unto himself, not imputing their trespasses unto them; and hath committed unto us the word of reconciliation.
2 Corinthians 5:19

"Behold, he calleth Elias"- Because part of the Hebrew name for God, *Eli,* is in the name of the great prophet *Elijah,* some of the people thought that Jesus was calling for the prophet to come to His rescue. This was also because of the darkness they saw and one of the last prophecies of the Old Testament:

Behold, I will send you Elijah the prophet before the coming of the great and dreadful day of the LORD.

Malachi 4:5

"And one ran and filled a spunge full of vinegar, and put it on a reed, and gave him to drink" - This was not the same kind of drink that was offered Jesus in vs. 23. It was an inexpensive beverage that was used in Bible times. **(Ruth 2:14)**

"And Jesus cried with a loud voice, and gave up the ghost" - Most of the victims spent their last moments being unconscious, but Jesus was able to speak up until the moment of His death. Most victims fought for their last breath, but Jesus dismissed His Spirit into the hands of the Father. *"No man taketh it from me, but I lay it down of myself."* **(John 10:18)** The death of Jesus the Messiah accomplished far more than our minds could ever comprehend, but here are a few accomplishments we do know:

* *The price for the sins of the world was paid in full* (I John 2:2)
* *This was the baptism that Jesus spoke about* (Mark 10:38)
* *The sinner could be justified and God still be just*
* *Righteousness could be imputed to all who believe*
* *Jesus was the only one who could have provided eternal redemption*
* *Demonstration of God's love for the world*

* *Jesus did not hang on the cross needlessly*
* *His work was finished*

The Torn Veil of the Temple

> **Mark 15:38** - *And the veil of the temple was rent in twain from the top to the bottom.*

It's worth mentioning here that the wording for the veil being rent in twain, or *torn,* is the very same word, *schizo,* as when the heavens opened at Jesus' baptism. **(Mark 1:10)**. The word means, *"divide, split, or torn."* The veil was 60 feet high and 30 feet wide, and the thickness as the palm of a man's hand. It took 300 priests to carry the veil. There were two veils in the Temple, but this was the *second veil* that separated the priests from the Holy of Holies. Only once a year could the priest enter to make an offering for the sins of the people. Notice the connection of these verses:

> *And thou shalt make a vail of blue, and purple, and scarlet, and fine twined linen of cunning work: with cherubims shall it be made: And thou shalt hang it upon four pillars of shittim wood overlaid with gold: their hooks shall be of gold, upon the four sockets of silver. And thou shalt hang up the vail under the taches, that thou mayest bring in thither within the vail the ark of the testimony: and the vail shall divide unto you between the holy place and the most*

holy. And thou shalt put the mercy seat upon the ark of the testimony in the most holy place.

Exodus 26:31-34

And after the second veil, the tabernacle which is called the Holiest of all; Which had the golden censer, and the ark of the covenant overlaid round about with gold, wherein was the golden pot that had manna, and Aaron's rod that budded, and the tables of the covenant; And over it the cherubims of glory shadowing the mercyseat; of which we cannot now speak particularly. Now when these things were thus ordained, the priests went always into the first tabernacle, accomplishing the service of God. But into the second went the high priest alone once every year, not without blood, which he offered for himself, and for the errors of the people.

Hebrews 9:3-7

While the Passover lambs were being sacrificed, *Yeshua,* the Messiah of Israel, died. The all-important veil of the Temple was torn from *top to bottom.* This meant that Jesus was the *Great High Priest,* and now sinful man could have access to the Holy Father in heaven. The blood of the Lamb of God had opened up a new and living way! Hallelujah! This did not mean that *all* of the Torah was abrogated. The *sacrificial system* had been fulfilled in the Messiah of Israel. The veil symbolized the body of Jesus the Son of God!

> *Having therefore, brethren, boldness to enter into the holiest by the blood of Jesus, By a new and living way, which he hath consecrated for us, through the veil, that is to say, his flesh.* Hebrews 10:19-20

The Confession of the Roman Centurion

> **Mark 15:39 - *And when the centurion, which stood over against him, saw that he so cried out, and gave up the ghost, he said, Truly this man was the Son of God.***

While the taunting mob and religious leaders mock Jesus, a Roman centurion confesses that *Jesus is the Son of God*. This is astounding! The major theme of Mark's gospel is confessed and spoken by a Gentile. What a message this must have been to Mark's readers who were mostly Gentiles! The centurion probably did not see the veil being torn, but he saw and heard all of the other phenomena that had happened.

The Women from Galilee

> **Mark 15:40-41 - *There were also women looking on afar off: among whom was Mary Magdalene, and Mary the mother of James***

the less and of Joses, and Salome; (Who also, when he was in Galilee, followed him, and ministered unto him;) and many other women which came up with him unto Jerusalem.

What a testimony of how the power of Jesus changes lives! These women from Galilee had felt His love and power and had followed Him the long journey from Galilee to Jerusalem. Not only did they stay in Jerusalem through the uncertain days of His arrest and trial, they stayed to see Him hang on the cross, and were even there after He had died. These women were true disciples, or the Hebrew *talmidot,* of our Lord. There was a strong Jewish custom called *shomer,* where certain people would keep a watch with a body until it was buried. What thoughts must have been going through their minds! They had remembered the springtime of Jesus when the crowds were running over themselves to see and to hear Him along the hills of Galilee. Some of the women no doubt believed that He would rise again, but they looked on from a distance with tear-stained faces. *Salome* was the mother of James and John, the sons of Zebedee.

The Entombment of Jesus the Messiah

Mark 15:42-47 - *And now when the even was come, because it was the preparation, that is, the day before the sabbath, Joseph of Arimathaea, * an honourable counsellor,* *which also waited for the kingdom of God, came, and went in boldly unto Pilate, and craved the body of Jesus. And Pilate marvelled if he were already dead: and calling unto him the centurion, he asked him whether he had been any while dead. And when he knew it of the centurion, he gave the body to Joseph. And he bought fine linen, and took him down, and wrapped him in the linen, and laid him in a sepulchre which was hewn out of a rock, and rolled a stone unto the door of the sepulchre. And Mary Magdalene and Mary the mother of Joses beheld where he was laid.*

★ *In* **John 19:38-39**, *we find that Nicodemus was also with Joseph of Arimathaea. Under Jewish law both of these men would have been considered unclean for handling a dead body, (Even though it was the sinless body of their Lord) therefore, prohibiting them from keeping the Jewish Passover. There was a law written in the Torah that provided a way for them to keep the Passover the next month. It was called Pesach Sheni, or the Second Passover:* **"Speak unto the children of Israel, saying, If any man of you or of your posterity shall be unclean by reason of a dead body, or be in a journey afar off, yet he shall keep the passover unto the LORD. The fourteenth day of the second month at even they shall keep it, and eat it with unleavened bread and bitter herbs."**

Numbers 9:10-11

As it was getting late and the *High Sabbath* was approaching, probably between 5:00–6:00 p.m., a secret disciple of Jesus named *Joseph of Arimathaea* went to Pilate and craved for the body of Jesus. *Joseph of Arimathaea* was part of the remnant of Israel who was *looking for the Messiah* to come. He knew that Jesus was the Messiah because God had revealed it to Him. It's also very interesting that *the centurion* who confessed that Jesus was the Son of God is mentioned here twice again. The *centurion* is the one who settled Pilate's mind that Jesus had indeed died. Jesus being buried by a rich man is fulfillment of part of Isaiah's prophecy concerning the *Suffering Messiah:*

> **And he made his grave with the wicked, and with the rich in his death; because he had done no violence, neither was any deceit in his mouth.**
>
> Isaiah 53:9

"And Mary Magdalene and Mary the mother of Joses beheld where he was laid" – According to **John 19:25** and the historical writings of *Papias of Heiropolis* (60–163AD), the *mother of Joses* was the sister to the *mother Mary* and the wife of *Cleopas*.

CHAPTER SIXTEEN

The Resurrection of the Lord Jesus Christ

Mark 16:1-4 - *And when the sabbath was past, Mary Magdalene, and Mary the mother of James, and Salome, had bought sweet spices, that they might come and anoint him. And very early in the morning the first day of the week, they came unto the sepulchre at the rising of the sun. And they said among themselves, Who shall roll us away the stone from the door of the sepulchre? And when they looked, they saw that the stone was rolled away: for it was very great.*

Since it was very *early in the morning* before the markets were open on Sunday, we can only speculate that the women went to the after-Sabbath market place sometime after the Sabbath ended that previous Saturday evening at 6:00 p.m. Possibly they had rested for a few hours and then made their way through Jerusalem to the tomb. The *first day of the week* became known as the *Lord's Day,* (**Rev.1:10**) when many of the early believers of Jesus gathered to worship. While most of the Jews who believed in Jesus still worshipped on the Sabbath Day, many of the Gentiles started worshipping on Sunday:

> *And upon the first day of the week, when the disciples came together to break bread, Paul preached unto them, ready to depart on the morrow; and continued his speech until midnight.*
>
> Acts 20:7

> *Upon the first day of the week let every one of you lay by him in store, as God hath prospered him, that there be no gatherings when I come.*
>
> I Corinthians 16:2

The women began to ask among themselves who was going to help them roll away the large stone in front of the door of the tomb? But when they came, they found the huge rounded *stone* rolled back from the tomb. We know this was a newly cut and expensive tomb because of the size of the stone. When we think that everything is hopeless and impossible, God rolls away the stone!

> **Mark 16:5-8 –** *And entering into the sepulchre, they saw a young man sitting on the right side, clothed in a long white garment; and they were affrighted. And he saith unto them, Be not affrighted: Ye seek Jesus of Nazareth, which was crucified: he is risen; he is not here: behold*

the place where they laid him. But go your way, tell his disciples and Peter that he goeth before you into Galilee: there shall ye see him, as he said unto you. And they went out quickly, and fled from the sepulchre; for they trembled and were amazed: neither said they any thing to any man; for they were afraid.

This is the greatest passage of scripture in the entire Word of God! Without the *risen Jesus,* there is no hope for a lost condemned world. There are many miracles recorded in the sacred pages of scripture, but the *crucified, buried,* and *risen Jesus of Nazareth* is the greatest miracle in history! Death could not hold the *Creator* of life!

The Father, Son, and Holy Spirit were all three working to bring about the resurrection:

(Father) *Therefore we are buried with him by baptism into death: that like as Christ was raised up from the dead by the glory of the __Father__, even so we also should walk in newness of life.*

Romans 6:4

(Son) *No man taketh it from me, but I lay it down of myself. I have power to lay it down, and __I__ have power to take it again. This commandment have I received of my Father.*

John 10:18

(Holy Spirit) ***But if the <u>Spirit</u> of him that raised up Jesus from the dead dwell in you, he that raised up Christ from the dead shall also quicken your mortal bodies by his Spirit that dwelleth in you.***

Romans 8:11

The Apostle Paul would later emphasize how important the resurrection of Jesus was to the believers in Corinth:

And if Christ be not risen, then is our preaching vain, and your faith is also vain. Yea, and we are found false witnesses of God; because we have testified of God that he raised up Christ: whom he raised not up, if so be that the dead rise not. For if the dead rise not, then is not Christ raised: And if Christ be not raised, your faith is vain; ye are yet in your sins. Then they also which are fallen asleep in Christ are perished. If in this life only we have hope in Christ, we are of all men most miserable.

I Corinthians 15:14-19

Mark mentions only one angel, or *messenger*, who had a message for the women. Notice the powerful, history-changing messages from the angel:

* *Be not affrighted*
* *Ye seek Jesus of Nazareth which was crucified*
* *He is risen; he is not here*

* *Behold the place where they laid him*
* *But go your way, tell his disciples and Peter*
* *He goeth before you into Galilee*
* *There shall ye see him, as he said unto you*

"tell his disciples and Peter" – Peter is being singled out as the leader of the disciples, and the angel's message seems to say that Peter had been forgiven for denying the Lord. Peter and the other disciples would see the risen Jesus back in Galilee where He first called them.

There could be an additional connection of the angel or angels guarding the tomb where Jesus had been buried in the garden, and the angels that guarded the Tree of Life in the *Garden of Eden*. Most of the time this connection is overlooked:

> **So he drove out the man; and he placed at the east of the garden of Eden Cherubims, and a flaming sword which turned every way, to keep the way of the tree of life.**
>
> Genesis 3:24

The *Cherubims* were placed in the *Garden of Eden* to keep Satan out until the *Seed of the Woman* came into the world and conquered death for mankind and removed the curse. The empty tomb brings us full circle from the book of Genesis. Now all of those who embrace the risen Jesus by faith will live in the New Jerusalem, or the so-called *Garden of Eden*. (**Rev.22:1-3**) The angels at the tomb of

Jesus were there to secure the place until the *three days and nights* were completed.

While mankind cannot be specifically sure about everything that happened, Jesus went down into the lower parts of the earth during that time. Many Hebrew scholars believe that Jesus went down to where the departed spirits went in the Old Testament *(sheol, where the righteous were separated from the unrighteous)* and proclaimed victory over the evil spirits, even from the days of Noah who had corrupted the seed of man:

> *For Christ also hath once suffered for sins, the just for the unjust, that he might bring us to God, being put to death in the flesh, but quickened by the Spirit: By which also he went and preached* (kerysso, proclaim something that has been done) *unto the spirits in prison; Which sometime were disobedient, when once the longsuffering of God waited in the days of Noah, while the ark was a preparing, wherein few, that is, eight souls were saved by water.*
>
> I Peter 3:18-20 (Also connect **Genesis 6:4**)

> ★ **Mark 16:9-11** – *Now when Jesus was risen early the first day of the week, he appeared first to Mary Magdalene, out of whom he had cast seven devils. And she went and told them that had been with him, as they mourned and wept.*

CARROLL ROBERSON

And they, when they had heard that he was
alive, and had been seen of her, believed not.

⋆ *The sudden change in style here has caused some scholars to*
*believe that Mark ended his gospel at **vs.8**. However, according to*
*the oldest transcripts, **verses 9-20** are part of the inspired gospel,*
so we will treat them as such.

Isn't it strange that Israel's Messiah would choose a
woman to be the first to witness His resurrection? Jesus
broke down the traditional beliefs about women being
inferior to men. The very first witness of the risen Christ
was *Mary Magdalene!* This proves that the four gospels were
not fables or fictionalized by the Jews. They would never
have placed a *woman* in that high of a position; furthermore,
a *woman* who had been demon-possessed. *Mary Magdalene*
not only saw the risen Lord first, she was commissioned
to *go and tell* the other disciples that Jesus was alive! Jesus
had foretold His resurrection to His disciples on several
occasions, **(Mark 8:31, 9:31, 10:33, 14:28)** but here they
refused to believe the message from Mary.

Mark 16:12-13 - *After that he appeared in*
another form unto two of them, as they walked,
and went into the country. And they went and
told it unto the residue: neither believed they
them.

Mark makes mention of the beautiful story of the two
men on the road to Emmaus that is covered more in detail

in **Luke 24:13-35**. Notice that the disciples did not believe their testimony either.

> **Mark 16:14** - *Afterward he appeared unto the eleven as they sat at meat, and upbraided them with their unbelief and hardness of heart, because they believed not them which had seen him after he was risen.*

Jesus now appears to the 11 disciples *(without Judas)* and begins to reprimand them for not believing the ones He had sent to tell them:

* ★ *Mary Magdalene*
* ★ *Two men on the Emmaus road*

> **Mark 16:15** - *And he said unto them, Go ye into all the world, and preach the gospel to every creature.*

The message of the gospel is the death, burial, and resurrection of Christ. Jesus Himself commands them to preach the gospel to *every creature,* or all of creation. This was unthinkable to the Jewish mind at that time, and it was a revolutionary command by Jesus to His disciples. The life-changing message of the Lord Jesus the Messiah not only was proclaimed into the known world of the disciples, but it has now encompassed the entire globe as a result of their faithful witness. The disciples gave their lives for preaching the gospel, and their names will be written on the 12 foundations of the New Jerusalem. **(Rev.21:14)**

> **Mark 16:16 -** *He that believeth and is baptized shall be saved; but he that believeth not shall be damned.*

Notice that the disciples were to administer water *baptism* to those who believed in Jesus the Risen Messiah as a sign of public identification. The ones who were not water *baptized* would not be damned, but those who did *not* believe. While water baptism is essential for obedience, it is not essential for salvation. Many churches have used this verse to try to prove that water baptism is necessary for salvation. One must see the overall truth of scripture concerning salvation, rather than choosing a random verse and taking it out of context. The Bible is clear that salvation is by faith alone in the finished work of Jesus!

> **Mark 16:17-18 -** *And these signs shall follow them that believe; In my name shall they cast out devils; they shall speak with new tongues; They shall take up serpents; and if they drink any deadly thing, it shall not hurt them; they shall lay hands on the sick, and they shall recover.*

* *Cast out demons* = Acts 16:16-18
* *New tongues* (languages) = Acts 2:4, 10:46
* *Serpents and poison* = Acts 28:3-5
* *Laying hands on the sick* = Acts 3:6-8, 28:8

These *signs* were not meant for people in future generations to *tempt* the Lord. These were *signs* that would *follow* the disciples as they went and preached the gospel for the very first time. Notice that the *signs* followed the preaching of the disciples, not that the disciples were to follow the *signs*.

> **Mark 16:19-20 –** *So then after the Lord had spoken unto them, he was received up into heaven, and sat on the right hand of God. And they went forth, and preached every where, the Lord working with them, and confirming the word with signs following. Amen.*

Jesus came into this world to be man's representative. He was born in Bethlehem, He was raised in Nazareth, He had His ministry in the Galilee, He died on a tree in Jerusalem, He arose from the grave in bodily form, and He ascended to heaven in the form of a man. He is now seated at the right hand of God interceding for His people. He will return as *King of Kings and Judge,* as the *Son of Man!* Notice this parallel passage concerning the ascension:

> *When they therefore were come together, they asked of him, saying, Lord, wilt thou at this time restore again the kingdom to Israel? And he said unto them, It is not for you to know the times or the seasons, which the Father hath put in his own power. But ye shall receive power, after that the Holy Ghost is come upon you: and*

ye shall be witnesses unto me both in Jerusalem, and in all Judaea, and in Samaria, and unto the uttermost part of the earth. And when he had spoken these things, while they beheld, he was taken up; and a cloud received him out of their sight. And while they looked stedfastly toward heaven as he went up, behold, two men stood by them in white apparel; Which also said, Ye men of Galilee, why stand ye gazing up into heaven? this same Jesus, which is taken up from you into heaven, shall so come in like manner as ye have seen him go into heaven.

Acts 1:6-11

The disciples did not stay together forever. This is a spiritual lesson for us today. We are not to gather together and stay within the walls of our local churches. The marching orders have been given, and we are to go as soldiers in God's army and share the truth of Jesus that contains the power to change other people's lives. The disciples separated and went to preach the gospel everywhere with the supernatural signs following them. We may not always see the same supernatural signs that the disciples saw, but we will see the results of God's Spirit touching lives when the gospel is preached in the power of the Holy Spirit. The gospel of Mark was a vital part in spreading the message of Christ in the first century. We are forever grateful to our Lord for inspiring Mark to write his gospel and to preserve it for us to have down through the centuries.

Printed in the United States
By Bookmasters

Printed in the United States
By Bookmasters